THE FACTS ON FILE
CHEMISTRY
HANDBOOK

Revised Edition

THE FACTS ON FILE
CHEMISTRY
HANDBOOK

Revised Edition

THE DIAGRAM GROUP

Facts On File
An imprint of Infobase Publishing

The Facts On File Chemistry Handbook, Revised Edition

Diagram Visual Information Ltd

Editorial directors	David Harding, Moira Johnston
Science editor	Eleanora von Dehsen
Editors	Nancy Bailey, Jean Brady, Paul Copperwaite, Eve Daintith, Bridget Giles, Jane Johnson, Reet Nelis, Jamie Stokes
Design	Richard Hummerstone, Edward Kinsey
Design production	Anthony Atherton, Carole Dease, Oscar Lobban, Lee Lawrence
Artists	Susan Kinsey, Lee Lawrence, Kathleen McDougall
Research	Peter Dease, Catherine & Neil McKenna,
Contributors	Michael Allaby, Martyn Bramwell, John Daintith, Trevor Day, John Haywood, Jim Henderson, David Lambert, Catherine Riches, Dr Robert Youngson

Facts On File, Inc.
An imprint of Infobase Publishing
132 West 31st Street
New York NY 10001

Library of Congress Cataloging-in-Publication Data

The Facts on File chemistry handbook / The Diagram Group. —Rev. ed.
    p. cm.
  Includes bibliographical references and index
  ISBN 0-8160-5878-4
  I. Chemistry—Handbooks, manuals, etc. I. Diagram Group.

  QD65.F33 2006
  540—dc22   2005055496

Facts On File books are available at special discounts when purchased in bulk quantities for businesses, associations, institutions, or sales promotions. Please call our Special Sales Department in New York at 212/967-8800 or 800/322-8755.

You can find Facts On File on the World Wide Web at
http://www.factsonfile.com

Cover design by Cathy Rincon

Printed in the United States of America

VB DIAG 10 9 8 7 6 5 4 3 2 1

This book is printed on acid-free paper.

INTRODUCTION

THE FACTS ON FILE CHEMISTRY HANDBOOK, Revised Edition offers students a full view of this vital branch of science, in the form of a one-stop reference.

The Revised Edition expands greatly on the information available in the previous edition, with the inclusion of four new sections—an A–Z of key advances in the field of chemistry; a list of Nobel Prize winners in chemistry; listings of important science and chemistry associations; and listings of key science and chemistry Web sites. The biography and chronology sections have been updated and the glossary expanded to include charts and graphs illustrating important concepts. Finally, the index has been extended and completely revised to make searching even easier. THE CHEMISTRY HANDBOOK, Revised Edition features the following components:

GLOSSARY
Almost 1,500 entries, many accompanied by illustrations and now with 14 new large diagrams and charts, are provided here, to aid students' understanding of the specialized terminology of chemistry.

BIOGRAPHIES
Biographies of more than 300 people are provided here—not only the giants of chemistry, but also many of those whose achievements may have gone unnoticed but whose discoveries have pushed forward the world's understanding of chemistry. Updated to 2005.

CHRONOLOGY
This section covers 9,000 years of events in the history of chemistry that have influenced our lives more than wars, political changes, and world rulers. Now extended to 2005.

KEY ADVANCES
This entirely new A–Z list of over 140 important advances in chemistry enables students to find quick information on who invented or discovered what and when.

NOBEL PRIZE WINNERS
The newly added list of Nobel Prize winners in chemistry is complete to 2005. Each entry includes the award citation as well as the nationality and dates of birth and death of the winners.

CHARTS & TABLES
This section brings together charts and tables in key areas of chemistry. Nine new pages have been added in the Revised Edition.

ASSOCIATIONS
This entirely new section provides the names, addresses, telephone numbers, and Web addresses of 30 important associations.

WEB SITES
Another entirely new section, listing 50 selected Web sites for students, teachers, and library patrons.

CONTENTS

SECTION ONE
ONE
GLOSSARY

absolute temperature (thermodynamic temperature) Based on absolute zero. The unit (the kelvin) is 1/273.16 of the temperature of the triple point of water and is equivalent to one degree Celsius (1°C).

absolute zero The lowest possible temperature. Zero on the Kelvin scale.

abundance A measure of the quantity of a substance occurring in a particular area (an element in the Earth's crust or an isotope in a sample of an element). It is expressed in percentage or parts per million.

Ac Symbol for the element actinium.

accelerator A chemical that increases the rate of a chemical reaction.

accumulator or **battery** A device that uses chemical energy to store electrical energy.

acetaldehyde *See* ethanal.

acetic acid *See* ethanoic acid.

acetone *See* propanone.

acetylene *See* ethyne.

acid Any substance that releases hydrogen ions when added to water. It has a pH of less than 7.

acid anhydrides Compounds that react with water, forming acids, for example, the acid anhydride SO_2 that reacts to make the acid H_2SO_4.

acid-base reaction An acid and a base react together to form a salt and water only.

acidic oxide The oxides of nonmetals that form acidic solutions in water. An acidic oxide reacts with a base to form salt and water only.

acidification The fall in pH in a solution caused by the addition of an acid. This is seen in nature in the pollution of lakes, rivers, and groundwater by acid rain.

acid, organic *See* organic acid.

acid rain A form of pollution where rain dissolves acidic gases (mainly sulfur dioxide) from the air. Sulfur dioxide is released into the atmosphere by the burning of fossil fuels.

acid salt A salt of a polybasic acid in which not all the hydrogen atoms have been replaced by a metal or metal-like group (e.g., ammonium group).

acid, standardization of *See* standardization of solutions.

actinides (**actinoids**) The name of the group of elements with atomic numbers from 89 (actinium) to 103 (lawrencium). All are radioactive and have similar properties to actinium. As their outer electronic structure is very similar (the f orbital in their fifth shell is being filled), they have similar chemical properties.

actinium Element symbol, Ac; silvery metallic element; Z 89; A(r) 227; density (at 20°C), 10.07 g/cm^3; m.p., 1,050°C; radioactive; name derived from the Greek *aktis*, "ray;" discovered 1899.

actinium series One of the naturally occurring radioactive series.

activated complex A short-lived association of atoms that is formed during a chemical reaction.

activation energy The energy barrier to be overcome in order for a reaction to occur. Many chemical reactions require heat energy to be applied to reactants to initiate a reaction.

active carbon Particles of carbon used widely as an adsorbent to remove impurities in gases and liquids.

addition polymerization A process by which molecules join together by a series of addition reactions to form larger molecules, or macromolecules, which consist of repeated structural units.

addition reaction A reaction in which a molecule of a substance reacts with another molecule to form a single compound. The term addition reaction is often used in organic chemistry to describe a reaction in which an atom is added to either side of the double or triple bond in an unsaturated compound to form a saturated compound.

additive A small quantity of a compound added to a bulk material to give it certain properties. For example, the colorings added to food and drink.

adsorption The process by which molecules of gases or liquids become attached to the surface of another substance. Desorption is the opposite process.

aerosol Extremely small liquid or solid particles suspended in air or another gas.

Ag Symbol for the element silver.

agrochemicals Chemicals used in agriculture, with the exception of fertilizers. The classification includes fungicides, herbicides, pesticides, growth regulators, and vitamin and mineral supplements.

air, a mixture Air is a mixture of several gases (*see* air, composition of). These can be physically separated by cooling (to remove water vapor) and by fractional distillation (to remove nitrogen). The properties of air are an average of its components.

air, composition of The composition of air varies but its average composition (given in percentages by volume) is nitrogen, 78; oxygen, 21; argon, 0.93; carbon dioxide, 0.03.

air, liquid Liquid air is a pale blue liquid that boils at –193°C. As its component parts have different boiling points (nitrogen boils at

Addition polymerization

Adsorption

Composition of air

actinium – air, liquid

GLOSSARY

-195.8°C, oxygen boils at -183°C), nitrogen and oxygen can be obtained by the fractional distillation of liquid air.

Al Symbol for the element aluminum.

alcohols *See* alkanols.

aldehydes A group of organic compounds containing the aldehyde group (–CHO). Names have the suffix -al.

algae A loose grouping of plant-like organisms including many single-celled forms and multicellular forms such as seaweeds.

algal bloom A rapidly growing layer of algae that floats on the surface of a body of water and whose growth is stimulated by nitrates and phosphates in fertilizers. This layer can cause plants growing at the bottom of the water to die as the light they need is shielded from them by the algal bloom.

aliphatic Organic compounds composed of carbon atoms in straight or branched chains.

alkali A solution of a substance in water that has a pH of more than 7 and has an excess of hydroxide ions in the solution.

alkali metals Metallic elements found in group 1 of the periodic table. They are very reactive, electropositive, and react with water to form alkaline solutions.

alkaline earth metals Metallic elements found in group 2 of the periodic table. They are less reactive and electropositive than alkali metals but also produce alkaline solutions when they react with water.

alkali, standardization of *See* standardization of solutions.

alkanal An aldehyde in which the radical attached to the aldehyde group is aliphatic.

alkanes A group of hydrocarbons whose general formula is C_nH_{2n+2}. They have single bonds between the carbon atoms and are thus said to be saturated and hence not very reactive.

alkanols (alcohols) A family of organic compounds whose structure contains the –OH functional group. General formula $C_nH_{2n+1}OH$.

alkenes A group of hydrocarbons, the general formula of which is C_nH_{2n}. They are unsaturated, having a double bond between a pair of carbon atoms. They are reactive and undergo addition reactions.

alkene, substituted An alkene in which one or more hydrogen atom has been replaced by a different atom (or group of atoms).

alkylation The insertion of alkyl groups into either hydrocarbon chains or aromatic rings.

Aldehyde

Alkane (ethane)

Alkanol (ethanol)

Alkene (ethene)

alkyl group A hydrocarbon group whose general formula is C_nH_{2n+1}.

alkynes A group of hydrocarbons whose general formula is C_nH_{2n-1}. They are unsaturated, having a triple bond between a pair of carbon atoms in each molecule and are thus reactive, undergoing addition reactions.

allo- A prefix to the name of a chemical compound that shows that the compound is a stereoisomer of a more common compound.

allotrope An element that can exist in more than one physical form while in the same state. Carbon can occur in two common allotropes, diamond and graphite (a third—buckminsterfullerene—has been discovered recently). The physical properties of these allotropes are very different.

alloy A metallic material made of two or more metals or of a metal and nonmetal. By mixing metals in certain proportions, alloys with specific properties can be made.

alpha particle A particle released during radioactive decay. It consists of two neutrons and two protons (the equivalent of the helium atom). Energy is released by this change; most is accounted for by the kinetic energy of the a particle that moves away at high speed but that rapidly loses energy by collision and ionization of other atoms and molecules and is easily stopped by a piece of paper. Alpha rays are streams of fast-moving a particles.

alumina A naturally occurring form of aluminum oxide also known as corundum.

aluminum Element symbol, Al; group 3; silvery white metallic element; Z 13; A(r) 26.98; density (at 20°C), 2.70 g/cm^3; m.p., 660.4°C; name derived from the Latin *alumen*; discovered 1825.

aluminum chloride $AlCl_3$. Anhydrous aluminum chloride fumes in moist air, reacting to form hydrogen chloride with water vapor.

aluminum hydroxide $Al(OH)_3$. A white crystalline compound. It appears as a white or yellowish gelatinous mass on precipitation from solutions of ammonium salts, in which form it contains coordinated water molecules and water molecules trapped in its structure. Partially dried gels of aluminum hydroxide are used as drying agents, catalysts, and absorbents.

aluminum nitride AlN. Formed (together with the oxide) when aluminum is heated strongly.

aluminum oxide Al_2O_3. A white or colorless crystalline compound. It is formed by heating aluminum hydroxide and has two main forms, the alpha form and the gamma form. The alpha form occurs naturally and is known as corundum. The gamma form (activated alumina) is used as a catalyst as it has adsorptive properties. Bauxite is a hydrated form of aluminum oxide. Aluminum oxide is amphoteric. It reacts with sodium hydroxide to form sodium aluminate ($NaAlO_2$) and water, and with hydrochloric acid to form aluminum chloride and water.

Am Symbol for the element americium.

amalgam An alloy containing mercury.

americium Element symbol, Am; Actinide; silvery radioactive metallic element; Z 95; A(r) 243; density (at 20°C), 13.67 g/cm^3; m.p., 994°C; name named for America; discovered 1944.

amide group $CONH_2$. A functional group consisting of a carbon atom joined to an oxygen atom with a double bond and to a nitrogen atom that is joined to two hydrogen atoms.

amides A group of organic compounds containing the amide group. Their general formula is $RCONH_2$. Amides are white solids that are soluble in alcohol and ether; some are soluble in water.

amines A group of organic compounds containing the amino functional group $-NH_2$.

amino acids A group of organic compounds containing both the carboxyl group ($-COOH$) and the amino group ($-NH_2$). (*See also* illustration on page 13.)

amino group $-NH_2$.

ammonia NH_3. Colorless, strong-smelling poisonous gas, very soluble in water, forming a weak alkaline solution. $NH_3 + H_2O = NH_4^+ + OH^-$. It burns in oxygen with a yellowish flame. It is used industrially in the manufacture of fertilizers and the production of nitric acid. Most ammonia used is produced by the Haber process.

ammonia, eighty-eight A concentrated solution of ammonia in water that contains about 35% by mass of ammonia. Its relative density is 0.880—hence the name. It softens water and helps to remove stains from clothes.

ammonia, liquor A solution of ammonia in water that is produced during coal-gas manufacture. It is used to make the fertilizer ammonium sulfate.

ammonia, oxidation If air is passed through a solution of ammonia in a flask and a red-hot platinum wire is placed at the top of the flask, the ammonia reacts with the oxygen in the air to form nitrogen monoxide. This then reacts with more oxygen to form brown fumes of nitrogen dioxide. As the reaction is exothermic, the platinum wire continues to glow red during the reaction.

ammonia, reactions Ammonia is very soluble in water, forming a weak alkaline solution. $NH_3 + H_2O = NH_4^+ + OH -$. Ammonia burns in

Amides (ethanamide)

Amino acid

Air →

Brown fumes of nitrogen dioxide

Red-hot platinum wire

Ammonia solution

Oxidation of ammonia

Amino acids: structure (see entry on page 12)

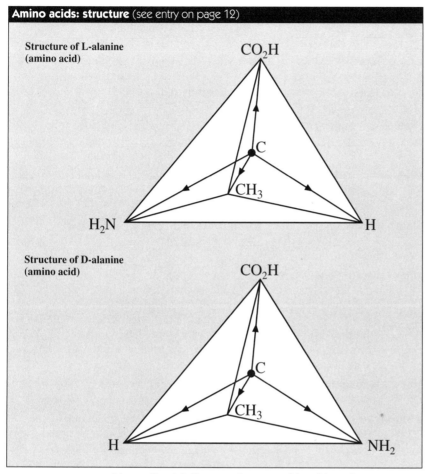

Structure of L-alanine
(amino acid)

Structure of D-alanine
(amino acid)

oxygen with a yellowish flame and reacts with acids to form
ammonium salts. Ammonium salts contain the ammonium ion NH_4^+.

ammonia, soda process *See* Solvay process.

ammonia, solution Ammonia solution is a weak alkali. It precipitates
insoluble hydroxides from metal salts in solution. (*See* ammonium
hydroxide.)

ammonium carbonate $(NH_4)_2CO_3$. Formed as a sublimate (mixed with
ammonium hydrogen carbonate) when calcium carbonate and
ammonium sulfate (or chloride) are heated together. It is very soluble
in water. Ammonium carbonate decomposes to form NH_3, CO_2, and
H_2O on heating and decomposes in moist air to form ammonium
hydrogen carbonate. It smells of ammonia, and the mixture of

Sublimation of ammonium chloride

Ammonium ion

Anaerobic production of biogas

ammonium carbonate and ammonium hydrogen carbonate is also called sal volatile. The mixture is used in smelling salts and baking powder.

ammonium chloride NH_4Cl (also called sal ammoniac) A white crystalline solid that is soluble in water. It sublimes on heating to form ammonia and hydrogen chloride (gas). It is used in dry cells, as a flux in soldering, and as a mordant.

ammonium hydrogen carbonate NH_4HCO_3. A white crystalline solid. It is more stable than ammonium carbonate and is therefore often used in its place both medicinally (smelling salts) and in baking powders.

ammonium hydroxide NH_4OH. It exists as an aqueous solution of ammonia and it contains ammonium ions, hydroxide ions, unionized ammonia, and water.

ammonium ion $NH_4{}^+$. Found in ammonia solution and in ammonium compounds. Ammonium salts are similar to the salts of monovalent metals.

ammonium nitrate NH_4NO_3. A colorless crystalline solid that dissolves readily in water. This is an endothermic reaction (the solution becomes cold), and a mixture of ammonium nitrate and water can be used as a freezing mixture (*see* freezing). When heated, ammonium nitrate forms dinitrogen oxide. Ammonium nitrate is used as a fertilizer and also as an explosive, with a suitable detonator, although it can detonate spontaneously.

ammonium nitrite NH_4NO_2. Very unstable; decomposes to form nitrogen and water.

ammonium salt, test for Into a test tube containing a small amount of an aqueous solution of a base, carefully add a small amount of the compound to be tested. Add more of the compound if there is no reaction. If the compound dissolves in cold alkali and liberates a gas that turns red litmus paper blue, this indicates that the gas is ammonia and that the compound tested is an ammonium salt. $NH_4{}^+ + OH^- = NH_3 + H_2O$.

ammonium sulfate $(NH_4)_2SO_4$. A colorless crystalline solid. It has been used as fertilizer but is now being replaced by fertilizers with higher nitrogen content. It is produced by passing ammonia and carbon dioxide into a suspension of calcium sulfate (gypsum).

amorphous Lacking form, shape, or crystal structure: amorphous substances have no fixed melting point.

amphoteric Exhibiting properties of both an acid and a base. An amphoteric compound reacts with both acids and bases to form salts.

anaerobic A process that takes place in the absence of free oxygen.

analysis A method of finding out what the component parts of a material are. *See* qualitative analysis and quantitative analysis.

anesthetic A substance used to relieve pain. General anesthetics affect the whole body, producing unconsciousness. Local anesthetics affect a specific part of the body.

anhydride The substance remaining when one or more molecules of water have been removed from an acid (or a base). Most anhydrides are good drying agents.

anhydrite Calcium sulfate ($CaSO_4$), which occurs naturally in an anhydrous state.

anhydrous Containing no water. Term applied to salts without water of crystallization.

anion An ion having a negative charge.

annealing A method of treating materials (metals and glass) to increase their strength and to relieve strain in their structure. The material is heated to a high temperature and then cooled slowly. In metals, this process causes large crystals to form, increasing the metal's malleability.

anode The electrode carrying the positive charge in a solution undergoing electrolysis.

anodize To coat the surface of a metal with a film of protective oxide. This can be done by making the metal the anode in an electrolysis cell.

antacid A substance such as milk of magnesia (MgO) and sodium bicarbonate ($NaHCO_3$) that is taken to neutralize excessive stomach acid in order to relieve indigestion.

anti-foaming powder A substance that is used in a number of processes to reduce the quantity of foam produced in order to increase the efficiency of the process. Polyamides are used in boiler systems. Low concentrations of silicones are also used widely.

antifreeze A substance that lowers the freezing point of water. Methanol and ethane-1,2-diol are examples of antifreeze agents that are added to the cooling systems of engines to prevent damage that would be caused by the formation of ice. A concentration of 30% methanol and water or 35% ethane-1,2-diol and water will remain liquid above $-20.6°C$.

antiknock In an internal combustion engine, gasoline and air must explode together at the correct moment or preignition occurs, making "knocking" sounds as the fuel explodes prematurely. Antiknock agents are added to the fuel to overcome this problem. They promote more efficient combustion (and increase the octane rating of the fuel). Lead(IV) tetraethyl has been an important antiknock agent, but

Anode

Anodizing

it is being withdrawn because of problems with lead pollution. *See* octane rating.

antimony Element symbol, Sb; group 5; most stable form has bluish white metallic appearance; derivatives very toxic; Z 51; A(r) 121.75; density (at 20°C), 6.68 g/cm^3; m.p., 630.7°C; Latin name, *antimonium-aktis*, "ray;" discovered before 1600; antimony compounds used in flame proofing, ceramics, and dyestuffs.

anti-oxidants Chemical additives that slow down the rate at which a substance is degraded by oxidation. When used in food, they increase the length of time a product can be kept. They are also added to paint and plastics.

aqua fortis Concentrated nitric acid.

aqua regia A mixture of one part concentrated nitric acid and three parts of concentrated hydrochloric acid. It dissolves all metals except silver.

aqueous solution A solution in which water is the solvent.

Ar Symbol for the element argon.

A(r) Symbol for relative atomic mass.

arene The general name for an aromatic hydrocarbon.

argon Element symbol, Ar; noble gas, group 8; Z 18; A(r) 39.95; density (at 20°C), 1.784 g/l at STP; m.p., –189.2°C; name derived from the Greek *argos*, "inactive;" discovered 1894; used in light bulbs.

aromatic compounds The group of hydrocarbons derived from benzene (C_6H_6), that have a ring structure.

arsenic Element symbol, As; group 5; a metalloid with bright metallic appearance; Z 33; A(r) 74.92; density (at 20°C), 5.73 g/cm^3; m.p., 817°C; arsenic compounds poisonous; name derived from the Greek *arsenikon*; discovered 1250; used in insecticides, semiconductors, and in alloys where it has a hardening effect.

aryl An aromatic hydrocarbon group formed by the removal of a hydrogen atom from an arene.

As Symbol for the element arsenic.

asbestos A naturally occurring fibrous material consisting mainly of calcium magnesium silicate. It has heat- (insulating and fire) proofing properties and was formerly widely used. It is now known to cause both asbestosis (a lung disease) and mesothelioma (a tumor of the epithelium lining the lungs, abdomen, or heart associated with exposure to asbestos) and its use has been greatly restricted.

association The process by which molecules of a substance combine to form a larger structure. This occurs in liquid ammonia where the liquid

Aromatic compound

consists of $(NH_3)x$ molecules rather than separate NH_3 molecules. An associated liquid is formed when molecules of one substance are held together with molecules of another by forces weaker than normal chemical bonds. For example, a mixture of ethanol and water forms an associated liquid in which the molecules are held together by hydrogen bonds.

astatine Element symbol, At; group 7, halogen; radioactive; Z 85; A(r) 210; m.p., 302°C; name derived from the Greek *astatos*, "unstable;" discovered 1940.

At Symbol for the element astatine.

atom The smallest particle of an element that can exhibit that element's properties. An atom has a small, massive nucleus of protons and neutrons surrounded by a cloud of electrons (equal in number to the number of protons in the nucleus and unique to the element).

atomic energy The energy liberated by changes in the nuclei of atoms. When the nuclei of radioactive elements break up and other elements are formed, matter is destroyed. This matter is converted to energy in the formula $E = mc^2$. (One kilogram of matter yields 9×10^{16} joules of energy.)

atomicity The atomicity of an element is the number of atoms in one molecule of the element. For oxygen (O_2) it is 2; for ozone (O_3) 3; for hydrogen (H_2) 2.

atomic mass Short for relative atomic mass.

atomic mass unit Defined as 1/12 the mass of one atom of carbon-12 isotope.

atomic number or **proton number (Z)** The number of protons in the nucleus of an atom. If not electrically charged, this is equal to the number of electrons in its shells.

atomic orbital *See* orbital.

atomic theory Matter consists of atoms, which are made of electrons, protons, and neutrons. Atoms can be created and destroyed in radioactive changes but not in chemical reactions. All atoms of an element contain the same number of protons. Atoms of an element may differ in mass because they contain different numbers of neutrons (*see* isotope). These do not affect their chemical properties. Chemical combination usually occurs between small, whole numbers of atoms (although it can occur between very large numbers of atoms, particularly with carbon compounds—*see* polymerization).

Au Symbol for the element gold.

Aufbau principle This governs the order in which orbitals are filled in successive elements in the periodic table: 1s, 2s, 2p, 3s, 3p, 4s, 3d,

Proton   Neutron   Electron

Atom

Aufbau principle

4p, 5s, etc. The number is the shell number and the letter denotes the orbital type.

autocatalysis The action as a catalyst by one of the products of a chemical reaction.

autoclave A strong vessel in which substances may be heated under pressure in order to carry out reactions at high temperatures and pressures. Autoclaves are also used for sterilization of equipment.

Avogadro constant or **number** (L) The number of particles (atoms, molecules, ions) present in a mole of substance. Specifically, it is the number of atoms present in 12 g of the carbon-12 isotope (6.023×10^{23}). (*See also* illustration on page 19.)

Avogadro's hypothesis or **law** Equal volumes of all gases at the same temperature and pressure contain the same number of molecules.

azeotrope (azeotropic mixtures) A mixture of liquids that boils without a change in composition, i.e. when it boils it gives off a vapor whose composition is the same as the liquid.

azides Compounds that contain the ion N_3^- or the group $-N_3$. Heavy metal azides are explosive.

azo compound A compound that contains two aromatic rings connected by an azo group. Many azo compounds are dyes.

azo group -N=N- An organic group containing two nitrogen atoms.

B Symbol for the element boron.

Ba Symbol for the element barium.

bakelite A phenol/methanal resin that was patented in 1909 by Leo Hendrik Baekeland. Bakelite is dark in color and has good electrical and heat insulation properties. It has been used as a covering for electric plugs and switches, for the handles of saucepans and other household items, jewelry, and more.

baking powder A mixture that produces carbon dioxide when heated or wetted. It is usually a mixture of sodium hydrogencarbonate and tartaric acid, or cream of tartar. If baking powder is mixed with other ingredients, the carbon dioxide produced causes the mixture to rise.

baking soda Sodium hydrogencarbonate. When heated, it decomposes to form sodium carbonate, carbon dioxide, and water. $2NaHCO_3 = Na_2CO_3 + CO_2 + H_2O$. If baking soda is mixed with other ingredients, the carbon dioxide produced causes the mixture to rise on cooking.

balance An instrument for comparing the masses of objects.

balanced equation A balanced chemical equation has equal numbers of each atom on each side of the equation. Such an equation can be used to

Azo compound

Bakelite

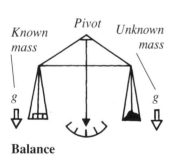

Known mass *Pivot* *Unknown mass*

g *g*

Balance

Avogadro's constant: apparatus for determination (see entry on page 18)

Apparatus for determining Avogadro's constant

a 6 volt DC supply
b Rheostat
c Hardboard or wooden electrode holder
d Copper foil cathode
e Copper foil anode
f Copper sulfate solution

calculate the masses of substances either reacting or being produced in a chemical reaction. To do this, it is assumed that each formula represents one mole of the substance, and weights can then be substituted where known to calculate the unknown quantities.

barite or **barytes** The mineral form of barium sulfate, a useful source of barium compounds.

barium Element symbol, Ba; group 2, alkaline earth metal; silver white metal; Z 56; A(r) 137.33; density (at 20°C), 3.5 g/cm^3; m.p., 725°C; compounds poisonous and opaque to X-rays; name derived from the

Greek *barys*, "heavy;" discovered 1808; used as a getter to remove oxygen, salts used in X-ray diagnosis.

barium carbonate $BaCO_3$. A white insoluble compound that occurs in the mineral witherite. It is used to make other barium salts, flux for ceramics, and in the manufacture of some types of optical glass.

barium chloride $BaCl_2$. A poisonous white compound that is used for the electrolytic production of barium.

barium chromate $BaCrO_4$. A yellow pigment that is fairly insoluble in water.

barium hydroxide $Ba(OH)_2$ (baryta) A white solid that is sparingly soluble in water. It is used in the laboratory as a weak alkali in volumetric analysis. It is also used as a plastic stabilizer and a gasoline additive.

barium peroxide BaO_2. A dense off-white solid that is used as a bleaching agent and in the manufacture of hydrogen peroxide.

barium sulfate $BaSO_4$. A poisonous white solid that is insoluble in water. Its mineral form is barytes. It is used as a pigment and as an additive in the glass and rubber industries. It is administered orally (barium sulfate is safe to use as it is very insoluble) for X-ray investigations.

base (usually a metal oxide or hydroxide) A substance existing as molecules or ions that can take up hydrogen ions. When a base reacts with an acid it forms a salt and water only.

base, equivalent of The mass in grams that reacts with the equivalent weight of an acid (1.08 g of hydrogen ions).

base, standardization of *See* standardization of solutions.

basic Having the properties of a base.

basicity of acids The number of hydrogen ions formed by a molecule of an acid. Hydrochloric acid (HCl) is monobasic. Sulfuric acid (H_2SO_4) is dibasic. Phosphoric acid (H_3PO_4) is tribasic.

basic oxide Many metal oxides are basic. Basic oxides react with acids, forming a salt and water only.

basic oxygen furnace A vessel in which a blast of oxygen is passed over the surface of, or through, molten iron to convert it to steel.

battery *See* accumulator.

bauxite The ore from which aluminum is extracted. It is a hydrated form of aluminum oxide ($Al_2O_3 . \times H_2O$).

Be Symbol for the element beryllium.

Benedict's solution A blue solution used to test for reducing sugars. It contains copper(II) sulfate, sodium, carbonate, and sodium citrate.

Benedict's test If a mixture of an aqueous solution of a reducing sugar and

Oxygen

Lining

Impurities

Molten iron

Solid base

Basic oxygen furnace

Benedict's solution is heated, when the temperature approaches boiling point, the color of the mixture changes from blue to green-yellow or orange. A brick red precipitate of copper(I) oxide is then formed.

benzene An aromatic hydrocarbon produced from naphtha. Its formula is C_6H_6, and each of the six hydrogen atoms is attached to one of the six carbon atoms that are arranged at the corners of a hexagon. This arrangement is called a benzene ring. Benzene is an important source of other organic compounds.

Benzene (abbreviated form)

berkelium Element symbol, Bk; actinide; Z 97; A(r) 247; density (at 20°C), 14 (est) g/cm^3; m.p., 986°C; named for Berkeley, California; discovered 1949.

beryllium Element symbol, Be; alkaline earth metal, group 2; gray, hard brittle metal; Z 4; A(r) 9.01; density (at 20°C), 1.85 g/cm^3; m.p., 1,287°C; compounds toxic; name derived from the Greek *beryllos*, "beryl;" discovered 1798; used in alloys and in nuclear reactors.

Bessemer converter A steel vessel lined with magnesium and calcium oxides. It has air holes in the base and can be tilted.

Bessemer process A process by which iron is converted to steel. Molten iron is added to a Bessemer converter while it is tilted to allow oxygen and superheated steam to be blown in. The converter is returned to the vertical position. Silicon, manganese, and carbon impurities burn off; carbon monoxide burns at the mouth of the converter. Phosphorus forms its oxide, which then combines with the lining, forming a basic slag of calcium and magnesium phosphates. Molten steel is tapped off from the base of the converter.

Bessemer converter

Hot waste gases

Slag on surface

Pivot

Molten iron and lime

Oxygen

beta particle A beta particle is a high-speed electron emitted by the nucleus of certain radioactive elements during β decay. When a neutron in the nucleus decays to a proton, an electron is emitted, thus the atomic number increases by one. A β ray is a stream of high-energy electrons. They will produce ions in matter through which they pass and will penetrate a layer of several millimeters of aluminum.

Bh Symbol for the element bohrium.

Bi Symbol for the element bismuth.

bimolecular reaction *See* molecularity.

binary compound A compound (such as carbon monoxide, CO) that contains two elements.

biochemistry The branch of chemistry that studies living things.

biodegradable A substance that can be broken down by microorganisms into simpler substances.

Ore + coke + limestone

Hot air   Hot air

Slag out   Molten iron out

Blast furnace

Thermometer

Vapor out

Bulb in vapor

Boiling liquid

Heat

Boiling point

biodegradable plastics Plastic with starch incorporated into its structure in order that it can be broken down when it comes into contact with soil.

bismuth Element symbol, Bi; Group 5; brittle reddish white metal; Z 83; A(r) 208.98; density (at 20°C), 9.8 g/cm³; m.p., 271.3°C; German name *wismut*, in Latin *bisemutum*; discovered around 1400; used in low melting alloys; some compounds have medical uses.

Bk Symbol for the element berkelium.

blast furnace A large tower (approximately 100 ft [30 m] high and 20 ft [6 m] wide) used to extract iron from its ores. Iron ore, coke, and limestone are added from the top, and pre-heated air is blown in through tubes (tuyeres) at the base. This causes the coke to burn and leads to several chemical processes, resulting in the reduction of the ore, which settles as a liquid at the base of the tower. A molten slag of calcium silicate floats on this and is removed separately.

bleach A substance that can remove the color from another substance, using either an oxidizing agent (such as chlorine) or a reducing agent (such as sulfur dioxide).

bleaching powder A white powder that consists of a mixture of hydrated calcium chloride, calcium hydroxide, and calcium chlorate(I) $(Ca(OCl)_2)$. When treated with a dilute acid, bleaching powder liberates chlorine. Chlorine is the bleaching agent (*see* bleach).

blue-ring test Test for the presence of thiosulfate (a salt containing the ion $(S_2O_3)^{2-}$). Take two test tubes. Pour 3 ml concentrated sulfuric acid in the first. In the second test tube add a small sample of the substance being tested to about 5 ml of aluminum molybdenate solution and shake to mix. While holding the first test tube at an angle of 45°, carefully pour some liquid from the second tube to form two liquid layers. If a deep blue ring is seen forming at the sulfuric acid/solution border, the solution contains a thiosulfate salt.

blue vitriol Hydrated copper sulfate $CuSO_4.5H_2O$. (Also known as copper sulfate pentahydrate.) Copper sulfate in this form exists as blue crystals.

bohrium Element symbol, Bh; transition element; Z 107; A(r) 262; named in honor of Danish physicist Niels Bohr; discovered 1981. Formerly known as unnilseptium.

boiling The process by which a substance changes from the liquid state to the gas state at a fixed temperature (the boiling point). At this point the vapor pressure of the liquid equals that of the atmosphere.

bond A bond is the chemical connection between atoms within a molecule. Bonds are forces and are caused by electrons. Covalent bonds form when two electrons are shared between two atoms (usually between two nonmetallic atoms), one contributed by each atom. Covalent double bonds form when four electrons are shared between the two atoms. Covalent triple bonds form when six electrons are shared between the two atoms. Coordinate bonds are a type of covalent bond and form when one of the atoms supplies both electrons. Ionic bonds (electrovalent or polar bonds) form when atoms form ions and electrons are transferred from one atom to another. The ions are held together by electrostatic attraction. *See* metallic bond.

bond energy During a chemical reaction, bonds between some of the atoms present are broken and new bonds are made. When bonds are broken, energy is absorbed; when bonds are formed, energy is evolved. The energy change in the reaction is the energy of a bond. Bond energies of multiple bonds are usually greater than those of single bonds. The energy of the hydrogen bond may be thought of as the energy absorbed when one mole of hydrogen molecules is split into free atoms. Bond energies can be calculated from the standard enthalpy of formation of the compound and from the enthalpies of atomization of the elements. Bond energies give the energy required to break the bonds and are hence a measure of the relative stabilities of the bonds.

bonding orbital *See* molecular orbitals.

borax $Na_2B_4O_7.10H_2O$ (disodium tetraborate-10-water, sodium tetraborate). A naturally occurring sodium salt. It is used in the glass industry and as a mild antiseptic.

boron Element symbol, B; group 3; very inert; Z 5; A(r) 10.81; density (at 20°C), 2.35 g/cm^3; m.p., 2,079°C; name derived from the Arabic *burak*; discovered 1808; used in nuclear reactors. Boron filaments are used in epoxy resins. Most of the boron used is in borosilicates in enamels and glasses.

boron carbide B_4C. A black solid that is very hard (9.5 on Mohs' scale). It is used as an abrasive.

boron nitride BN. A very hard solid that is insoluble in cold water. It sublimes above 3,000°C. It has high electrical resistance and high thermal conductivity and is used in the electrical industry.

borosilicate glass Glass made by the addition of boron oxide (B_2O_3) to the normal silicate network of glass. It forms a glass (such as Pyrex) that has a low coefficient of thermal expansion that allows it to be exposed to rapid heating or cooling without cracking.

borosilicates Substances in which BO_3 and SiO_4 are linked to form networks that have many structures.

Bosch process The production of hydrogen from water gas by passing a mixture of water, gas, and steam over an iron catalyst at about 500°C.

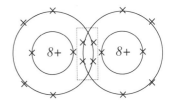

Bond + double covalent bond in oxygen

Boron

Borosilicate glass

Pressure increases →

← *Volume increases*

Boyle's law

$CO + H_2O = CO_2 + H_2$. The carbon dioxide is removed by washing with water or with potassium carbonate solution under pressure. $K_2CO_3 + CO_2 + H_2O = 2KHCO_3$.

Boyle's law The volume of a given mass of gas varies inversely with its pressure at constant temperature. One of the three ideal gas laws.

Br Symbol for the element bromine.

branched chains A line of carbon atoms having side groups attached to the chain.

brass An alloy of copper and up to 40% of zinc. It is harder and has more corrosion resistance than copper. It is used for electrical components and ornaments.

breeder reactor A nuclear reactor that produces more material capable of nuclear fission than it consumes.

brine A strong solution of sodium chloride in water.

bromides Compounds derived from hydrobromic acid (HBr). Silver bromide is used in photography and some bromides are used medicinally as sedatives.

bromine Element symbol, Br; halogen, group 7; dark red liquid, vapor is red and poisonous; Z 35; A(r) 79.9; density (at 20°C), 3.12 g/cm^3; m.p., −7.2°C; very reactive oxidizing agent; name derived from the Greek *bromos*, "stench;" discovered 1826; used to make ethylene dibromide and manufacture photographic materials, fumigants, water-purifying materials, and flame-proofing agents.

bromine test To test for an unsaturated hydrocarbon. Add bromine solution (orange in color) to the hydrocarbon being tested. If the hydrocarbon contains unsaturated bonds, the bromine solution is decolorized. This test uses the ability of bromine molecules to add on to a double bond, forming a colorless halocarbon compound.

bronze An alloy of copper and tin (less than 10%). It is much stronger than copper and its discovery was important in the history of human civilization. Its uses now are in gear wheels and engine bearings.

brown-ring test The chemical test for the presence of nitrates. The sample is dissolved in water in a test tube. A solution of iron(II) sulfate is added and the two solutions are mixed. Concentrated sulfuric acid is added slowly so that it sinks to form a layer beneath the aqueous solution. If nitrate is present in the sample, a brown ring is formed at the junction between the sulfuric acid and the aqueous solution. This disappears if the tube is shaken.

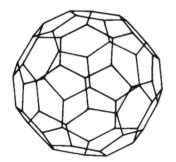

Buckyball molecule

buckyball molecule or **buckminsterfullerene** An allotropic form of carbon. It has a cage-like structure and has the formula C50, C60, and C70.

buffer solution A solution that can maintain an almost constant pH value when dilute acids or alkalis are added to it. It is made up of a dilute acid or base with a solution of one of its salts and can "mop up" excess hydrogen ions from acids or excess hydroxide ions from bases, maintaining a constant pH. Buffers are present in body fluids such as blood.

bunsen A burner used in the laboratory. It burns a variable mixture of gas and air, the proportions of which can be changed by changing the air hole on the side of the burner.

burette A long, graduated glass tube with a tap at the lower end. It is used to measure a volume of liquid accurately.

burning *See* combustion.

butane C_4H_{10}. A flammable, colorless gas with a slight smell; m.p., $-138.4°C$; b.p., $-0.5°C$. It is a saturated hydrocarbon belonging to the alkane homologous series. Butane is used as a fuel. It is isomeric with 2-methylpropane (formerly called isobutane). $CH_3CH(CH_3)CH_3$.

butanol C_4H_9OH. An aliphatic alcohol with four isomeric forms:

1-butanol, $CH_3CH_2CH_2CH_2OH$, b.p., $117°C$.

Isobutanol or 2-methylpropanol, $(CH_3)_2CHCH_2OH$, b.p., $108°C$.

Secondary butyl alcohol or 2-butanol, $CH_3CH_2CH(CH_3)OH$, b.p., $100°C$.

Tertiary butyl alcohol or 2-methyl-2-propanol, $(CH_3)_3COH$, which occurs as colorless prisms, m.p., $25°C$, b.p., $83°C$.

butene C_4H_8. An unsaturated hydrocarbon belonging to the alkene homologous series. Three isomers are possible:

1-butene, $CH_3CH_2CH=CH_2$

2-butene, $CH_3CH=CHCH_3$

isobutene or 2-methylpropene$(CH_3)_2C=CH_2$

They are all normally colorless gases (b.p. between $-6°C$ and $+3°C$) with unpleasant odors.

byproduct A substance produced in a reaction in addition to the required product. (Slag is produced as a byproduct of iron manufacture.)

C Symbol for the element carbon.

Ca Symbol for the element calcium.

cadmium Element symbol, Cd; transition element; white shiny metal; Z 48; A(r) 112.41; density (at 20°C), 8.65 g/cm^3; m.p., 320.9°C; compounds very toxic; name derived from the Greek *kadmeia*,

Bunsen burner

Butene

"calamine," from Cadmus (founder of Thebes); discovered 1817; used for electroplating and in alloys. Compounds used in pigments and in color TV tubes.

calcium Element symbol, Ca; alkaline earth metal, group 2; soft silvery white metal; Z 20; A(r) 40.08; density (at 20°C), 1.54 g/cm^3; m.p., 839°C; name derived from the Latin *calx*, "lime;" discovered 1808; used as a reducing agent and as a getter.

calcium carbide *See* calcium dicarbide.

calcium carbonate $CaCO_3$. A white solid that is sparingly soluble in water. It forms calcium oxide and carbon dioxide when heated. Calcium carbonate occurs naturally in marble, limestone, chalk, and calcite. It dissolves in dilute acids (in rainwater that is used as public water supply, this causes temporary hardness). It is a raw material in the Solvay process and is also used in manufacture of lime (CaO), cement, and glass.

calcium chloride $CaCl_2$. This exists as an ionic compound ($Ca_2^+ \, 2Cl^-$). It is nonvolatile and soluble in water. Its aqueous solution is an electrolyte.

calcium dicarbide CaC_2 (calcium carbide, carbide) A colorless solid; r.d., 2.22; m.p., 450°C; b.p., 2,300°C. It is produced industrially by a reaction between coke and calcium oxide (CaO) at a temperature of about 2,000°C in an electric furnace. Ethyne (C_2H_2) is produced when water is added to calcium dicarbide.

calcium hydrogencarbonate $Ca(HCO_3)_2$ (calcium bicarbonate) This is only stable in aqueous solution. It is formed in nature when water containing carbon dioxide (rainwater) attacks rocks containing calcium carbonate. The insoluble calcium carbonate forms soluble calcium hydrogencarbonate. $CaCO_3 + CO_2 + H_2O = Ca(HCO_3)_2$. Calcium hydrogencarbonate forms temporary hardness in water because, when heated, the insoluble carbonate is formed and is precipitated in vessels used to boil water.

calcium hydroxide $Ca(OH)_2$ (slaked lime) A white powder that dissolves sparingly in water. It absorbs carbon dioxide to form calcium carbonate. It is manufactured by adding water to calcium oxide, the process is known as slaking and is highly exothermic. $CaO + H_2O = Ca(OH)_2$.

calcium nitrate $Ca(NO_3)_2$. A white deliquescent compound; r.d., 2.5; m.p., 561°C. It is very soluble in water. It is formed by reacting nitric acid with a calcium salt (oxide, carbonate or hydroxide). The tetrahydrate form ($Ca(NO_3)_2.4H_2O$) can be crystallized from a solution of calcium nitrate. The anhydrous form can be obtained from the hydrate by heating, but it decomposes easily to form calcium oxide,

Rain

Chalk hills | *Streams containing dissolved solids*

Chalk (calcium carbonate) dissolves in rainwater

nitrogen dioxide, and water. It is used as a fertilizer and in the manufacture of explosives and matches.

calcium oxide CaO (quicklime, lime) A white, hygroscopic powder; r.d., 3.5; m.p., 2,600°C; b.p., 2,850°C. It has a giant structure and is formed when calcium carbonate is heated strongly. It becomes incandescent at high temperatures. Calcium oxide is used in the manufacture of calcium hydroxide, as a cheap soil conditioner on acid soils, and in the production of iron ore to remove impurities.

calcium phosphate(V) $Ca(PO_4)_2$. A white insoluble powder; r.d., 3.14. It is found in the mineral apatite and is the main component of animal bones. Calcium dihydrogenphosphate(V) and calcium sulfate are formed when calcium phosphate is treated with sulfuric acid. $Ca(PO_4)_2 + 2H_2SO_4 = Ca(H_2PO_4)_2 + 2CaSO_4$. Superphosphate is the name given to this mixture of calcium dihydrogenphosphate and calcium sulfate. It is an important fertilizer.

calcium silicate $CaSiO_3$. It is formed as a slag in a blast furnace during the extraction of iron from iron ore and is used to make cement.

calcium stearate $Ca(CH_3(CH_2)_{16}COO)_2$. An insoluble solid that is formed on the surface of water when soap has been used in hard water that contains calcium sulfate $(CaSO_4)$.

calcium sulfate $CaSO_4$. A white solid that is sparingly soluble in water (it is a cause of permanent hardness of water). It occurs naturally as anhydrite and (as $CaSO_4.2H_2O$) as gypsum. It is used as a drying agent.

Gypsum, heated at 130°C forms plaster of Paris $(2CaSO_4.H_2O)$.

Anhydrite and gypsum are used in the manufacture of sulfuric acid.

californium Element symbol, Cf; actinide; silver-gray metal; Z 98; A(r) 251; named for California; discovered 1950.

calorific value The energy value of a food or fuel, given by the heat produced when a unit amount (1 g or 1 kg) is completely burnt in oxygen.

calorific value of a gas The heat produced by unit volume of the gas when completely burnt.

cane sugar Sucrose $(C_{12}H_{22}O_{11})$ which is extracted in a solution of hot water from crushed sugar cane.

carbide A compound that contains carbon and an element with lower electronegativity. (Compounds containing carbon and oxygen, sulfur, phosphorus, nitrogen or the halogens are not, therefore, carbides, and nor are compounds containing carbon and hydrogen.) Examples of carbides are calcium dicarbide (CaC_2); silicon carbide (SiC); aluminum carbide (Al_4C_3); boron carbide (B_4C). Carbides are

Test pipette · *Rubber* · *Steam evolved* · *Water* · *Calcium hydroxide powder* · *Crucible* · *Becomes hot*

Calcium oxide

formed by heating the components in an electric furnace. Some carbides are very hard. Carbides formed by elements close to carbon in size are covalent, while those formed by highly electropositive elements are ionic.

carbohydrate One of a large group of organic compounds that contain carbon, hydrogen, and oxygen. They have the general formula $C_x(H_2O)_y$. There are three groups of carbohydrate:

simple sugars (monosaccharides), such as the isomers glucose and fructose ($C_6H_{12}O_6$);

complex sugars (disaccharides), such as the isomers sucrose and maltose ($C_{12}H_{22}O_{11}$);

complex carbohydrates (polysaccharides), such as starch, dextrins, and cellulose. Their formulas are $(C_6H_{10}O_5)n$ where n is a large number.

carbohydrates, tests for For a reducing sugar such as glucose (*see* test for reducing sugar). For starch, add iodine solution. If starch is present, the solution will turn blue-black.

carbolic acid *See* phenol.

carbon Element symbol, C; group 4; three isomers, diamond—clear, crystalline; graphite—black, shiny; buckminsterfullerene; Z 6; A(r) 12.01; density (at 20°C) in g/cm^3, 2.25 (graphite), 3.51 (diamond); m.p., 3,550°C; name derived from the Latin *carbo*, "charcoal;" known since prehistoric times; active carbon used in industry; carbon 14 isotope(^{14}C) is radioactive and is used in radiocarbon dating. Carbon compounds occur widely in nature, in living organisms, and in fossilized hydrocarbons.

carbonate The carbonate ion CO_3^{2-} has a valency of 2. Group 1 metal carbonates are soluble in water, but all others are insoluble. Carbonates produce carbon dioxide when heated strongly or treated with dilute acid. Thus the test for a carbonate is to add acid and test the resulting gas with limewater. If a carbonate is present there will be a milky precipitate.

carbonation The process of dissolving carbon dioxide in a liquid under pressure. Water is carbonated to make soda water and other fizzy drinks.

carbon bonds Carbon forms four covalent bonds that are arranged symmetrically in three dimensions. *See* tetrahedral compound.

carbon cycle The circulation of carbon through the biosphere. Plants use atmospheric carbon dioxide to make food, which is eaten by animals. Breathing, burning, and decay return carbon dioxide to air.

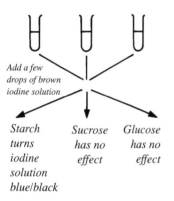

Starch solution   Sucrose solution   Glucose solution

Add a few drops of brown iodine solution

Starch turns iodine solution blue/black   *Sucrose has no effect*   *Glucose has no effect*

Carbohydrate test

carbon dating (radiocarbon dating). The way in which the age of previously living animal or vegetable life can be determined. Carbon is present in the atmosphere and in all living tissue in a mixture (the proportions of which are constant while the tissue is living) of isotopes, one of which, ^{14}C, is radioactive with a half-life of 5,730 years. When the tissue (animal or vegetable) dies, the proportion of ^{14}C decreases as radioactive decay occurs. The age of a sample of dead material can thus be measured by measuring the radioactivity of the sample.

carbon dioxide CO_2. A dense, colorless, odorless gas that does not support combustion; m.p., –56.6, b.p., –78.5. It exists in the atmosphere (0.03%) and is instrumental in the carbon cycle. There is concern that the level of carbon dioxide in the atmosphere is rising and causing global warming (*see* greenhouse effect). Carbon dioxide is soluble in water, forming carbonic acid. Solid carbon dioxide is known as dry ice. To test for the presence of carbon dioxide, pass the gas through limewater; if the gas is carbon dioxide, it forms a white precipitate.

carbonic acid H_2CO_3. A very weak acid formed by dissolving carbon dioxide in water.

carbonization Anaerobic destructive distillation. Coal forms coke in this process; wood forms charcoal.

Air *Carbon dioxide*

Burned candle is extinguished

Carbon dioxide

Carbon dioxide

Laboratory preparation of carbon dioxide

a Marble chips
b Dilute hydrochloric acid
c Carbon dioxide
d Water

a   b   c   d

Reaction: $CaCO_3 + 2HCl = CaCl_2 + H_2O + CO_2$

---

carbon monoxide CO. A colorless, odorless, very poisonous gas; m.p., –199°C; b.p., –191.5°C. It is sparingly soluble in water and burns in air with a blue flame (this is a test for carbon monoxide). Its toxicity is caused by its ability to bond with hemoglobin in the blood, forming carboxyhemoglobin, which is unable to transport oxygen around the body. Carbon monoxide forms carbonyls with metals because it has vacant p-orbitals that are used to form bonds.

carbon tetrachloride *See* tetrachloromethane.

carbonyl group A carbon atom that is attached to an oxygen atom by a double bond and that combines with two other groups of atoms with single bonds.

carboxyl group The organic radical –CO.OH.

carboxylic acid An organic acid that contains one or more carboxyl groups.

carcinogen A substance that can cause cancer.

cast iron Iron obtained from a blast furnace. It contains many impurities, including about 3% of carbon, in addition to phosphorus, silicon, manganese, and sulfur. These impurities make it brittle and it cannot be welded. It is used for objects that are not put under great strain. The Bessemer process and the basic oxygen furnace are two processes of converting cast iron to steel.

Castner-Kellner cell The cell used in the Castner-Kellner process.

Castner-Kellner process The process of electrolysis of brine between graphite anodes and a flowing mercury cathode in a cell.

At the anode the following reactions occur, $2Cl^-_{(aq)} = Cl_{2(g)} + 2e^-$.

At the cathode, $Na^+_{(aq)} + 2e^- = 2Na$.

Followed by Na + mercury = amalgam. This amalgam is mixed with water and enters a second cell where the amalgam reacts with water to form hydrogen and sodium hydroxide solution. The mercury is reused. This process was formerly used for the production of sodium hydroxide, used in the chemical industry, but is now more important for the production of chlorine, which is widely used in the manufacture of plastics.

catalysis The alteration of the rate of a chemical reaction because of the presence of a catalyst.

catalyst A substance that alters the rate of a chemical reaction. It takes part in the reaction but remains chemically unchanged by it. Enzymes are the organic catalysts present in animals and plants.

catalytic converter A component of the exhaust system of a car with a gasoline engine. It uses a catalyst of platinum and rhodium to convert

inlet gases *outlet gases* *catalyst*

Catalytic converter

various waste products of gasoline combustion (carbon monoxide, nitric oxide, and hydrocarbon compounds that have not undergone complete combustion) to carbon dioxide, nitrogen, and nitrous oxide, thus reducing air pollution.

catalytic cracking *See* cracking.

catalytic reforming *See* reforming.

cathode The electrode carrying the negative charge in a solution undergoing electrolysis.

cation An ion having positive charge, which is attracted by the negatively charged electrode, the cathode, during electrolysis.

caustic An alkaline substance that burns or corrodes organic material.

caustic potash The common name for potassium hydroxide (KOH).

caustic soda The common name for sodium hydroxide (NaOH).

Cd Symbol for the element cadmium.

Ce Symbol for the element cerium.

cell A vessel, used either to produce electricity or to perform electrolysis, containing an electrolyte in which are dipped two electrodes. There are three main types of cell:

(1) the primary cell, which produces electricity by chemical action (usually irreversible);

(2) the secondary cell, which can be charged by passing electricity through in a direction opposite to the discharge. This reverses the chemical action that produces electricity.

(3) the electrolytic cell in which electrolysis takes place.

cellulose A complex carbohydrate $(C_6H_{10}O_5)_n$ (*n* is a large number) that is insoluble in water. Cellulose is the main component of the cell walls of plants. Animals can digest cellulose but human beings cannot. Cellulose is used to manufacture paper, cellophane (sheet cellulose manufactured in sheets and used as wrapping material), cellulose ethanoate, and rayon.

cellulose acetate *See* cellulose ethanoate.

cellulose ethanoate (cellulose acetate) A solid flammable substance used in the manufacture of lacquers, magnetic tape, photographic film, and rayon. It is formed by the reaction of cellulose with ethanoic acid using sulfuric acid as catalyst.

Celsius (**C**) A scale of temperature that has 100 divisions between the lower fixed point (the melting point of pure ice) and the upper fixed point (the boiling point of pure water). $1° = 1K$.

Primary cell

Celsius

cement A gray powder that is a mixture of calcium silicate and calcium aluminate made by heating limestone (calcium carbonate) and clay (containing silicon dioxide and aluminum oxide). A corrosive alkaline mixture is produced when cement is mixed with water. Cement is used as a bonding material in building.

centrifuge A machine that rotates an object at high speed. Under the action of centrifugal force, the rate of sedimentation in a suspension is increased, and particles of different densities can be separated.

ceramics Ceramics such as pottery, stoneware, bricks, tiles, and pipes are made by shaping clay (a mixture of silica and hydrated aluminum silicate $Al_2O_3.2SiO_2.2H_2O$) into the required form and then firing it in a kiln. This renders it hard, durable, and resistant to most chemicals. A surface glaze of a glass (sodium or lead silicate) is usually applied to the object, as it would otherwise be porous. Ceramics are good electrical insulators.

cerium Element symbol, Ce; rare earth/lanthanide; Z 58; A(r) 140.12; density (at 20°C), 6.77 g/cm^3; m.p., 799°C; named for the asteroid Ceres; discovered 1803; used in alloys to improve properties of cast iron and magnesium alloys. Compounds used in ceramic coatings.

cesium Element symbol, Cs; alkali metal, group 1; very reactive metal; Z 55; A(r) 132.91; density (at 20°C) 1.88 g/cm^3; m.p. 28.4°C; name derived from the Latin *caesius*, bluish gray; discovered 1860; used as getter in photoelectric cells (removal of oxygen); isotope 137 used in deep-ray therapy.

Cf Symbol for the element californium.

CFC *See* chlorofluorocarbons.

chain length A measure of the number of atoms linked to form a hydrocarbon chain.

chain reaction A reaction where one event leads to a second, and so on. It is often used to describe a nuclear reaction in which energy is released constantly because neutrons emitted by the fission of an atomic nucleus proceed to cause further fissions, which in turn emit more neutrons.

chamber process (lead-chamber process) One of the processes used for sulfuric acid production. Sulfur dioxide, oxygen, and nitrogen dioxide react within a large, lead-sheathed brick tower. Sulfuric acid forms as fine droplets that fall to the base of the tower.

change of state The physical process where matter moves from one state to another. Examples of such changes are melting, evaporation, boiling, condensation, freezing, crystallization, and sublimation. A change of state is associated with energy changes.

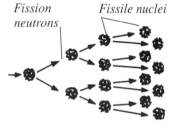

Fission neutrons *Fissile nuclei*

Chain reaction

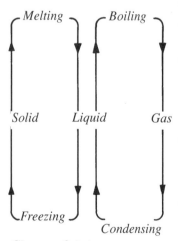

Melting *Boiling*

Solid *Liquid* *Gas*

Freezing *Condensing*

Change of state

charcoal The result of the destructive distillation of wood or animal bones. It consists of carbon and has a very open structure with a very large surface area. Gases are easily adsorbed onto the surface of charcoal.

Charles' law The volume (V) of a fixed mass of gas at constant pressure (P) is dependent on its temperature (T).

chemical compound A substance composed of two or more elements linked by chemical bonds which may be ionic or covalent. The properties of a compound can be very different from the properties of the elements from which it is made.

chemical energy The energy stored in the bonds between atoms and molecules that is released during a chemical reaction.

chemical equation *See* balanced equations.

chemical equilibrium A chemical reaction that reaches a dynamic equilibrium.

chemical reaction The process in which one or more substances reacts to form new substances. During the process, bonds between atoms are broken and formed as at least one of the original substances is changed to another.

chemiluminescence Light radiated during a chemical reaction.

Chile saltpeter A naturally occurring compound containing sodium nitrate ($NaNO_3$) and some sodium iodate ($NaIO_3$). There are large deposits in Chile. It is used as a fertilizer and in nitric acid manufacture.

china clay A white powder composed of complex aluminum salts used in manufacture of pottery and as a filler in textiles and paper. It is also known as kaolin and is a very pure form of clay.

chlorides Compounds containing chlorine and another element. If the element combined with chlorine is a nonmetal, such as carbon or hydrogen, its chloride is a covalent compound and will be either a liquid with a low boiling point or a gas. If the element is a metal, its chloride will be an ionic solid. Silver nitrate is used to test for the presence of a chloride. If a white precipitate is formed on mixing a solution of a compound with silver nitrate solution and the precipitate dissolves in ammonia solution, the compound being tested contains a chloride.

chlorination Term refers to two processes. (1) The use of chlorine to disinfect water used for drinking or in swimming pools. (2) Reactions introducing one or more chlorine atoms into a hydrocarbon structure to form a chlorinated hydrocarbon (*see* halogenation).

chlorine Element symbol, Cl; halogen, group 7; greenish poisonous gas; Z 17; A(r) 35.45; density (at 20°C), 3.214 g/l at STP; m.p., –101°C; powerful oxidizing agent; name derived from the Greek *khloros*,

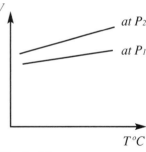

V

at P_2

at P_1

$T°C$

Charles' law

"green;" discovered 1810; used widely in chemical industry in manufacture of chlorinated hydrocarbons; also used in water sterilization and bleaching compounds.

chlorine, isotopes Chlorine has two isotopes. Chlorine-35 contains 18 neutrons and 17 protons in its nucleus; chlorine-37 contains 20 neutrons and 17 protons in its nucleus. Chlorine gas contains approximately three times more chlorine-35 than chlorine-37; this gives chlorine the relative atomic mass of approximately 35.5.

chlorine water A yellow solution made by passing chlorine gas into ice-cold water. The water absorbs about two and a half times its volume of gas. Chlorine water is a mixture of hydrochloric acid (HCl) and hypochlorous acid ($HClO$).

chloroethene C_2H_3Cl (also known as vinyl chloride). A gas with m.p. $-153.8°C$ and b.p. -13.37. It is made by chlorinating ethene to form dichloroethane and then removing hydrogen chloride. It is the monomer from which polychloro(ethene) (formerly polyvinyl chloride or PVC) is made.

chlorofluorocarbons Compounds formed when some or all of the hydrogen atoms in a hydrocarbon (typically an alkane) have been replaced with chlorine and fluorine. They are inert substances that have been used widely as refrigerants and as propellants in aerosol cans. Their use is being discontinued as they have been implicated in the destruction of the ozone layer above the Earth and have contributed to the greenhouse effect.

chloroform *See* trichloromethane.

chlorophyll A green pigment normally found in plant leaves. It traps energy from the Sun, which is used by the plant to form glucose by photosynthesis.

chromatography A way of separating and identifying mixtures of solutes in a solution. The method depends on the affinity of the different solutes in the mixture for the medium through which solution moves.

chromium Element symbol, Cr; transition element; hard silvery white metal; Z 24; A(r) 52; density (at 20°C), 7.2 g/cm^3; m.p., 1,857°C; very resistant to oxidation; name derived from the Greek *khroma*, "color;" discovered 1798; used extensively as a steel additive and for electroplating.

chromophore A group of atoms responsible for the color of a compound—the azo group is a chromophore.

citric acid $C_6H_8O_7$. A white crystalline solid. It is a weak organic acid that contains three carboxyl groups and one hydroxyl group. Citric acid is found in the juice of lemons and some other fruits.

Oxygen

Sunlight

Chlorine water

Chlorine water

Cl Symbol for the element chlorine.

clay A fine-grained deposit formed by weathering of rocks. It is mainly composed of hydrated aluminum silicates and usually contains some impurities, such as iron, calcium, and magnesium oxides. Very pure clay is white (*see* china clay).

Cm Symbol for the element curium.

Co Symbol for the element cobalt.

coagulation The grouping together of small particles in a solution into larger particles. Such a solution eventually coagulates with the particles forming either a precipitate or a gel.

coal A fossil fuel containing (approximate percentages) carbon, 80%; oxygen, 8%; hydrogen, 5%; and sulfur, 1%, with some nitrogen and phosphorus.

coal gas A mixture of hydrogen, methane, and carbon monoxide produced by the destructive distillation of coal.

coal tar One of the products of the destructive distillation of coal. It is a black liquid containing hundreds of organic compounds (such as benzene, toluene, naphthalene, and phenol), which can be separated by fractional distillation. Coal-tar derivatives are important in the manufacture of dyes, drugs, insecticides, and other organic chemicals.

cobalt Element symbol, Co; transition element; silvery white metal; Z 27; A(r) 58.93; density (at 20°C), 8.83 g/cm^3; m.p., 1,495°C; name derived from the German *kobold*, "goblin;" discovered 1735; used in alloys.

cobalt chloride $CoCl_2$. Its anhydrous form is blue and its hydrated form is pink. Anhydrous cobalt chloride is used to test for the presence of water.

coenzyme A small organic nonprotein molecule that acts with an enzyme in many enzyme-catalyzed reactions.

coke The solid residue produced by the destructive distillation of coal.

colloid A substance made of very small particles whose size (1–100 nm) is between those of a suspension and those in solution.

combining mass *See* equivalent mass.

combining power (valency) *See* valency.

combustion The chemical term for burning, usually in oxygen.

common salt *See* sodium chloride.

complex ion A cation formed when an atom or group of atoms (*see* ligand) donate electrons to form coordinate bonds with a metal ion or atom.

Clay

Carbon dioxide up chimney

Blue flames of burning carbon monoxide

Air

Air

Coke

Many complex ions are formed by transition metals because they are able to accept the donated electrons. The ammonium ion (NH_4^+) and the hydroxonium ion (H_3O^+) are also complex ions.

compound *See* chemical compound.

concentration A measure of the quantity of solute dissolved in a solution at a given temperature. Units used are grams of solute per liter of solution, molarity, and percentage.

concrete A mixture of cement with sand and gravel. It sets to a rock-like mass when mixed with water because the silicates and aluminates in the cement form long thread-like crystals when hydrated.

condensation The process by which a liquid forms from its vapor.

condensation polymerization A process by which molecules join together in a series of condensation reactions. When molecules join together in this way, a small molecule (usually water) is eliminated and larger molecules, or macromolecules, are formed that consist of repeated structural units.

condensation reaction The joining together of two or more molecules with the elimination of a small molecule (usually water).

condenser An apparatus in which a vapor is converted to a liquid. In a condenser (Liebig condenser), the tube through which the vapor flows is surrounded by a jacket in which water flows.

conduction (1) (*electrical*) The movement of free electrons from atom to atom in a metallic conductor, which transfers electrical energy. The current (flow of charge per second) depends on the circuit's resistance (Ohm's law). (2) (*thermal*) *see* thermal conduction.

conductor A material that is able to conduct heat and electricity.

conformation A particular three-dimensional shape taken by a molecule. Many shapes are possible, given that part of the molecule can rotate about a single bond.

conjugated structure A structure that has alternate single and double (or triple) bonds between carbon atoms in an organic compound.

conjugate solutions Solutions of two substances that are partially miscible will form two conjugate solutions in equilibrium at a certain temperature.

constant boiling mixture *See* azeotrope.

contact process The industrial process used to manufacture sulfuric acid. It uses iron pyrites.

control experiment (control) An experiment that is performed at the same time as an experiment investigating the operation of a particular

Water to waste

Water in

Condenser

Carbon electrodes

Molten compound

Crucible

Heat

Conduction

Conjugated structure

factor. In the control experiment this factor remains constant in order that the effect of the particular factor may be studied.

coordinate bond *See* bond.

copolymer A polymer formed by the polymerization of more than one monomer.

copper Element symbol, Cu; transition element; pinkish metal; Z 29; A(r) 63.55; density (at 20°C), 8.92 g/cm^3; m.p., 1,083.4°C; brightly colored salts; name derived from the Latin *cuprum*; known from prehistoric times; used widely in alloys (brass, bronze); used in wire and piping; compounds used in pigments, paints, and fungicides.

copper(II) carbonate Its formula is $CuCO_3$, but it is unknown in this state. It occurs as $CuCO_3.Cu(OH)_2$, a green insoluble solid. It is soluble in both dilute acids and ammonia solution. It decomposes to form copper oxide, carbon dioxide, and water vapor when heated.

copper(II) hydroxide $Cu(OH)_2$. A blue-green insoluble gelatinous base that decomposes to form copper(II) oxide and water vapor when heated. It is formed by the action of an aqueous solution of a copper(II) salt with sodium hydroxide.

copper(II) nitrate $Cu(NO_3)_2$. (Usually, $Cu(NO_3)_2.3H_2O$). A blue, deliquescent soluble salt that decomposes to form copper(II) oxide, nitrogen dioxide, and oxygen when heated.

copper(II) sulfate $CuSO_4.5H_2O$. A blue, soluble salt that can be formed by the action of hot concentrated sulfuric acid on copper $Cu + 2H_2SO_4 = CuSO_4 + SO_2 + 2H_2O$ or by the reaction between copper(II) oxide and dilute sulfuric acid. $CuO + H_2SO_4 = CuSO_4 + H_2O$. Copper(II) sulfate is used as a wood preservative and as a fungicide and insecticide for plant diseases (in Bordeaux mixture). Anhydrous copper sulfate is white and can be used to test for the presence of water, when it turns blue.

copper chlorides CuCl (copper(I) chloride) A white insoluble solid that is formed by boiling copper with copper(II) chloride solution and concentrated hydrochloric acid. The solution is then poured into water.

$CuCl_2$ (copper(II) chloride) An anhydrous soluble brown solid. A concentrated aqueous solution of copper(II) chloride is brown. The color of the solution changes to green ($CuCl_2.2H_2O$), then blue as more water is added.

copper oxides (1) Cu_2O (copper(I) oxide). An insoluble red solid that is made by reducing copper(II) sulfate solution. (2) CuO_2 (copper(II) oxide) An insoluble black solid obtained by heating $Cu(NO_3)_2$.

copper plating To plate an item with copper, it should be thoroughly cleaned, then immersed in a solution of copper sulfate solution. A copper rod

Copper rod is the anode

DC supply

Object to be plated is the cathode

Solution of copper sulfate

Copper plating

is also placed in the solution, and the item to be plated is connected to an electrical source together with the copper rod (the copper rod being the anode and the item to be plated the cathode). If the item is rotated in the solution while a small current flows, it will be coated evenly with copper.

copper pyrites The copper ore $CuFeS_2$. To extract copper, the ore is roasted in air to form a molten mixture of copper(I) sulfide and iron(II) oxide. This is heated with sand, and the iron(II) oxide forms a silicate slag. Some of the copper(I) sulfide forms copper(I) oxide and this reacts with the remaining copper(I) sulfide to form copper.

core charge In a molecule having covalent bonds, such as water, where the oxygen nucleus is more massive than the hydrogen nucleus, electrons in the shared pairs are closer to the oxygen nucleus because of its larger attractive charge than the electrons in the lone pairs.

corrosion The process by which the surface of a metal turns from being an element to being a compound and is thus gradually destroyed. For example, iron corrodes to form rust (hydrated iron oxide) and the surface of copper becomes green when exposed to the atmosphere. *See* electrical protection, sacrificial protection.

covalency The number of covalent bonds an atom is able to make when forming a molecule.

covalent bond *See* bond.

covalent compounds Compounds consisting of molecules where the atoms in the molecules are held together by covalent bonds. They are liquids and gases with low melting and boiling points.

covalent network (covalent crystal) A structure in which millions of atoms are linked by single covalent bonds. Such structures have high melting and boiling points.

Cr Symbol for the element chromium.

cracking The process used in the petroleum industry to convert large-chain hydrocarbon molecules to smaller ones. The process uses heat and catalysts.

cream of tartar $C_4H_5O_6K$ (Potassium hydrogen tartarate) A white crystalline solid used in baking powder and medicine.

cross-linking Chemical bonds between adjacent polymer molecules.

crude oil or **petroleum** A mixture of solid, liquid, and gaseous hydrocarbons. It tends to be a thick black liquid that has to be converted to useful products by refining. The different components are separated by fractional distillation, and larger molecules are split into more useful smaller ones by cracking.

Covalent network structure

Cross-linking

cryoscopic constant A constant used in the calculation of freezing-point depression.

crystal A substance with an orderly arrangement of atoms, ions, or molecules in a regular geometrical shape. *See* crystal structure.

crystallization The process of forming crystals from a solution which is concentrated above its saturation point (supersaturated) at a certain temperature.

crystallization, water of *See* water of crystallization.

crystal structure The orderly geometric arrangement, or lattice, of atoms, molecules, or ions in a structure that has a particular regular three-dimensional structure. There are several basic shapes taken by a crystal lattice, depending on the component particles. Shapes can be cubic, tetragonal, rhombic, hexagonal, trigonal, monoclinic, or triclinic. In addition, they can have close-packed structures, in which the shape is said to be face-centered, or more loosely packed, in which case the shape is body-centered.

Cs Symbol for the element cesium.

Cu Symbol for the element copper.

curium Element symbol, Cm; actinide; silvery metal; Z 96; A(r) 247; density (at 20°C), 13.5 (est.) g/cm^3; m.p., 1,340°C; rapidly oxidized; named in honor of the scientists Marie and Pierre Curie; discovered 1944.

cyanides Compounds derived from hydrocyanic acid containing the –CN group or the CN$^-$ ion. They are very poisonous.

cycloalkanes Homologous series with the formula C_nH_{2n}. Cycloalkanes have a ring structure and are saturated (they contain no double bonds).

Dacron A polyester fiber made by condensation polymerization between ethane-1,2-diol (ethylene glycol) and the aromatic acid benzene-1,4-dicarboxylic acid (terephthalic acid) $C_6H_4(COOH)_2$. It is used widely in the manufacture of textile fibers, and its texture is similar to that of wool.

Dalton's atomic theory John Dalton, an English schoolmaster, was the first person to formulate a theory of matter. In 1808 he made the following assertions. Matter consists of atoms, which are tiny indivisible particles. Atoms cannot be created or destroyed. The atoms of one element are all identical, particularly in mass, and are different from atoms of other elements. "Compound atoms" (now called molecules) are formed when small numbers of atoms combine chemically. "Compound atoms" within a compound are identical and differ from those of other compounds. Modern atomic theory has superseded this theory.

Cubic

Octahedral

Tetrahedral

Crystal structure

Copper sulfate solution

Zinc rod

Zinc sulfate solution

Copper vessel / *Porous pot*

Daniell cell

Dalton's law of partial pressure For a mixture of gases at constant temperature, the total pressure is equal to the sum of the individual pressures (partial pressures) each gas would exert if it were the only gas present in the volume occupied by the entire mixture.

Daniell cell A primary cell where a zinc rod (the negative electrode) is immersed in a saturated solution of either zinc sulfate or dilute sulfuric acid contained within a porous pot. This pot is immersed in a solution of copper(II) sulfate, contained in a copper vessel, which forms the positive electrode. The cell produces an e.m.f. of 1.1 volts.

darmstadtium Element symbol, Ds; transition element; Z 110; A(r) 271; name derived from the city of Darmstadt, Germany, where the element was discovered in 1994.

Db Symbol for the element dubnium.

DDT $(C_6H_4Cl)_2CHCCl_3$ (dichlorodiphenyltrichloroethane) It is a double cyclic organic compound that is insoluble in water. It is a very powerful insecticide and has been successful in controlling malaria. Its use is now restricted as it is not biodegradable and it concentrates in the fatty tissue of animals, where it acts as a poison.

decomposition The process of breakdown of a chemical compound into less complex substances.

dehydrating agent A substance that has an attraction for water and is therefore used as a drying agent. Dehydrating agents can be of different types—a liquid such as concentrated sulfuric acid, a compound such as calcium oxide, which reacts with water to form calcium hydroxide, or an anhydrous salt, which absorbs water.

dehydration A chemical reaction to remove a water molecule from a compound.

dehydrogenation The chemical process of removal of hydrogen atoms from a molecule (a form of oxidation), increasing its degree of unsaturation. For example, the dehydrogenation of ethanol (C_2H_5OH) produces ethanal (CH_3CHO).

deliquescence The way in which a solid substance absorbs water from the atmosphere. The process can continue until the substance passes into solution.

delocalized electron Each atom in a metal has one or more outer electrons that are free to move between atoms. These are delocalized electrons.

depression of freezing point The reduction of the freezing point of a pure liquid when a substance is dissolved in it. The amount of reduction is proportional to the quantity of substance dissolved and not on the type of molecule. The reduction of freezing point ($\Delta t = K_f C_M$ [C_M is the molar concentration of dissolved solute] K_f is the cryoscopic constant).

desiccator A container used to dry and to keep substances dry. It is made of glass or plastic with a close-fitting lid. The substance to be dried is placed on a perforated plate above a dehydrating agent (often silica gel in the laboratory). It can have a tap to remove air.

Desiccator

desorption *See* adsorption.

destructive distillation The process of breaking down complex organic substances into a mixture of volatile products in the absence of air. These are condensed and collected.

destructive distillation of coal The products are coke, ammonia liquor, coal tar, and coal gas.

desulfurization Removal of sulfur, using hydrogen and a catalyst, from fossil fuels to prevent the release of sulfur dioxide when the fuel is burnt.

detergent The term is usually used for a synthetic soap substitute. Detergents lower the surface tension of water (*see* surfactant), allowing the thorough wetting of objects. They emulsify oils and fats. An emulsion is formed because one end of the detergent molecule is hydrophilic and is attracted to water, the other end, the hydrocarbon chain, is hydrophobic and is attracted to the oil or fat molecules. The oil or fat is thus broken up into small particles and forms an emulsion. The calcium and magnesium salts of detergents are soluble in water and hence do not form a scum. Detergents are made from petroleum.

Lumps of coal (or wood)

Heat

Gas

Cold water

Ammonia liquor

Tar

Destructive distillation

deuterium An isotope of hydrogen. Its nucleus contains one proton and one neutron and thus has a relative atomic mass of two.

di- A prefix meaning "two."

diamond Naturally occurring transparent, colorless crystalline allotrope of carbon. It is very hard (10 on Mohs' scale). Artificial diamonds are manufactured from graphite (another allotrope of carbon) using intense heat and pressure.

Diamond

diaphragm cell An alternative to the Castner-Kellner method of producing chlorine and sodium hydroxide from brine. In the cell, the anode (a ring of graphite rods) is separated from the cathode (an iron gauze cylinder) by a diaphragm of porous asbestos. Brine passes from the anode, through the diaphragm to the cathode.

Anode reaction $2Cl^- 2e^- \rightarrow Cl_2$.

Cathode reaction $2H_2O + 2e^- \rightarrow 2OH^- + H_2$. Chlorine gas is released at the anode and hydrogen gas at the cathode where hydroxide ions are also formed.

diatomic molecule A molecule that consists of two like (H_2) or unlike (HCl) atoms.

dibasic acid An acid that has two replaceable hydrogen atoms. A dibasic acid can form both a normal salt (if both hydrogen atoms are replaced) and an acid salt (if only one hydrogen atom is replaced). *See* basicity of acids.

1,2-dibromoethane $BrCH_2.CH_2Br$ (ethylene dibromide) A colorless liquid with a sweet odor; m.p., 10°C; b.p., 132°C. It is used widely in gasoline as an antiknock additive (it combines with the lead from lead tetraethyl).

diesel fuel (diesel oil, gas oil, DERV [diesel engine road vehicle]) A petroleum fuel consisting of alkanes with a chain length of 14–20 in the boiling range 200–350°C. It is used in diesel engines where it is mixed with air and compressed. This mixture explodes.

diffusion The process of rapid random movement of the particles of a liquid or gas that eventually form a uniform mixture.

dilute solution A solution containing a low concentration of solute. To increase dilution, more solvent is added to the solution.

dimer A compound formed by the combination of two identical molecules (monomers). The resulting compound can contain exactly twice the atoms of the monomer. This is addition dimerization. If another molecule (such as water) is formed when two monomers combine to form a dimer, this is condensation dimerization.

Dimer (of NO_2)

dimorphism A substance having two crystal forms.

dinitrogen oxide N_2O (nitrous oxide) (dinitrogen monoxide) A colorless gas with a pleasant smell; m.p., –90.8°C; b.p., –88.5°C. It is moderately soluble in water, forming a neutral solution. It decomposes above 600°C, forming a mixture of nitrogen and oxygen (one-third oxygen by volume). Dinitrogen oxide is used as a mild anesthetic (laughing gas) in dental and other minor operations and as an aerosol propellant.

dinitrogen tetroxide N_2O_4. A colorless solid that melts at 9°C, forming a yellow liquid whose boiling point is 22°C, at which point a brown vapor of nitrogen dioxide (NO_2) is formed.

dipeptide Two amino acids linked by a peptide bond.

disaccharide A sugar molecule formed by a condensation reaction between two monosaccharide molecules (a water molecule is eliminated). Sucrose (a disaccharide) is formed from a molecule of glucose (a monosaccharide) and a molecule of fructose (a monosaccharide) by a condensation reaction. *See* carbohydrate.

HOCH₂   *HOCH₂*

Disaccharide   *HOH*

displacement reaction A metal rod is placed in a solution of a metal salt. The metal rod consists of an element lower in the electrochemical series than the metal ions in solution. The rod will become coated with the ions in solution, and some of the atoms from the metal rod will go into solution as ions. This is a displacement reaction: the ions in the original solution displace the ions in the rod.

dissociation The breaking down of a molecule into smaller molecules, atoms or ions. *See* strengths of acids and bases.

dissolve To add a solute to a solvent to form a uniform solution.

distillation A process in which a solution (or a mixture of liquids whose boiling points are widely differing) is heated to a particular temperature to produce a vapor. This vapor is condensed, forming a pure liquid that has a single boiling point.

Displacement reaction

Distillation

Simple distillation when boiling points are widely separated

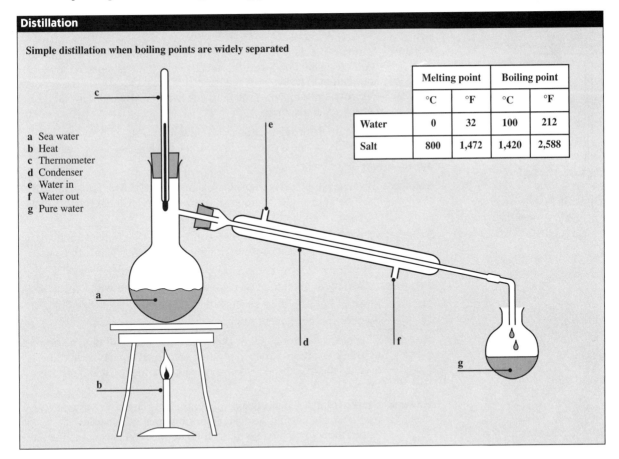

a Sea water
b Heat
c Thermometer
d Condenser
e Water in
f Water out
g Pure water

	Melting point		Boiling point	
	°C	°F	°C	°F
Water	0	32	100	212
Salt	800	1,472	1,420	2,588

d orbitals

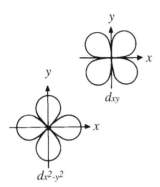

Dry cell

Metal terminal

Sealing material

Steel case

Zinc cup

Carbon rod

Powdered carbon and manganese oxide

Ammonium chloride jelly

divalent Having a valency of two.

d orbital A type of orbital; five types are possible. Each type of d orbital can hold two electrons.

double bond *See* bond, multiple bonds.

double decomposition (metathesis) A chemical reaction between two solutions of ionic salts where an insoluble solid is precipitated. For example, if silver nitrate solution is added to sodium chloride solution, a precipitate of silver chloride is formed. $AgNO_3(aq) + NaCl(aq) \rightarrow AgCl (s) + NaNO_3 (aq)$. Some insoluble salts are produced in this way.

Downs cell Chlorine is extracted by electrolysis of molten sodium chloride in a Downs cell. There is a central graphite anode and a cylindrical steel cathode. Chlorine is collected in a hood over the anode.

Dow process Extraction of magnesium from sea water. Magnesium hydroxide is precipitated by adding slaked lime.

dry cell A form of Leclanché cell where the ammonium chloride solution in the zinc casing that forms the negative electrode is replaced by ammonium chloride jelly and the cell is sealed to prevent the electrolyte drying out. (The individual chemicals used may vary between manufacturers.)

dry ice Solid carbon dioxide. Carbon dioxide solidifies at –78.5°C. Dry ice turns directly into a gas (sublimes) if it is heated above this temperature.

drying agent *See* dehydrating agent.

dubnium Element symbol, Db; transition element; Z 105; A(r) 262; named for the Dubna Institute, Moscow; discovered 1967. (Formerly known as hahnium, then unnilpentium.)

Dulong and Petit's law The product of a solid element's relative atomic mass and its specific heat capacity is approximately 6.4. This can be used to find a solid's valency if its equivalent mass has been determined.

duralumin An alloy of aluminum containing 95% aluminum with copper and magnesium. It is much stronger than pure aluminum.

Dy Symbol for the element dysprosium.

dyes Chemicals, either natural or synthetic (and usually of organic origin), used to color fabrics, paper, plastics, etc. Dyed objects have color because the dye absorbs some of the light falling on it and reflects the rest.

dynamic equilibrium A balanced state of continual change in a system. A reversible chemical reaction may reach a state of dynamic equilibrium when the rate of the forward reaction is equal to the rate of the backward reaction.

dynamite Nitroglycerine (unstable in handling) mixed with a type of clay to produce a stick of dynamite, which is safe to handle and explodes only if detonated.

dysprosium Element symbol, Dy; rare earth element/lanthanide; Z 66; A(r) 162.5; density (at 20°C), 8.55 g/cm^3; m.p., 1,412°C; name derived from the Greek *dysprositos*, "hard to get at;" discovered 1886; compounds used in lasers.

effervescence The production of bubbles of gas or air that rise to the surface in a liquid.

efflorescence The way in which a hydrated crystal loses water of crystallization to the atmosphere, making its surface become powdery.

effusion The process by which a gas under pressure moves through a small aperture into a region of lower pressure (*see* Graham's law).

einsteinium Element symbol, Es; actinide; Z 99; A(r) 254; named in honor of Albert Einstein; discovered 1952.

elastomer A substance that can stretch and return to its former shape.

electrical protection Protection of a metal surface against corrosion. A metal loses electrons when it corrodes. If the metal surface is connected to the negative terminal of a direct source of electricity, electrons are supplied to it and corrosion of the surface is inhibited. The bodies of cars and trucks are connected to the negative terminal of the battery to give them some electrical protection.

electrochemical series (electromagnetic series, displacement series, electromotive series) Metallic elements arranged in order of increasing electrode potential (or readiness to release electrons and form cations). The highest elements in the table are the most reactive or electropositive (the most likely to release electrons and form cations).

The series can be used to predict reactions between metals by comparing their positions in the series (*see* displacement reaction).

The values assigned to the elements in the series (large negative values at the top of the table) can be used to calculate the voltage of a cell consisting of two different metal electrodes with an electrolyte between them by using the values of the two metals. The highest voltages are attained when there is a large gap between the two elements in the table.

electrode A conductor that allows current to flow through an electrolyte, gas, vacuum, dielectric, or semiconductor.

electrolysis The process by which an electrolyte is decomposed when a direct current is passed through it between electrodes. Positive cations

Platinum anode receives electrons

+ve   – ve

Cathode loses electrons

Solution of CuCI$_2$

Electrolysis

move to the cathode to gain electrons, negative anions move to the anode to lose electrons. Substances are either deposited or liberated at the electrodes depending on the nature of the electrodes and electrolyte.

electrolysis of brine *See* Castner-Kellner cell.

electrolyte A substance that forms ions when molten or dissolved in a solvent and that carries an electric current during electrolysis. Strong electrolytes contains many ions.

electromotive series *See* electrochemical series.

electron One of the three basic subatomic particles. It is very light (its mass is 9.109×10^{-31} kg) and orbits round the nucleus of an atom. It has a negative charge, and in neutral atoms the number of electrons is equal to the number of protons in the nucleus.

electron arrangements *See* electronic structure of atom.

electronegativity A measure of the ease with which an atom can attract electrons. Group 7 of the periodic table contains electronegative elements, fluorine being the most electronegative.

electronic structure of atom (electronic configuration). This gives an indication of the position of electrons around the nucleus of an atom and is useful in showing how the element forms bonds. Electrons are arranged in shells around a nucleus. Each shell can contain a maximum number of electrons, depending on the number of orbitals in the shell (each orbital can contain two electrons). The further from the nucleus a shell is, the more orbitals it can contain. The first shell can contain up to two electrons (in one s orbital), the second up to eight (in one s and three p orbitals), the third up to 18 (in one s, three p and five d orbitals), and the fourth up to 32 (in one s, three p, five d and seven f orbitals). The *nth* shell contains 2^{-2} orbitals.

In the periodic table, elements are arranged in order of increasing atomic number (number of electrons). The shells of electrons around the nucleus of each atom are filled in turn; the Aufbau principle governs the order in which the orbitals are filled. The shell closest to the nucleus is filled first, as it has the lowest energy level. The degree to which these shells are full affects the properties of the element. Elements that have a full outer shell tend to be more stable (the noble gases have a full outer shell). The electronic configuration of each element can be represented. For example, in group 1 of the periodic table (the alkali metal group), lithium is represented as 2.1 (the first shell is full and there is one electron in the second shell); sodium can be represented as 2.8.1 (the first and second shells are full and there is one electron in the third shell). Group 1 elements have an electronic configuration ending in 1, group 2 elements 2, etc.

electrophoresis (cataphoresis) The movement of charged particles, colloidal particles or ions through a fluid under the influence of an electric field. It is a method of analyzing protein mixtures and it can be done using specially prepared paper or on a glass slide coated in a gel.

electroplating Electrolytic coating of a metal with a less reactive one. The metal to be plated is used as the cathode in an electrolyte containing ions of the metal that is used for the plating. These ions are deposited firmly on the surface of the cathode.

electropositivity A measure of the ease with which an atom loses electrons. Elements from group 1 of the periodic table are all very electropositive.

electrovalent bond *See* bond.

element A substance that cannot be split into simpler substances using chemical methods. An element contains atoms that have the same numbers of protons and electrons (the numbers of neutrons may vary between atoms of an element). Over one hundred and ten elements have been discovered, although only 92 occur naturally.

elementary particles The particles from which atoms are made. Neutrons and protons are found in the nucleus of the atom. Electrons form a cloud around the nucleus. *See* fundamental particles.

element, families of Elements in the same group of the periodic table have similar properties—they have the same number of electrons in their outer shell.

elimination reaction A chemical reaction in which an organic molecule loses certain atoms and a double or triple bond is formed. For example, a water molecule can be removed from a molecule of ethanol (using sulfuric acid) leaving a molecule of ethene.

empirical formula The simplest ratio of atoms in a compound.

emulsifier A substance that both assists the formation of an emulsion and stabilizes it when formed.

emulsion A colloidal dispersion of small droplets of one liquid dispersed within another, such as oil in water or water in oil.

enantiotropy The transformation of one allotrope, or form, of a substance into another by a change in temperature. Such a change is reversible.

endothermic change A chemical reaction that absorbs heat from the surroundings.

end point The point at which a reaction is complete. The end point of a titration is the point at which one of the reactants has been completely used and it can be seen using an indicator.

energy change *See* exothermic change, endothermic change, enthalpy.

Nickel electrode

Copper object

Solution containing Ni^{2+} (aq) ions

Electroplating

Water *Oil*

Cloudy mixture forming emulsion when shaken

When left to stand the liquids separate

Emulsion

energy-level *See* electronic structure of atom.

energy-level diagrams These show the energy levels of reactants and products of a chemical reaction. They can be used to show changes in enthalpy.

enol A type of organic compound containing a hydroxyl group adjacent to a carbon atom that also has a double bond.

enthalpy A measure of the stored heat energy of a substance. During a chemical reaction, change in enthalpy can be measured. If energy is released (ΔH is negative), the reaction is exothermic; if energy is absorbed (ΔH is positive), the reaction is endothermic. $H = U + pV$, where H is the enthalpy, U the internal energy of the system, p its pressure, and V its volume.

Enzyme action

enzyme An organic catalyst made of proteins. They are produced by living cells and increase the rate of a specific biochemical reaction. Enzymes can be manufactured using microorganisms or animals and plants, and are used in industrial processes.

Epsom salts *See* magnesium sulfate.

equation *See* balanced equation, ion–electron equation, ionic equation, word equation.

equilibrium The state of a reversible chemical reaction where the forward and backward reactions take place at the same rate (i.e. equilibrium is reached when there is no apparent change in the amounts of reactants and products with time).

equilibrium constant *See* law of mass action.

equivalent mass (equivalent mass or combining mass) The mass of an element or compound that will combine with or replace 8 g of oxygen (or 1 g of hydrogen or 35.5 g of chlorine) in a chemical reaction. For an element, it is the element's relative atomic mass divided by its valency.

equivalent weight of acid An alternative to using molarities in calculations of acid/alkali titrations. The mass (in grams) of an acid that can produce 1.008 g of hydrogen ions when dissolved in water is its equivalent weight.

equivalent weight of base The mass (in grams) of an alkali which reacts with the equivalent weight of an acid.

Er Symbol for the element erbium.

erbium Element symbol, Er; rare earth element/lanthanide; Z 68; A(r) 167.26; density (at 20°C), 9.07 g/cm³; m.p., 1,529°C; named for Ytterby, a town in Sweden; discovered 1843; oxide is used in glass manufacture.

Es   Symbol for the element einsteinium.

esterification The formation of an ester formed by the reaction of an organic acid and an alcohol.

esters   A group of hydrocarbons that are formed by a reaction between a carboxylic acid and an alcohol. Esters are used in flavorings and perfumes because they have a sweet fruity smell.

ethanal CH_3CHO (acetaldehyde) A colorless liquid; b.p., 20.8°C. It is soluble in water.

ethane C_2H_6. An alkane. A colorless flammable saturated gas; m.p., −183°C; b.p., −89°C. It occurs in natural gas.

ethane-1,2-diol CH_2OHCH_2OH (ethylene glycol) A dihydric alcohol. A colorless, water-soluble, viscous hygroscopic liquid; m.p., −13°C; b.p., 197°C. It is used as antifreeze and in the manufacture of polyesters.

ethanoic acid CH_3COOH (acetic acid) A weak organic acid. Its salts are ethanoates (acetates).

ethanol C_2H_5OH (ethylalchol) An alkanol. A volatile, colorless water-soluble liquid; m.p., −117°C; b.p., 78.5°C. It is manufactured by the fermentation of certain carbohydrates in the alcoholic drinks industry. Industrial ethanol is manufactured by the hydrolysis of ethane. It is used as a solvent.

ethanoyl group The organic group CH_3CO-.

ethene C_2H_4 (ethylene). An alkene. A colorless flammable unsaturated gas; m.p., −169°C; b.p., −102°C. It is manufactured by cracking petroleum gas, and it is used in ethanol and poly(ethene) production.

ethers   A group of organic compounds containing the group –O–. They are volatile liquids with a pleasant smell and they are insoluble in water but soluble in alcohol. Diethyl ether ($C_2H_5OC_2H_5$) is the simplest ether and is known as *ether*. It was formerly used as an anesthetic and is now used as a solvent.

ethoxyl group –O.C_3H_5.

ethyl acetate *See* ethyl ethanoate.

ethyl alcohol *See* ethanol.

ethylene *See* ethene.

ethylene dibromide *See* 1,2–dibromoethane.

ethylene glycol *See* ethane-1,2-diol.

ethyl ethanoate $CH_3COOC_2H_5$. A sweet-smelling ester produced by the reaction between ethanoic acid and ethanol. It is used in glues and paint as a solvent.

Ethanal

Ethanol

Ethene

H−C≡C−H

Ethyne

Some molecules have enough energy to escape

Molecules moving at different speeds in the liquid

Evaporation

Energy

Reactants

ΔE

Products

Exothermic

ethyl group or **radical** $C_2H_5^-$. It is present in many organic compounds.

ethyne C_2H_2 (acetylene) An alkyne. A colorless flammable unsaturated (contains a triple bond between the carbon atoms) gas; m.p., −82°C, b.p., −84°C. It was formerly made by the action of water on calcium carbide and is now made from cracking petroleum products. When combined with oxygen and burnt, high temperatures (3,000°C) are reached; this mixture is used in the oxyacetylene torch for cutting and welding metals.

Eu Symbol for the element europium.

europium Element symbol, Eu; rare earth element/lanthanide; Z 63; A(r) 151.96; density (at 20°C), 5.24 g/cm^3; m.p., 822°C; named for the continent of Europe; discovered 1901; used as neutron absorber in nuclear reactor and compounds used in color televisions.

eutectic alloy An alloy consisting of at least two metals in proportions that gives the lowest melting point of any composition of the metals.

eutectic mixture A mixture of two or more substances that melts at the lowest freezing point of any mixture of the components. This temperature is the eutectic point. The liquid melt has the same composition as the solid.

eutrophic Containing too many nutrients. If land has been overfertilized, water running over it will carry large amounts of nitrates and phosphates into rivers and lakes. These nutrients cause rapid growth of weeds, which choke the water, removing oxygen and preventing sunlight from penetrating to the lower levels of the water. This affects the ability of the river or lake to support animal and plant life and it is said to be suffering from eutrophication.

evaporation The process in which a liquid changes state to vapor. It can occur at any temperature up to the boiling point of the liquid. An evaporator is a system in which evaporation can take place.

exothermic changes A chemical reaction that releases heat to the surroundings.

F Symbol for the element fluorine.

Faraday constant The amount of electricity needed to liberate one mole of a monovalent ion during electrolysis ($9.648\ 670 \times 10^{-4}$ C mol^{-1}).

Faraday's laws of electrolysis (1) The amount of chemical change (or mass of a substance liberated at an electrode) produced by a current is proportional to the quantity of electricity passed. (2) The quantities of different substances deposited or liberated by a given quantity of electricity are in the ratio of their chemical equivalent weights.

fat (lipid) The general name for mixtures of triglycerides (*see* glycerides) of fatty acids. They have a melting point above room temperature.

fatty acid (alkanoic acid) The general formula is $C_nH_{2n+1}COOH$. A fatty acid is a straight chain saturated or unsaturated monocarboxylic acid (having one carboxyl group). The higher (longer-chain) fatty acids occur in nature and combine with glycerol to form esters such as oils and fats.

Fe Symbol for the element iron.

Fehling's solution An aqueous solution prepared by mixing copper(II) sulfate ($CuSO_4$) solution with an alkaline solution of potassium sodium tartarate sodium hydroxide. It is used to test for estimating and detecting reducing sugars.

Fehling's test If a mixture of an aqueous solution of a reducing sugar and Fehling's solution is boiled, a brick red precipitate of copper (I) oxide confirms that the solution contained a reducing sugar.

fermium Element symbol, Fm; actinide; Z 100; A(r) 257; very radioactive; named in honor of Enrico Fermi; discovered 1952.

ferroxyl indicator A pale yellow solution that turns blue in the presence of Fe^{2+} ions. It is used to test for rust.

fertilizers Natural (farmyard manure, compost) or synthetic substances (such as ammonium nitrate and superphosphate) added to the soil to replace nutrients used by crops. Synthetic fertilizers are manufactured to contain the elements nitrogen, phosphorus, and potassium, which are required by plants.

film Any thin layer of a substance.

filter A device, containing a porous material such as paper or sand, that removes suspended solid particles from a fluid.

filtrate Clear liquid that has passed through a filter.

fire-damp Common name for methane found in coal mines.

fire extinguisher Carbon dioxide is used in fire extinguishers as it does not support burning and therefore smothers a fire. Some fire extinguishers contain an acid and sodium carbonate (or sodium hydrogen carbonate), and when these reactants mix, carbon dioxide is produced. Alternatively, a fire extinguisher can contain pressurized carbon dioxide.

fission A process (spontaneous or induced) during which a heavy atomic nucleus disintegrates into two lighter atoms that together have less mass than the total initial material. This lost mass is converted to energy, the amount of which is given by Einstein's equation $E = mc^2$.

flame A burning mass of gas that gives out heat and light energy.

Sulfuric acid

Sodium hydrogen-carbonate solution

Fire extinguisher

flame test This test allows salts containing metal ions to be identified, due to the observation that the presence of certain metal ions causes a coloration in a flame in which these ions are burnt.

In order to test a solution, a clean nichrome or platinum wire is bent and cleaned. This is done by dipping it into concentrated hydrochloric acid, putting it in the hottest part of a Bunsen flame until it no longer colors the flame, and dipping it into concentrated hydrochloric acid again. The wire is then dipped into a sample of the solid to be tested and placed in the flame.

If the flame burns yellow/orange, the sample contains sodium ions; lilac denotes potassium ions; brick red denotes calcium; apple green denotes barium; green/blue denotes copper; bright red denotes lithium; red denotes strontium.

flocculation The grouping together of colloidal particles to form a precipitate that may float in the liquid.

fluid A substance that can flow because its particles are not fixed in position. Liquids and gases are fluids.

fluorescence The emission of light from an object that has been irradiated by light or other radiations. Energy is absorbed by the object and then re-radiated at a longer wavelength than the incident light.

fluoridation Very small amounts of fluorides (1 part per million of fluoride ions) added to drinking water to prevent dental disease.

fluorine Element symbol, F; halogen, group 7; very reactive gas; Z 9; A(r) 19; density (at 20°C), 1.696 g/l at STP; m.p., −219.6°C; name derived from the Latin *fluere*, also fluorspar; discovered 1886; used in manufacture of plastics and toothpaste and in water treatment.

flux A substance that combines with another substance (usually an oxide) forming a compound with a lower melting point than the oxide.

Fm Symbol for the element fermium.

foam A dispersion of gas in a liquid or solid. Small bubbles of gas are separated by thin films of the liquid or solid.

f orbital A type of orbital, of which seven types are possible, each of which can hold two electrons.

formaldehyde *See* methanal.

formalin A solution of methanal in water. It is used as a preservative.

formic acid *See* methanoic acid.

formula (often used to refer to the molecular formula) A way in which the composition of a chemical compound may be represented using symbols to represent the atoms present. *See* empirical formula, full structural formula, general formula, molecular formula, perspective formula, shortened structural formula, simple formula.

formula mass The relative molecular mass of a compound calculated using its molecular formula. It is also the mass of a mole of the substance.

fossil fuel Coal, oil, and natural gas are fossil fuels. Coal was formed about two hundred million years ago by the bacterial decomposition of plants, such as large tree ferns and giant reeds, followed by exposure to heat and pressure. Oil and natural gas were formed in the oceans millions of years ago from microscopic plants and animals that sank to the bottom of the sea. They were covered with layers of sand and other materials that subjected them to pressure and helped to turn them into oil and gas.

fountain experiment Demonstration of the solubility of ammonia. If a large dry flask full of ammonia, closed with a stopper and containing a glass tube, is inverted in a tall jar of water colored with red litmus solution, the ammonia in the glass tube dissolves and the water rises up the tube. When a drop of water reaches the flask, it dissolves most of the ammonia, leaving a partial vacuum in the flask. Water from the jar is forced up the glass tube by atmospheric pressure, fountaining into the flask. The water turns blue on entering the flask because of the presence of the dissolved ammonia.

Fr Symbol for the element francium.

fractional distillation The separation of a mixture of liquids that have differing but similar boiling points. The fractionating column allows the separate liquids (or fractions) to be collected at different temperatures. The temperature is higher in the lower regions of the fractionating column, which is where the less volatile compounds condense and are removed. The more volatile compounds progress up the column to condense at lower temperatures. (*See also* illustration on page 54.)

fractional distillation of oil The use of fractional distillation to separate oil into different fractions.

The least volatile compound (the residue with a boiling point above 400°C) is bitumen; it is used for road surfaces and roofing material.

Heavy oil is collected in the boiling range 350–400°C; it is used for lubricating oil, fuel oil for furnaces, Vaseline, and paraffin wax.

Gas oil and diesel oil are collected in the boiling range 250–350°C and they are used as fuel.

Kerosene (paraffin oil or naphtha) is collected in the boiling range 175–250°C. This fraction is cracked to form gasoline.

Gasoline is collected in the boiling range 50–175°C. This is used as motor fuel.

Jet
Fountain
Ammonia
Thick-walled flask
Water + red litmus

Fountain experiment

Fractional distillation (see entry on page 53)

Fractional distillation when boiling points are close together

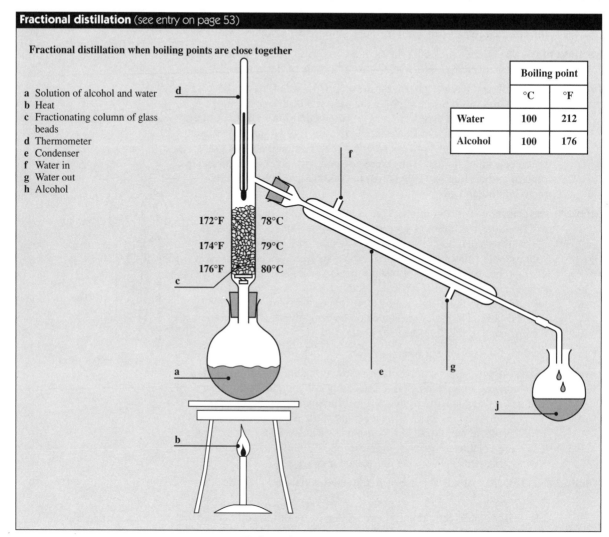

a Solution of alcohol and water
b Heat
c Fractionating column of glass beads
d Thermometer
e Condenser
f Water in
g Water out
h Alcohol

	Boiling point	
	°C	°F
Water	100	212
Alcohol	100	176

Hydrocarbon gases are collected at temperatures below 40°C. They are used as "bottled gas."

fractionating column *See* fractional distillation.

francium Element symbol, Fr; alkali metal group 1; radioactive (half-life of most stable isotope is 21 minutes), occurs in the radioactive series; Z 87; A(r) 223; density (at 20°C), 2.4 g/cm³; m.p., 27°C; named for France; discovered 1939.

Frasch process The process in which sulfur is extracted from deep underground deposits. It consists of three concentric pipes that are sunk to the level of the deposit. Superheated water is forced down the outermost pipe and hot compressed air through the innermost pipe. As the steam melts the sulfur, it is forced up the middle pipe with air and water. Sulfur solidifies in large tanks on the surface.

freeze-drying The removal of water from a frozen substance by reducing the pressure and allowing the water to sublime. This process is used for the dehydrating of heat-sensitive substances such as blood plasma and food.

freezing The process by which a change of state from liquid to solid occurs. The freezing point is the temperature at which this change occurs (it is also the temperature of the melting point, when the state changes from solid to liquid). It is the point at which the solid and liquid are in equilibrium. A freezing mixture is used to create a low temperature for chemical reactions. The mixture absorbs heat, producing lower temperatures than the original components of the mixture.

Freon *See* chlorofluorocarbons.

fructose $C_6H_{12}O_6$ (fruit sugar). The sweetest sugar. It occurs in fruits and honey.

fuel A substance that can produce large quantities of heat by either burning or undergoing nuclear fission.

fuel cell A type of primary cell that operates in the opposite way to electrolysis. It converts chemical energy directly to electrical energy. One type of fuel cell passes hydrogen and oxygen over porous electrodes where electricity is produced and the gases are converted to water.

full structural formula This represents the atoms in a molecule and the bonds between them, giving an indication of their position in relation to each other, although it does not always show the actual positions.

functional group (organic chemistry). The atom (or group of atoms) present in a molecule, which determines the characteristic properties of that molecule.

fundamental particles The large number of subatomic particles making up the universe. Many subatomic particles have been discovered and they are of three main types:

(1) leptons: particles of low mass, such as electrons, muons, tauons, and associated neutrinos;

(2) mesons: unstable particles of medium mass consisting of two quarks;

(3) baryons: more massive particles consisting of three quarks. The proton and neutron are baryons.

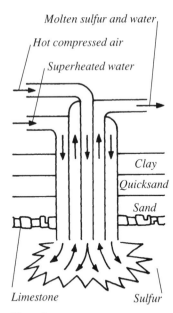

Molten sulfur and water
Hot compressed air
Superheated water

Clay
Quicksand
Sand

Limestone   Sulfur

Frasch process

Full structural formula

freeze-drying – fundamental particles   GLOSSARY

Each particle has an anti-particle (a particle with the same mass but opposite charge). The fundamental particles in the nucleus are quarks.

fundamental units Internationally agreed, independently defined units of measurement used to form the basis of a system of units. As a base for such a system, three mechanical units, such as length, mass, and time, and one electrical unit are required. SI units (using the meter, kilogram, and second, together with the kelvin, candela, and mole) are the standard. Formerly, the c.g.s. (using the centimeter, gram, and second) and the m.k.s. (meter, kilogram, second) and the f.p.s. (foot, pound, second) systems have been used (*see* SI).

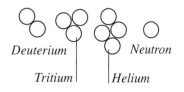

Deuterium   Neutron

Tritium   Helium

Fusion reaction

fusion   (1) (*melting*) The process by which a change of state from solid to liquid occurs.

(2) (*nuclear*) The process (which requires extremely high temperatures to initiate) by which two or more light atomic nuclei join, forming a single heavier nucleus. The products of fusion are lighter than the components. The mass lost is liberated as energy, given by Einstein's equation $E = mc^2$.

Ga   Symbol for the element gallium.

gadolinium Element symbol, Gd; rare earth element/lanthanide; Z 64; A(r) 157.25; density (at 20°C), 7.9 g/cm³; m.p., 1,313°C; named in honor of Gadolin, a Finnish chemist; discovered 1880; used in electronics industry; compounds used as catalysts.

galena   Metallic looking, naturally occurring ore consisting of PbS.

gallium   Element symbol, Ga; Group 3; Z 31; A(r) 69.74; density (at 20°C), 5.9 g/cm³; m.p., 29.8°C; name derived from the Latin name for France, *Gallia*; discovered 1875; used in semiconductors.

galvanizing The coating of iron or steel plates with a layer of zinc to protect against rusting. It is done either by dipping the iron or steel into a bath of molten zinc or by electrolysis.

Electrons flow towards iron (steel) as zinc corrodes

Water

Zinc

Steel

Galvanizing

gamma radiation Very short-wave electromagnetic radiation emitted as a result of radioactive decay. It is the least ionizing and most penetrating of the three types of radiation emitted in radioactive decay. It will penetrate a thick metal sheet and is only stopped by over 15 cm of lead or by thick layers of concrete.

gas   One of the three states of matter. In a gas, the particles can move freely throughout the space in which it is contained. Gas is the least dense of the states of matter.

gas law   The equation combining Boyle's law and Charles' law, $PV = nRT$, where P is the pressure, V is the volume, n is the number of moles of gas present, T is the temperature measure in Kelvin, and R is the universal gas constant.

gasoline A mixture of alkanes with chain lengths of between five and ten carbon atoms used as a fuel for internal combustion engines. It is obtained from the fractional distillation of petroleum and from cracking and reforming of hydrocarbons. *See* octane rating.

Gay-Lussac's law Volumes of gases that react do so in simple whole number ratios to each other and to the volumes of any gaseous products. (The volumes are measured at constant temperature and pressure.)

Gd Symbol for the element gadolinium.

Ge Symbol for the element germanium.

gel A colloidal solution that has formed a jelly. The solid particles are arranged as a fine network in the liquid phase.

general formula A formula showing the relative numbers of atoms present using the variable "n" for members of a homologous series.

germanium Element symbol, Ge; group 4; grayish white metalloid; Z 32; A(r) 72.59; density (at 20°C), 5.36 g/cm^3; m.p., 937.4°C; has excellent semiconductor properties; name derived from the Latin name for Germany, *Germania*; discovered 1886; used in manufacture of electronic components.

getter A substance that is evaporated on the inside surface of a vacuum tube to adsorb residual gas.

giant structure Atoms or ions present in very large numbers in a lattice. Each particle has a strong attractive force for those around it; this spreads the effect of the forces through the structure. Ionic compounds have giant structures, as do most elements (all metals and several nonmetals). Giant structures have high melting and boiling points. *See* covalent network.

Gibbs function or **Gibbs free energy** The energy absorbed or released in a reversible reaction at a constant temperature or pressure. It is calculated for a system from the enthalpy minus the product of the entropy and absolute temperature.

glass or **soda glass** A transparent substance formed by the fusion of silicon dioxide (white sand) with carbonates or oxides of calcium, sodium, potassium, or lead. Hard glass is a mixture of potassium and calcium silicates.

glucose $C_6H_{12}O_6$ (grape sugar, blood sugar). It is found in fruit juices, plant leaves, and in animal blood, and it is formed in plants by photosynthesis.

$6CO_2 + 6H_2O$ + energy (chlorophyll catalyst) = $C_6H_{12}O_6$ +$6O_2$.

The enzyme zymase in yeast causes glucose to ferment to ethanol.

Molten glass

Rollers

Glass

Glass manufacture

glycerides These are esters that are formed between glycerol and one or more organic acids. Depending on the number of hydroxyl groups that have reacted with the fatty acids, the glyceride may be a mono-, di-, or triglyceride. Glycerides made from unsaturated fatty acids usually have lower melting points than those made with saturated fatty acids, which have the same number of carbon atoms.

glycerol (propane-1,2,3-triol) $CH_2OH–CHOH–CH_2OH$. A trihydric alcohol. It is a colorless, water-soluble, viscous, hygroscopic liquid.

glycol *See* ethane-1,2-diol.

gold Element symbol, Au; transition element; shiny yellow metal; Z 79; A(r) 196.97; density (at 20°C), 19.32 g/cm^3; m.p., 1,064.4°C; good conductor of heat and electricity; Old English name, *gold*, Latin *aurum*; known since prehistoric times; used in coins, jewelry, and electrical contacts.

Graham's law The velocity with which a gas will diffuse is inversely proportional to the square root of its density.

gram-equivalent mass The equivalent mass expressed in grams. It is the number of grams of the element (or compound) that combines with or replaces 8 g of oxygen (or 35.5 g of chlorine, or 1 g of hydrogen) during a chemical reaction.

gram-formula mass An alternative way of describing a mole of a substance.

graphite An allotrope of carbon; m.p., 3,650°C. It is an opaque, grayish black solid with a metallic luster. It has a structure of hexagonal crystals arranged in giant layers that slide over each other because the forces between the layers are weak. It is a good conductor of heat and electricity.

gravimetric analysis A method of quantitative analysis in which accurate results are obtained by determining the weights of the components of a compound. For example, if the compound whose components were to be measured was in solution, an insoluble salt of one of the components could be precipitated and then weighed.

greenhouse effect Atmospheric warming caused by gases that act like a greenhouse roof, trapping solar heat below them. Waste gases produced by human industrial and agricultural activity are arguably intensifying the natural greenhouse effect.

green vitriol Hydrated iron(II) sulfate. $FeSO_4.7H_2O$ (iron sulfate heptahydrate). It is also known as copperas. *See* iron sulfates.

ground state The lowest energy state of an atom in which the electrons occupy the orbitals of lowest available energy. If an atom has more energy than it would possess in the ground state, it is said to be in an excited state.

Graphite sliding

Solar radiation

Heat trapped within atmosphere

Earth

Greenhouse effect

group The vertical columns of elements in the periodic table. Elements in a group react in a similar way. There is a gradation in properties from one member of the group to the next. They have the same number of electrons in their outer shell and an increasing number of shells. Elements lower in a group have increased metallic character.

group 1 or **I elements** The alkali metals. The elements lithium, sodium, potassium, rubidium, cesium, francium. These elements have one electron in their outer shell. They are very electropositive, soft, less dense than water, and have low melting points. They form strong alkalis and have a valency of one.

group 2 or **II elements** The alkaline earth metals. The elements beryllium, magnesium, calcium, strontium, barium, radium. These elements have two electrons in their outer shell. They are electropositive and are harder and less dense than the group 1 elements.

group 3 or **III elements** The elements boron, aluminum, gallium, indium, and thallium. These elements have a full s orbital and one electron in a p orbital in their outer shell. Their inner shells are full. There is more variation in properties in this group than in groups 1 and 2. Elements lower in the group are more metallic than those higher in the group and are more likely to form ions with a positive charge of 3.

group 4 or **IV elements** The elements carbon, silicon, germanium, tin, and lead. These elements have a full s orbital and two electrons in two p orbitals in their outer shell. Their inner shells are full. The character of the group changes from nonmetallic at the top to metallic at the bottom. The elements have a valency of 4, although the larger atoms (lower in the group) tend to form divalent compounds.

group 5 or **V elements** The elements nitrogen, phosphorus, arsenic, antimony, bismuth. These elements have a full s orbital and three electrons in three p orbitals in their outer shell. Their inner shells are full. The two lightest elements are nonmetals and the others are metalloids. Nitrogen has a valency of 3 and forms covalent compounds. The character of the group increases in its metallic nature further down the group. The elements in this group form compounds with the 3 oxidation state. The larger elements can also form compounds with the 5 oxidation state by using the available d orbitals in their outer shell (they promote an s electron from the outer shell to a d orbital).

group 6 or **VI elements** (the chalcogens) The elements oxygen, sulfur, selenium, tellurium, and polonium. These elements have a full s orbital, one full p orbital, and two half-full p orbitals in their outer shell. Their inner shells are full. As the outer shells of these elements are only two electrons short of the noble gas structure they tend to be electronegative (this tendency decreases in the larger elements) and nonmetallic. These elements form covalent bonds with a variety of other elements and they all form hydrides with two atoms of hydrogen.

group 7 or **VII elements** (the halogens) The elements fluorine, chlorine, bromine, iodine, astatine. These elements have a full s orbital, two full p orbitals, and one half-full p orbital in their outer shell. Their inner shells are full. As the outer shells of these elements are only one electron short of the noble gas structure, they tend to be very electronegative, having high electron affinities and forming compounds by gaining an electron to form a stable outer shell. They can also share their outer electrons to form covalent compounds with single bonds, and all exist as diatomic molecules.

group 8 or **VIII elements** (the noble or inert gases) The elements helium, neon, argon, krypton, xenon, radon. The outer shell of the atoms in these elements is complete, rendering these elements unreactive.

H   Symbol for the element hydrogen.

Haber process This is used in the industrial manufacture of ammonia. Nitrogen and hydrogen are dried, mixed, and reacted together at high temperature and pressure in the presence of a catalyst to form ammonia. As only about 15% of the reactants combine under typical conditions, the unreacted nitrogen and hydrogen are recycled for further reaction.

hafnium Element symbol, Hf; transition element; shiny silvery metal; Z 72; A(r) 178.49; density (at 20°C), 13.3 g/cm³; m.p., 2,227°C; name derived from *Hafnia*, the Latin name for Copenhagen; discovered 1923; used in alloy with tungsten to make filaments and electrodes. Used in control rods of nuclear reactors to absorb neutrons.

half-cell A metal in contact with a solution of its own ions. If two half-cells (each using a different metal) are connected together, electricity is produced. To do this, the metals are connected by wires and the solutions in the cells are joined by an ion bridge. A strip of filter paper soaked in a solution of sodium chloride can form an ion bridge. The wires between the metal rods and the ion bridge connecting the solutions completes the circuit.

half-life A substance that undergoes exponential decay decays by the same ratio in equal intervals of time. The constant ratio is the half-life. The rate of radioactive decay of a substance is defined by its half-life.

half-reaction A representation of a reaction that is particularly useful when considering redox reactions. A complete reaction between two substances is viewed as two separate reactions of each of the substances. For example, the displacement of zinc ions from solution by magnesium

Nitrogen from air

Hydrogen from methane

Reactor vessel with iron catalyst

Unreacted nitrogen and hydrogen recycled

Condenser produces liquid ammonia

Haber process

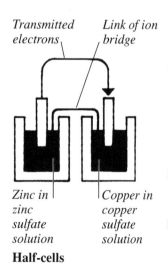

Transmitted electrons

Link of ion bridge

Zinc in zinc sulfate solution

Copper in copper sulfate solution

Half-cells

$$Zn^{2+} (aq) + Mg(s) \rightarrow Mg^{2+} + Zn(s).$$

This may be seen as $Zn^{2+}(aq) + 2e^- \rightarrow Zn(s)$
and $Mg(s) \rightarrow Mg^{2+} + 2e^-$

halide A compound that a halogen makes with another element. Metal halides are ionic; nonmetal halides are formed by covalent bonding.

halogen *See* group 7 elements.

halogenation The introduction of one or more halogen atoms into the structure of an organic molecule. If the halogen introduced is chlorine, the process is termed chlorination; if the halogen is bromine, the process is bromination, etc.

$CH_4 + Cl_2 \rightarrow CH_3Cl + HCl$

$C_6H_6 + Br_2 \rightarrow C_6H_5Br + HBr$

Halogenation

hardness *See* Mohs' scale.

hardness in water The presence of calcium and magnesium ions in water, which restricts the ability of soap to form a lather and leaves deposits in pipes. There are two types. In temporary hardness, soluble hydrogencarbonate compounds of calcium, magnesium, and iron are dissolved in cold water. When the water is heated, these salts form insoluble carbonates that are precipitated. Permanent hardness is caused largely by calcium sulfate and cannot be easily removed.

hassium Element symbol, Hs; transition element; Z 108; A(r) 265; name derived from the Latin name for Hess (the German state), *Hassias*; discovered 1984. Formerly known as unniloctium.

He Symbol for the element helium.

heat capacity The heat capacity of an object is the product of its mass and its specific heat capacity.

heat energy A system has heat energy because of the kinetic energy of its atoms and molecules (due to translation, rotation, and vibration). It is transferred by conduction, convection, and radiation.

heat exchange A process of transferring energy from one material to another. If a process is well designed, the heat produced in one part of a system can be used in another.

heat of combustion The heat change when one mole of a substance is completely burnt in oxygen (both products and reactants being at 25°C and one atmosphere). The value is negative when heat is given out (the change is exothermic).

heat of formation The heat change when one mole of a compound is formed from its elements at 25°C and one atmosphere.

heat of neutralization The heat change when acid that produces one mole of hydrogen ions is neutralized by an alkali (both acid and alkali being in dilute solution). The heat of neutralization of a strong acid by a strong alkali.

The reaction $H^+(aq) + OH^-(aq) \rightarrow H_2O(l)$ is usually about –57 kJ.

heat of reaction The difference between the enthalpy of the products of a reaction and the enthalpy of the reactants. (The heat of reaction is negative if the reaction is exothermic and positive if the reaction is endothermic.)

heat of solution The heat change when one mole of solute dissolves in a large volume of solvent (usually water) until no further heat change is observed.

heavy metals High-density metals such as cadmium, lead, and mercury. Heavy metals are poisonous, and careless dumping of heavy-metal wastes can create local health hazards.

heavy water D_2O. Water containing two atoms of deuterium (the isotope of hydrogen whose relative atomic mass is twice that of hydrogen) in place of hydrogen.

helium Element symbol, He; noble gas, group 8; Z 2; A(r) 4; density (at 20°C), 0.178 g/l at STP; m.p., –272.2°C; chemically inert; name derived from the Greek *helios* (sun); discovered 1868; used to fill balloons, as an inert atmosphere for arc welding, and in gas lasers.

hemoglobin A red oxygen-carrying pigment found in the red blood cells of vertebrates and in the blood plasma of some invertebrates.

Henry's law The mass of a gas that dissolves in a given volume of solvent at a constant temperature is proportional to the pressure of the gas (assuming that the gas does not react with the solvent).

Hess's law The total heat change during a complete chemical reaction is the same regardless of how many intermediate stages take place in the reaction.

heterocyclic compound An aromatic organic compound where one or more atoms other than carbon form part of the ring structure.

heterogeneous catalyst The catalysis of a reaction by a substance that is in a different state (solid, liquid, or gas) from the reactants.

heterogeneous reaction A chemical reaction taking place between substances in different physical states—solids, liquids, and/or gases.

Hf Symbol for the element hafnium.

Hg Symbol for the element mercury.

Ho Symbol for the element holmium.

holmium Element symbol, Ho; rare earth/lanthanide; Z 67; A(r) 164.93; density (at 20°C), 8.8 g/cm^3; m.p., 1,474°C; name derived from *Holmia*, the Latin name for Stockholm; discovered 1878.

homogeneous catalyst The catalysis of a reaction by a substance that is in the same state (solid, liquid, or gas) as the reactants.

homogeneous reaction A chemical reaction taking place between substances that are in the same physical state—solid, liquid, or gas.

homologous series A series of related organic compounds. The formula of each member differs from the preceding member by the addition of a –CH_2– group. Each series has a general formula; for example, the general formula for alkanes is C_nH_{2n+2}. The properties of each series, though similar, change gradually and regularly with increasing molecular weight.

Hs Symbol for the element hassium.

humidity The measure of the amount of water vapor in air, expressed as either the absolute or relative humidity.

Hund's principle When electrons are filling the orbitals of one type in a shell (for example the three p orbitals), they tend to distribute themselves in different orbitals because they repel each other (if an atom had three p electrons they would each be in a different p orbital).

hydrate A salt containing water of crystallization, for example $CuSO_4.5H_2O$.

hydration A type of solvation. Molecules or ions of solute become surrounded by water molecules to which they are attached by coordinate bonds or by a type of electrostatic force.

hydride A compound formed between hydrogen and one other element. Electropositive elements form salt-like hydrides containing the hydride ion (H^-), which are very reactive. nonmetals and transition metals form covalent hydrides such as methane (CH_4), ammonia (NH_3), and water (H_2O).

hydriodic acid Aqueous solution of hydrogen iodide. A strong acid.

hydrobromic acid Aqueous solution of hydrogen bromide. It is a strong acid.

hydrocarbon chain A line of carbon atoms in a molecule. In polymers these chains can be thousands of atoms long. Molecules can consist of a straight chain or a branched chain.

hydrocarbon An organic compound that contains carbon and hydrogen only. Hydrocarbons can be aliphatic or aromatic and be saturated or unsaturated.

hydrochloric acid HCl. A strong acid. In dilute solution it reacts with most metals to form hydrogen. With carbonates it forms carbon dioxide and with sulfites it forms sulfur dioxide. With alkalis and insoluble bases it forms a salt and water. It contains hydrogen ions. The concentrated acid is a strong reducing agent.

hydrofluoric acid An aqueous solution of hydrogen fluoride. It is a weak acid that attacks glass and is used for glass etching.

Anions surrounded by water molecules

Cations surrounded by water molecules

Hydration

hydrogen Element symbol, H; the lightest element; colorless gas; Z 1; A(r) 1.01; density (at 20°C), 0.09 g/l at STP; m.p., −259.1°C; explodes readily in oxygen; name derived from the Greek words *hydor*, "water," and *genes*, "producing;" discovered 1766; used in the synthesis of ammonia and the hydrogenation of oils. (*See also* illustration on page 65.)

hydrogenation The addition of hydrogen to another compound, usually an unsaturated organic compound. Nickel is a good catalyst for such reactions. Ethane is formed if ethene is hydrogenated. Hydrogenation is a very important process in the formation of margarine, in which unsaturated oils are hydrogenated to form saturated fats. The hydrogenation of vegetable and animal oils was first carried out in 1910, when the oils were heated to about 200°C and hydrogen was bubbled through them in the presence of finely divided nickel. The oils changed to fats which could be converted to margarine and other products.

hydrogen, atomicity of The hydrogen molecule is diatomic. *See* atomicity.

hydrogen bond This occurs in compounds in which a hydrogen atom makes a covalent bond with an electronegative element, for example, in water, H_2O. The bond is polarized because the electrons are attracted towards the electronegative oxygen atom, leaving the hydrogen atom with a positive charge.

If another water molecule approaches this hydrogen atom, the oxygen atom of the second water molecule forms a weak electrostatic bond, called a hydrogen bond, with the hydrogen atom in the first water molecule.

Hydrogen bonds are weaker than covalent or ionic bonds, but they do affect the physical properties of compounds in which they occur. *See* polar molecule.

hydrogen bromide HBr. A colorless gas; m.p., −86°C; b.p., −66.4°C.

hydrogencarbonates Acid salts of carbonic acid containing the ion $^-HCO_3$. *See* baking powder for sodium hydrogen carbonate. *See* hardness in water for other hydrogencarbonates.

hydrogen chloride HCl. A colorless gas with a pungent smell. It fumes in moist air, forming tiny drops of hydrochloric acid solution; m.p., −114°C; b.p., −85°C. It is very soluble in water.

hydrogen fluoride HF. A colorless liquid; m.p., −83°C; b.p., 19.5°C. Hydrogen bonds are formed in the liquid state. It is very corrosive (it is used in glass etching) and is a good fluorinating agent (*see* halogenation).

hydrogen iodide HI. A colorless gas (m.p., −51°C; b.p., −36°C) that is very soluble in water.

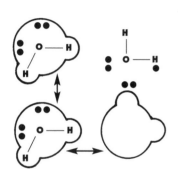

● *Electron pair*

Hydrogen bond

Hydrogen: laboratory preparation (see entry on page 64)

Laboratory preparation
in Kipps apparatus

Collection of dry hydrogen

a Dilute hydrochloric acid
b Impure zinc
c Hydrogen gas

Reaction:
$$Zn + 2HCl \rightarrow ZnCl_2 + H_2$$

a Hydrogen from Kipps apparatus
b Anhydrous calcium chloride
c Dry hydrogen gas

hydrogen ion H^+. This is usually regarded as being a single proton. In aqueous solution, the hydrogen ion exists in a hydrated form such as the oxonium (hydroxonium) ion H_3O^+.

hydrogen, isotopes of Hydrogen has three isotopes: the normal hydrogen atom (protium), whose nucleus contains one proton and thus has a relative atomic mass of one; deuterium, whose nucleus contains one proton and one neutron and thus has a relative atomic mass of two; tritium, whose nucleus contains one proton and two neutrons and thus has a relative atomic mass of three.

hydrogen peroxide H_2O_2. A colorless or pale blue viscous liquid; m.p., $-0.89°C$; b.p., $151.4°C$. It decomposes in light to form water and oxygen. It is available in solutions designated by the volume of oxygen that can be liberated. For example, 20-volume hydrogen peroxide yields 20 volumes of oxygen from one volume of solution.

It is a strong oxidizing agent, but it can also act as a reducing agent, depending on the substance with which it reacts. With lead(II) sulfide (PbS), it acts as an oxidizing agent, forming lead(II) sulfate ($PbSO_4$) and water. With lead(IV) oxide (PbO_2) it acts as a reducing agent, forming lead(II) oxide (PbO) oxygen and water).

hydrogen sulfide H_2S. A colorless poisonous gas smelling of bad eggs; m.p., −85.5°C; b.p., −60.7°C. It is moderately soluble in water; the solution is a weak acid (hydrosulfuric acid). Hydrogen sulfide is a reducing agent.

hydrolysis The interaction of water with a salt to form an acid and a base. The water dissociates to H^+ and OH^- ions.

hydrometer An instrument used to measure the densities or relative densities of liquids.

hydrophilic Water-loving. In solution, it refers to a chemical or part of a chemical that is highly attracted to water.

hydrophobic Water-hating. It refers to a chemical or part of a chemical that repels water.

hydroxide ion (**hydroxyl ion** or deprotonated water) The negative ion (OH^-) present in alkalis. It forms water with the addition of a hydrogen ion (H^+) or proton.

hydroxides A compound containing the hydroxide ion or the hydroxyl group bonded to a metal atom. Metal hydroxides are bases.

hydroxonium ion (hydronium ion or protonated water) The positive ion $(H_3O)^+$. It is the hydrated form of the hydrogen ion (H^+) or proton.

hydroxy A compound that contains one or more hydroxyl (OH^-) group.

hydroxyl group −OH. A monovalent functional group that consists of an oxygen atom and a hydrogen atom. In metal hydroxides it exists as the hydroxide (or hydroxyl) ion. *See* hydroxide ion.

hygroscopic A substance that absorbs moisture from the air without becoming liquid.

hypochlorous acid HClO (chloric(I) acid) A weak acid that acts as a strong oxidizing agent. It forms salts called chlorates. Chlorates are used as bleaches and in water purification.

I Symbol for the element iodine.

ice The solid state of water, H_2O. It is less dense than water and therefore floats on water.

ideal gas A gas that obeys the gas laws and in which molecules have negligible volume and the forces of molecular attraction are negligible. No known gas is completely ideal.

Start with white sulfate

After several minutes, blue copper sulfate forming

After several hours, no further change

Hygroscopic substance

ideal solution A solution in which there is no chemical interaction between the solvent and the solute molecules.

immiscible Substances that do not mix and form more than one phase when brought together.

In Symbol for the element indium.

incandescence The emission of light by a body that is strongly heated. For example, the filament of an electric light bulb and the "limelight" obtained by heating lime.

indicator A substance that indicates, by a change in its color, the degree of acidity or alkalinity of a solution or the presence of a given substance.

indium Element symbol, In; group 3; soft silvery metal; Z 49; A(r) 114.82; density (at 20°C), 7.31 g/cm^3; m.p., 156.6°C; compounds are toxic; named after the indigo line in its spectrum; discovered 1863; forms alloys with low melting points; compounds used in semiconductors and electric motors.

inert A substance that is either very or completely unreactive. Nitrogen and the noble gases are inert.

inert gases *See* group 8 elements.

inhibitor The reverse of a catalyst, a compound that slows down the rate of a chemical reaction. *See* antiknock for the action of lead(IV) tetraethyl in slowing down the ignition of a petrol-air mixture.

inorganic chemistry The study of the chemistry of all the elements excluding the organic compounds made by carbon (it includes the study of carbon-containing compounds such as carbonates, hydrogencarbonates, and carbon dioxide).

insoluble A substance that does not dissolve in a particular solvent under certain conditions of temperature and pressure.

insulator A material that does not conduct energy, e.g., electricity, heat, or sound.

iodides Salts of hydriodic acid.

iodine Element symbol, I; halogen, group 7; black solid, producing iodine vapor (violet); Z 53; A(r) 126.9; density (at 20°C), 4.94 g/cm^3; m.p., 113.5°C; name derived from the Greek *iodes*, "violet;" discovered 1811; essential element in diet; used in disinfectants, photography, halogen light bulbs.

iodoform test Test for the presence of an ethanoyl group in ketones or aldehydes. Pour 2 ml of a solution of iodine in potassium iodide solution into a test tube and carefully add sodium hydroxide until the brown color of the solution has almost gone. Add two drops of the solution to be tested. If a fine yellow precipitate is produced, it confirms the presence of an ethanoyl group in the sample.

○ Cl⁻
● Na⁺

Ionic crystal

$$OH^-(aq) + H^+(aq) \rightarrow H_2O(l)$$

Ionic equation

ion   An electrically charged atom or group of atoms. An atom (or group of atoms) tends to lose or gain one or more electrons to form an ion that has a noble gas configuration.

ion bridge *See* half-cell.

ion-electron equation representation of a chemical reaction showing the gain or loss of electrons from an element or ion as the charge on the element or ion changes during the reaction.

ion-exchange A process in which ions of the same charge are exchanged between ions in a solution and ions in a solid in contact with the solution. *See* Permutit.

ionic bond *See* bond.

ionic compound Compounds consisting of ions held together by strong ionic bonds. They tend to be hard solids. Their melting points are high because of the strength of the ionic bonds. Ionic compounds are electrolytes; their ions can move when the compound is melted or dissolved in a suitable solvent.

ionic crystal A type of crystal where ions of two of more elements form a regular three-dimensional arrangement (crystal structure). The ions are held strongly in place by ionic bonds between positive and negative ions.

ionic equation A representation of a chemical reaction where the reactants and products taking part in a reaction are shown as ions. Other ions may be present but do not take part; they are known as spectator ions. For example, in the reaction between nitric acid and sodium hydroxide, forming sodium nitrate and water:

$$HNO_{3(aq)} + NaOH_{(aq)} = NaNO_{3(aq)} + H_2O_{(l)}$$

If this is written in ionic form

$$H^+ NO_3^-{}_{(aq)} + Na^+ OH^-{}_{(aq)} = Na^+NO_3^-{}_{(aq)} + H_2O_{(l)}$$

the sodium and the nitrate ions appear on both sides of the equation, and are said to be spectator ions and the ionic equation is

$$H^+{}_{(aq)} + OH^-{}_{(aq)} = H_2O_{(l)}$$

ionic formula This shows the charges of the ions in an ionic substance, for example, Na^+Cl^- or $Ca^{2+}(Cl^-)_2$.

ionic lattice An ionic crystal of two or more elements that is held together by the electric forces (ionic bonds) between negative and positive ions in a regular structure.

ionic theory Substances that separate into oppositely charged particles (ions) when electricity is passed through a solution of the substance, or a molten sample of the substance.

ionization The process by which an atom becomes an ion by either losing or gaining one or more electrons.

ionization energy The energy needed to remove completely an electron from a neutral gaseous atom or ion against the attraction of the nucleus. The energy needed to remove the first electron is the first ionization energy; the energy for the second is the second ionization energy. These become progressively larger.

ion migration The movement of ions in an electrolyte under the influence of an applied voltage. If ions forming compounds of certain colors are used, it is possible to study the process of ion migration by observing color changes in different parts of the electrolyte (or in filter paper soaked in an electrolyte).

Ir Symbol for the element iridium.

iridium Element symbol, Ir; transition element; silvery metal; Z 77; A(r) 192.22; density (at 20°C), 22.42 g/cm^3; m.p., 2,410°C; name derived from the Latin and Greek word *iris*, "rainbow;" discovered 1803.

iron Element symbol, Fe; transition element; silvery malleable and ductile metal; Z 26; A(r) 55.85; density (at 20°C), 7.87 g/cm^3; m.p., 1,535°C; Old English name *iren*; Latin name *ferrum*; known since prehistoric times; used in construction, usually converted to steel for strength.

iron(II) disulfide FeS_2. A yellow crystalline mineral occurring in many rocks. It is often mistaken for gold.

iron chloride $FeCl_2$ (iron(II) chloride, ferrous chloride) Anhydrous iron(II) chloride is a white solid. It is deliquescent and becomes green-yellow on absorbing water; m.p., 670°C; r.d., 3.16. It also exists as $FeCl_2.2H_2O$, a green crystalline compound; r.d., 2.36; and as $FeCl_2.4H_2O$, a blue crystalline compound; r.d., 1.93.

$FeCl_3$ (iron(III) chloride, ferric chloride) Anhydrous iron(III) chloride is a black-brown solid; m.p., 306°C; r.d., 2.9. It forms a brownish yellow solution. It also exists as $FeCl_3.6H_2O$, a brown-yellow deliquescent crystalline substance.

iron, extraction of *See* blast furnace.

iron hydroxide $Fe(OH)_2$ (iron(II) hydroxide, ferrous hydroxide) A solid that is white when pure. It is formed as a dirty green precipitate when an alkali is added to an aqueous solution containing Fe^{2+} ions.

$Fe(OH)_3$ (iron (III) hydroxide, ferric hydroxide) A rust-colored gelatinous solid precipitated by adding an alkali to a solution containing Fe^{3+} ions.

iron oxides FeO (iron(II) oxide, ferrous oxide) r.d., 5.7; m.p., 369°C. A black

Dry hydrogen chloride enters
Clamp
Iron
Hydrogen burns

Iron chloride | *Heat*

solid formed by heating iron(II) ethanedioate (FeC_2O_4) in a vacuum. It dissolves in dilute acids.

Fe_2O_3 (iron(III) oxide, ferric oxide) A red-brown insoluble solid, r.d., 5.24, m.p., 1,565°C. It is formed when $Fe(OH)_3$ is heated. For the hydrated form ($Fe_2O_3.\times H_2O$), *see* rust.

(Fe_3O_4 iron(II) di-iron(III) oxide, tri iron tetroxide) A magnetic oxide of iron; it occurs naturally as magnetite. It is formed as a black solid when steam is passed over red-hot iron.

iron pyrites *See* iron(II) disulfide.

iron sulfates $FeSO_4.H_2O$ (iron(II) sulfate, ferrous sulfate) An off-white crystalline compound; r.d., 2.97.

$FeSO_4.7H_2O$. A blue-green crystalline compound; r.d., 1.898, m.p., 64°C; known as green vitriol or copperas.

$Fe_2(SO_4)_3$ (iron(III) sulfate, ferrous sulfate) A yellow hygroscopic crystalline compound; r.d., 3.097. It decomposes above 480°C.

isocyanates Substances that contain the group –N=C=O.

isomers Different (usually organic) compounds having the same molecular formula and relative molecular mass but some different properties, as they have different three-dimensional structures. *See* structural isomer, stereoismer.

isometric (1) In the study of crystals, isometric describes cubic crystal systems where the axes are perpendicular to each other.

(2) In the graphic representation of temperature, pressure, and volume, an isometric line shows how the temperature and pressure of a gas relate to each other at constant volume.

isomorphism The existence of two or more different substances (isomorphs) that have the same crystal structure.

isotonic Solutions that have the same osmotic pressure.

isotope Atoms of the same element (all chemically identical) having the same atomic number but containing different numbers of neutrons, giving different mass number. Some elements occur naturally as a mixture of different isotopes. All elements can produce radio isotopes artificially.

isotropic A substance whose physical properties do not change with direction, such as a cubic crystal.

K　　Symbol for the element potassium.

kaolin　*See* china clay.

Kelvin scale A temperature scale that has no negative values. Its lower fixed point is absolute zero. The size of the unit, the kelvin, is the same as the degree Celsius, and the triple point of water is 273.16 K.

kerosene (paraffin oil) A mixture of hydrocarbons mainly consisting of alkanes with between 10 and 16 carbon atoms. It is used in jet engine fuel and in paraffin heaters. It is obtained from petroleum refining. It boils between 160 and 250°C.

keto- A prefix denoting that the substance contains a carbon atom attached to an oxygen atom by a double bond and to two other carbon atoms by single bonds, i.e. it contains a carbonyl group.

ketone A family of organic compounds that contain two organic radicals connected to a carbonyl group. Names have the suffix -one. General formula: R–CO–R, where R represents an aliphatic or aromatic hydrocarbon group. Ketones are very reactive.

kinetic theory All matter consists of particles, such as atoms, ions, or molecules, which are in a state of continual motion, and this motion is dependent on temperature. The theory explains some of the physical properties of materials, and it is particularly useful in explaining the behavior of gases, because gas molecules are relatively unaffected by forces of attraction between molecules. In solids and liquids, the amount of movement is less, due to bonds between particles.

Kr Symbol for the element krypton.

krypton Element symbol, Kr; noble gas, group 8; Z 36; A(r) 83.3; density (at 20°C), 3.743 g/l at STP; m.p., −157.3°C; name derived from the Greek *kryptos*, "hidden;" discovered 1898; used in fluorescent lights.

La Symbol for the element lanthanum.

lactose A disaccharide with the formula $C_{12}H_{22}O_{11}$; it is an isomer of maltose. Lactose is a white crystalline solid occurring in the milk of mammals. It is a reducing carbohydrate.

lanthanides (lanthanoids, lanthanons, rare earths) A series of elements comprising lanthanum, cerium, praesodymium, neodymium, promethium, samarium, europium, gadolinium, terbium, dysprosium, holmium, erbium, thulium, ytterbium, and lutetium. As their outer electronic structure is very similar (the f orbital in their fourth shell is being filled), they have similar chemical properties. The metals are shiny and are attacked by water and acids. Their usual oxidation number is +3.

lanthanum Element symbol, La; lanthanide; silvery metal; Z 57; A(r) 138.91; density (at 20°C), 6.15 g/cm^3; m.p., 921°C; name derived from the Greek *lanthanein*, "to lie unseen;" discovered 1839; used in alloys with magnesium and aluminum and in steels.

latent heat The amount of heat that is absorbed or released by a substance

Ketone

Lattice

during a change of state (fusion or vaporization) at constant temperature.

lattice The orderly three-dimensional arrangements of atoms, molecules, or ions seen in crystals.

law A rule describing certain natural observable phenomena or the relationship between effects of variable quantities.

law of combining masses Elements combine in the ratio of their combining masses or in a simple multiple of that ratio.

law of constant composition or **law of definite proportions** or **Proust's law** A pure chemical compound always contains the same elements combined in the same proportions by mass.

law of definite proportions *See* law of constant composition.

law of mass action This applies to a reversible chemical reaction such as aA + bB ⇌ cC+dD at chemical equilibrium where the rate of the forward reaction is equal to the rate of the back reaction. The equilibrium constant

$$K = \frac{[C]^c[D]^d}{[A]^a[B]^b}$$

where [A] etc. are the active masses of the substances. These are often taken as their molecular (molar) concentrations. For gas reactions, partial pressures are used rather than concentrations.

The equilibrium constant shows the position of equilibrium; if it has a low value, it shows that [C] and [D] are low compared with [A] and [B]. It also indicates how the equilibrium would shift if one of the concentrations changed.

law of multiple proportions If two elements (A and B) combine to form more than one compound, the different masses of A that combine with a fixed mass of B are in a simple ratio.

H	Li	Be	B	C	N	O
F	Na	Mg	Al	Si	P	S
Cl	K	Ca	Cr	Ti	Mn	Fe
(doh	ray	me	fah	soh	lah	te)

Law of octaves

law of octaves or **Newlands' law** An arrangement of 56 elements in order of ascending atomic weight made by John Newlands in 1863. He found that if the elements were arranged in order of ascending atomic weight and placed in a table so that the first eight were aligned above the second eight (and so on), the elements in a column had similar properties.

law of reciprocal proportions *See* law of combining masses.

lawrencium Element symbol, Lr; actinide; Z 103; A(r) 256; no solid compounds are known; named in honor of the physicist Ernest O. Lawrence; discovered 1961.

laws of chemical combination The laws representing the way in which elements combine in the formation of chemical compounds. There are three laws: the law of constant composition, the law of multiple proportions, and the law of combining masses.

lead Element symbol, Pb; group 4; silvery white metal; Z 82; A(r) 207.2; density (at 20°C), 11.35 g/cm^3; m.p., 327.5°C; compounds are toxic; Old English name *lead*; Latin name *plumbum*; known since prehistoric times; used in batteries and in water, noise, and radiation shielding. It is also used in high-quality glass production and the manufacture of storage batteries.

lead(II) carbonate hydroxide $2PbCO_3.Pb(OH)_2$ (white lead, lead(II) carbonate hydroxide) It occurs naturally in hydroxycerussite. It decomposes at 400°C. White lead was used widely in paint, but it discolored on contact with hydrogen sulfide in the atmosphere. Fears of lead poisoning also led to the decline in use of white lead in paint.

lead bromide $PbBr_2$. A white crystalline, poisonous solid; m.p., 373°C. It is almost insoluble in cold water, but fairly soluble in hot water.

lead carbonate $PbCO_3$. A poisonous white salt that is insoluble in water. It occurs naturally in the mineral cerussite and is used as a pigment.

lead chamber process *See* chamber process.

lead chloride $PbCl_2$. A white crystalline solid that is almost insoluble in cold water. It is fairly soluble in hot water.

lead iodide PbI_2. It is formed as a golden yellow precipitate in solution.

lead nitrate $Pb(NO_3)_2$. Lead nitrate exists as colorless crystals that are used as a mordant in dyeing and in the manufacture of chrome-yellow pigment.

lead oxides PbO (lead(II) oxide, lead monoxide) A yellow compound that is amphoteric and insoluble in water; m.p., 886°C. It exists in two crystalline forms: litharge, obtained when the oxide is heated above the melting point; and massicot, when it is heated to temperatures below the melting point. It is used in the manufacture of paint and glass.

PbO_2 (lead(IV) oxide, lead dioxide) A dark brown solid that decomposes to form lead(II) oxide and oxygen on heating. It is a powerful oxidizing agent. It is used in lead-acid cells.

$Pb_3O_4.(Pb_2PbO_4)$ (di-lead(II) lead(IV) oxide, tri-lead tetroxide, red lead) A red solid produced on heating lead(II) oxide in oxygen at 400°C. It decomposes at 500°C to form lead(II) oxide and oxygen. It is used in paint manufacture and in the manufacture of lead(IV) oxide.

lead sulfate $PbSO_4$. A white insoluble crystalline solid; m.p., 1,170°C. It has been used in paint because it is less susceptible to discoloration than lead(II) carbonate hydroxide, but it is now less used because of fears about lead poisoning.

lead sulfide PbS. A brownish black insoluble crystal; m.p., 1,114°C; occurs naturally as the mineral galena.

Le Chatelier's principle If a chemical reaction is at equilibrium and a change is made to any of the conditions, further reaction will take place to counteract the changes in order to re-establish equilibrium.

Leclanché cell A primary cell with an e.m.f. of 1.5 volts and internal resistance of 1 ohm. The positive electrode is a carbon rod that is surrounded by a mixture of powdered carbon and manganese dioxide in a porous pot. The pot stands in ammonium chloride solution contained in a zinc pot, which forms the negative electrode.

Li Symbol for the element lithium.

ligand An atom (or group of atoms) surrounding the central atom in a complex.

lime *See* calcium oxide.

limestone *See* calcium carbonate.

limewater A solution of calcium hydroxide that is used to test for the presence of carbon dioxide. If carbon dioxide is bubbled through limewater, a solid precipitate of calcium carbonate is formed.

linear molecules Molecules whose atoms are in a line. For example, ethyne, carbon dioxide.

lipid General name for a loosely defined group of organic compounds that are considered to be the esters of long-chain carboxylic acids and various alcohols. Oils, fats, and waxes are lipids.

liquid A state of matter between solid and gas. Particles are loosely bonded, so can move relatively freely. A liquid has low compressibility.

lithium Element symbol, Li; alkali metal, group 1; silvery white metal; Z 3; A(r) 6.94; density (at 20°C), 0.53 g/cm³; m.p., 180.5°C; reacts with water; name derived from the Greek *lithos*, "stone;" discovered 1817; used in low-melting alloys; compounds have many uses, including ceramics and fungicides.

lithium carbonate Li_2CO_3. A white solid; m.p., 735°C. It decomposes above 1,200°C. Lithium carbonate is used in the prevention and treatment of manic depressive disorders.

lithium chloride $LiCl$. A very deliquescent soluble white solid that is used in mineral waters and as a flux in soldering.

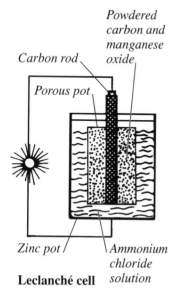

Powdered carbon and manganese oxide

Carbon rod

Porous pot

Zinc pot

Ammonium chloride solution

Leclanché cell

lithium oxide Li_2O (lithia). A white crystalline compound; m.p., 1,700°C; used in lubricating greases, ceramics, and glass.

litmus A soluble purple compound extracted from lichens. It can be used as an acid-base indicator because its color changes are dependent on the pH of a solution with which it is mixed. It is red in acid solutions (pH less than 5) and blue in alkaline solutions (pH more than 8). Paper that has been soaked in a solution of litmus and dried is called litmus paper.

lone pair A pair of electrons in a filled atomic orbital in the outermost shell of an atom. They are not involved in the formation of covalent bonds but have an effect on the shape of molecules (by affecting the angles of the bonds formed) and also cause the molecule to become strongly polar. *See* polar molecule.

Lr Symbol for the element lawrencium.

Lu Symbol for the element lutetium.

luminescence Light emission from a substance caused by an effect other than heat. Fluorescence and phosphorescence are forms of luminescence.

lutetium Element symbol, Lu; rare earth/lanthanide; silvery metal; Z 71; A(r) 174.97; density (at 20°C), 9.84 g/cm^3; m.p., 1,663°C; named for *Lutetia*, the Latin name for Paris; discovered 1907; used as a catalyst.

M *See* molarity.

macromolecules Very large molecules, such as polymers and proteins, whose relative molecular mass is larger than 1000.

magnesite Mineral containing magnesium carbonate.

magnesium Element symbol, Mg; alkali earth metal, group 2; silver-white metal; Z 12; A(r) 24.31; density (at 20°C), 1.74 g/cm^3; m.p., 648.8°C; will burn in air; named after Magnesia, a district in Thessaly; discovered 1755; used in alloys and castings. Some compounds have medicinal uses; also used in sugar, cement, paper manufacture, and many other industries.

magnesium carbonate $MgCO_3$. A white compound that is slightly soluble in water. It is used in making magnesium oxide and as a drying agent (particularly in table salt as an anti-caking agent). It is used medically as laxative and antacid.

magnesium chloride $MgCl_2$. A white solid compound; m.p., 714°C; b.p., 1,412°C. It is deliquescent, forming the hexahydrate $MgCl_2.6H_2O$. Magnesium chloride is used in fireproofing and fire-extinguishing materials, and in the textile industry.

magnesium hydrogen carbonate $Mg(HCO_3)_2$. A soluble magnesium salt that is only stable in solution. It decomposes on heating to form

Lone pair of electrons in ammonia

Carbon dioxide

Burning magnesium ribbon

Add diluted hydrochloric acid and shake

Black specks float in acid, which disolves the magnesium oxide

Magnesium oxide

magnesium carbonate, carbon dioxide, and water. It is formed by the action of carbon dioxide and water on calcium carbonate and is one of the causes of temporary hardness in water (*see* hardness in water).

magnesium hydroxide $Mg(OH)_2$. A slightly soluble crystalline white powder that decomposes at 350°C. It occurs naturally in the mineral brucite or it can be prepared by adding a strong alkali to a solution containing magnesium ions. It is used medically as an antacid (milk of magnesia).

magnesium oxide MgO (magnesia). A white solid (m.p., 2,800°C) occurring naturally in the mineral periclase. It is prepared industrially by the thermal decomposition of magnesite. It has many uses, including reflective coatings and as a component of semiconductors.

magnesium sulfate $MgSO_4$. A white soluble salt that exists in both anhydrous form and in hydrated crystalline form. $MgSO_4.H_2O$ magnesium sulfate monohydrate is found as the mineral kieserite. The heptahydrate ($MgSO_4.7H_2O$) is found as the mineral epsomite and is known as Epsom salts. Epsom salts are used medically as a laxative, in the manufacture of fertilizers and matches, in sizing and fireproofing textiles, and in tanning leather.

magnetite Fe_3O_4. A mineral containing iron(II) di-iron(III) oxide. It is a black solid that is a natural magnet or "lodestone."

malachite A copper ore formed of hydrated copper carbonate. Its formula can be written either $Cu_2(OH)_2CO_3$ or $CuCO_3.Cu(OH)_2$. Its color ranges from dark to light green, and the mineral is found with these colors forming striking patterns of bands.

malleability of metals Metals can be rolled into flat sheets and hammered into different shapes because they are malleable.

maltose A disaccharide with the formula $C_{12}H_{22}O_{11}$. An isomer of lactose, it is a reducing carbohydrate.

manganese Element symbol, Mn; transition element; soft gray metal; Z 25; A(r) 54.94; density (at 20°C), 7.3 g/cm^3; m.p., 1,244°C; name derived from medieval translation of the Latin *magnesia*; discovered 1774; used in steel manufacture and in alloys. Compounds have many industrial uses.

manganese(IV) oxide MnO_2 (manganese dioxide). It is an insoluble black powder that is made by heating manganese(II) nitrate. It is a powerful oxidizing agent.

margarine *See* hydrogenation.

marsh gas More commonly known as methane (CH_4), it is found in marshy districts, where it is formed by the anaerobic bacterial decomposition of vegetable (and animal) material.

mass number The total number of protons and neutrons (nucleons) in the nucleus of an atom.

Md Symbol for the element mendelevium.

meitnerium Element symbol, Mt; transition element; Z 109; A(r) 266; named in honor of Austrian physicist Lise Meitner; discovered 1982. Formerly known as unnilennium.

melamine $C_3H_6N_6$ (cyanuramide, 2,4,6-triamino-1,3,5-triazine). A white or colorless crystalline compound (m.p., 354°C) produced from urea. It forms strong thermosetting polymers, which are stable to heat and light, on undergoing condensation polymerization with methanal.

melting The change of state from solid to liquid. It occurs when the particles in the solid lattice have gained sufficient energy to break the bonds that hold them in the lattice.

mendelevium Element symbol, Md; actinide; Z 101; A(r) 258; no solid compounds known; named in honor of Dmitry Mendeleyev, Russian chemist; discovered 1955.

Mendeleyev classification Scientists in the 19th century found that there were elements that had similar properties, and formulated the idea that there were families or groups of elements. The Russian chemist Dmitry Mendeleyev suggested in 1869 that "The properties of the elements are in periodic dependence upon their atomic weights" and related the chemical properties of each group to those of the other groups. In his table of elements, elements in the same group were placed in the same vertical column and these columns were arranged in the order given by the elements' gradual change in chemical reactivity and increasing atomic weight.

mercury Element symbol, Hg; transition element; silver liquid metal; Z 80; A(r) 200.59; density (at 20°C), 13.55 g/cm³; m.p., −38.8°C; mercury and many of its compounds are toxic and tend to accumulate in the bodies of higher animals; named for the planet Mercury, Latin *hydrargyrum*, "liquid silver;" known since prehistoric times; used in dental fillings, thermometers.

mercury(II) oxide HgO (mercuric oxide). A red solid when formed by heating mercury in oxide, a yellow precipitate formed by the addition of a strong alkali to a solution containing mercury(II) ions. The color difference is caused by particle size. Both forms decompose to form mercury and oxygen when strongly heated.

mercury cathode cell *See* Castner-Kellner cell.

metallic bond The bonding formed in metallic crystals where there is a lattice formation of positively charged ions within a sea of electrons that binds them together. There are insufficient electrons in this "sea" to

Melamine

Lattice (solid)

Melting

Lattice breaks down

(Liquid)

Melting

Metallic bond

form individual bonds between atoms. Atoms that have more electrons in their outer shell can contribute more electrons to the electron sea. The bonding is thus stronger and the metallic crystal formed is harder and denser as the ions are held more tightly. Thus alkali metals are softer and less dense than transition elements.

metallic crystal Metals form a giant crystalline structure with high melting and boiling points. The structure is formed of metal ions. Metal atoms have excess electrons in their outer shell (sodium has one, calcium two); these are mobile within the giant structure of ions and allow the solid to be a good conductor.

metalloid An element that has both metallic and nonmetallic properties.

metal properties Metals are strong, dense, and malleable, and they are good conductors of heat and electricity.

metals and acids All metals higher in the reactivity series than copper react with a dilute acid to form a salt and hydrogen.

metals and oxygen All metals higher in the reactivity series than silver combine with oxygen when heated.

metals and water All metals higher in the reactivity series than aluminum react with water to give hydrogen gas and the metal hydroxide.

metals, extraction of Most metals are not found naturally as the pure metal, exceptions being very unreactive metals such as gold and silver. Most metals are found combined with other elements in ores. Ores have to be processed to extract the metal. An example of this is the extraction of iron from iron ore (where iron is present as Fe_2O_3) in the blast furnace (*see* blast furnace). Metal oxides are reduced to the metal during extraction. (*See also* illustration on page 79.)

metals recycling Waste steel and aluminum can be recycled. This reduces energy use because making an object from recycled aluminum uses about 5% of the energy that would be used if new aluminum were used. Recycling is also of value because of the finite nature of the world's resources of metals.

metastable Describes a system that appears to be stable but that can undergo a rapid change if disturbed. For example, if water is slowly cooled below 0°C (supercooled water), it appears to be a stable liquid, but if a piece of ice is added, the water freezes rapidly as the system attains a lower energy state. This condition is also seen in supersaturated solutions.

methanal HCHO (formerly formaldehyde) The simplest aldehyde. It is a colorless gas with a pungent smell; m.p., –92°C; b.p., –21°C.

methane CH_4. The simplest alkane. A colorless, tasteless, odorless flammable gas; m.p., –182°C; b.p., –162°C. It is found in natural gas and in coal

Metals recycling

Methanal

Metal	Main ore from which obtained	Main method of extraction
Aluminum	Bauxite ($Al_2O_3.2H_2O$)	Electrolysis of Al_2O_3 in molten cryolite (Na_3AlF_6)
Copper	Copper pyrites ($CuFeS_2$) (CuS + FeS)	Controlled heating with correct amount of air $\rightarrow$ Cu + SO_2
Iron	Haematite (Fe_2O_3)	Reduce Fe_2O_3 with carbon monoxide
Lead	Galena (PbS)	Heat sulfide in air $\rightarrow$ oxide. Reduce oxide with carbon
Magnesium	Magnesite ($MgCO_3$) and Mg^{2+} ions in sea water	Electrolysis of molten $MgCl_2$
Mercury	Cinnabar (HgS)	Heat in air $\rightarrow$ Hg + SO_2
Sodium	Rock salt (NaCl)	Electrolysis of molten NaCl
Tin	Tinstone (SnO_2)	Reduce SnO_2 with carbon
Zinc	Zinc blende (ZnS)	Heat sulfide in air $\rightarrow$ oxide. Dissolve oxide in H_2SO_4, electrolyze

Metals, extraction of (see entry on page 78)

gas and can be formed by the anaerobic decomposition of vegetable and animal compounds. It is used as a fuel. It is slightly soluble in water, forming a neutral solution. Methane is used in the formation of many organic compounds.

methanoic acid HCOOH (formic acid) The simplest carboxylic acid. A colorless liquid with a pungent smell. It is used in textile dyeing, electroplating, and in some pesticides. Salts of methanoic acid are called methanoates (formerly formates).

methanol CH_3OH (methyl alcohol, wood alcohol) The simplest alkanol. It is a volatile, colorless, flammable, poisonous liquid that is produced by reacting methane with steam over a nickel catalyst at high temperature and pressure. This produces synthesis gas, which is converted to methanol when passed over a zinc oxide and chromium(III) oxide catalyst at 300°C under pressure. Methanol is used as a solvent and in methanal production.

methyl alcohol *See* methanol.

methylated spirits A form of ethanol (90% of the mixture) that has been rendered unfit for human consumption (and thus escapes taxation) by the addition of methanol (9.5%) and pyridine (0.5%) and a trace of blue dye. It is used as a solvent.

methylbenzene $C_6H_5CH_3$ (toluene) An aromatic hydrocarbon found in coal tar. It is a colorless insoluble flammable liquid used as a solvent and in the synthesis of other organic compounds.

Methylbenzene

methyl group or **radical** The organic group CH_3^-.

methyl orange Water-soluble, acid-base indicator. It is red in solutions where the pH is less than 3.2 and yellow in solutions having a pH above 4.4. Between 3.2 and 4.4 it is orange. It is used in titrations of a weak base with a strong acid, giving a weak acidic end point.

methyl tertiary butyl ether (MTBE) An additive in unleaded gasoline.

Mg   Symbol for the element magnesium.

mineral   A natural inorganic substance with distinct chemical composition and internal structure. Various kinds of minerals form the ingredients of rocks. Quartz is the most plentiful rock-forming mineral.

mineral processing The processes by which elements found in the Earth's crust in minerals and metallic ores are changed into more useful forms.

The mineral ore is extracted, crushed, and then purified by chemical means. For examples of purification, *see* blast furnace (for the smelting of iron ore); Castner-Kellner process (for the production of chlorine); Frasch process (for the production of sulfur).

miscible   Liquids that mix together completely. The result of mixing looks like a single liquid and requires fractional distillation to separate the liquids.

mixture   A system that consists of two or more substances (solid, liquid, or gas) present in any proportions in a container. There is no chemical bonding between substances. A mixture can be separated using physical methods. The formation of a mixture does not involve a change in temperature.

Mn   Symbol for the element manganese.

Mo   Symbol for the element molybdenum.

Mohs' scale A scale that measures the hardness of minerals by their ability to scratch one another. A mineral is given a number on Mohs' scale according to its ability to scratch one of the reference materials. In order of increasing hardness: 1, talc; 2, gypsum; 3, calcite; 4, fluorite; 5, apatite; 6, feldspar; 7, quartz; 8, topaz; 9, corundum; 10, diamond.

molality (m) Concentration of solution giving the number of moles of solute dissolved in 1 kg of solvent.

molar gas constant or **universal gas constant** (R) It is used in the gas equation $PV=nRT$. Its value is 8314 JK^{-1} mole^{-1}.

molarity (M) Concentration of solution giving the number of moles of solute dissolved in 1 dm^3 of solution.

molar solution A solution containing one mole of a solute in one liter of solution.

molar volume (gram molecular volume) (V_m) The volume occupied by one mole of a substance.

molar volume of gas At STP all gases have approximately equal molar volumes, 22.4 cubic decimeters.

mole The amount of a substance that contains the same number of entities (atoms, molecules, ions, any group of particles), but the type must be specified, as there are atoms in 0.012 kg of the carbon-12 isotope. The actual number is known as the Avogadro number. Its value is 6.023×10^{23}.

molecular crystal A type of crystal where molecules form a regular three-dimensional arrangement (crystal structure). The atoms within the molecule are held firmly in place but the molecules are held together by weak bonds, such as van der Waal's bonds and hydrogen bonds, and are easily separated. Molecular crystals have low melting points and they do not conduct electricity (there are no mobile electrons in the structure). Organic compounds tend to form molecular crystals.

molecular formula This indicates both the type of atom present (using the symbols that represent each element in the periodic table) and the number of each atom in the molecule. The molecular formula may be a multiple of its empirical formula.

molecularity The number of molecules taking part in a chemical reaction, which form an activated complex during one step of a process. A reaction is unimolecular if one molecule takes part, bimolecular if two molecules take part, and so on. *See* order of reaction.

molecular mass or **weight** *See* formula mass.

molecular orbitals The orbitals belonging to a group of atoms forming a molecule. Only the outer electrons are usually considered as forming molecular orbitals.

In the formation of a molecule, the valence electrons (electrons that make the bond between the atoms) are affected by both nuclei, and they move in molecular orbitals whose shape is governed by the shape of the individual atomic orbitals. For example, in a bond between two hydrogen atoms, each of the electrons that is to form the bond between the atoms is in an s orbital; these s orbitals overlap to form a molecular orbital between the two nuclei. This orbital is known as a sigma orbital. If bonding takes place between p orbitals, the bond is in two parts (at the end of each lobe of the p orbital) and is known as a pi orbital.

The shape of molecular orbitals can be seen in terms of hybrid orbitals, when the electrons forming a bond are in different types of

Two carbon atoms

Six hydrogen atoms

Molecular formula
Ethane shown as an example

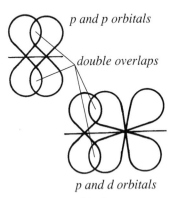

p and p orbitals

double overlaps

p and d orbitals

Molecular orbitals

orbitals in a shell. Carbon, for example, has one s orbital and three p orbitals in its outer shell, and when forming tetrahedral molecules (i.e. making four bonds), it is considered that rather than forming one bond with an electron in an s orbital and three with electrons in p orbitals, it forms four sp^3 hybrid orbitals.

molecule The smallest part of an element or chemical compound that can exist independently with all the properties of the element or compound. It is made up of one or more atoms bonded together in a fixed whole number ratio.

molecules, shapes of The shape of molecules is governed by the arrangement of the bonds within them. For example, the four bonds of carbon are arranged tetrahedrally around the carbon atom and the angle between bonds is about 109.5°. The nitrogen atom in the ammonia molecule forms three covalent bonds with hydrogen atoms, but this leaves an unshared pair of lone electrons around the nitrogen atom. This lone pair repels the shared electrons in the covalent bonds and reduces the angle between the covalent bonds to about 108°. In the water molecule, the oxygen atom has two lone pairs of electrons and these repel the shared electrons in the oxygen-hydrogen bonds even more, reducing the angle between these bonds to 104.5°.

Shapes of molecules

mole fraction A measure of the amount of one of the components in a mixture. It is calculated by dividing the number of moles of the component present in the mixture by the total number of moles of substances present. The sum of the mole fractions of the components of a mixture is one.

molybdenum Element symbol, Mo; transition element; silvery hard metal; Z 42; A(r) 95.94; density (at 20°C), 10.22 g/cm^3; m.p., 2,617°C; chemically unreactive; name derived from the Greek *molybdos*, "lead;" discovered 1781; used in steel alloys; compounds are used in pigments.

monatomic molecule A molecule that consists of one atom. Noble gases are monatomic; they have a full outer shell of electrons, and it is difficult for them to share electrons to form bonds with other atoms.

mono- A prefix meaning "one."

monobasic acid An acid that has one replaceable hydrogen atom. Normal salts only can be formed. *See* basicity of acids.

monomer A basic unit from which a polymer is made, either naturally (where glucose [$C_6H_{12}O_6$] is the basic unit of polysaccharides, *see* carbohydrate) or, more usually, synthetically (where a monomer is used in the production of plastic polymers).

monosaccharides *See* carbohydrate.

monotrope Allotropes of an element that exhibit monotropy.

monotropy An element that can exist in more than allotrope but one is always more stable under all conditions. The other forms are metastable (*see* metastable).

monovalent (univalent) Having a valency of one.

mordant A substance used in dyeing to fix the color of the dye onto the fiber.

mortar A mixture of slaked lime and sand made into a paste with water. It sets to a hard mass as the water evaporates and the slaked lime slowly reacts to form calcium carbonate.

Mt Symbol for the element meitnerium.

multiple bonds Covalent bonds that contain more than two electrons. Double bonds contain four electrons. The first two electrons are considered to form a normal bond and the second two electrons are considered to be in p orbitals in the outer shells of the atoms forming the bond. These are brought close enough by the first bond to interact and form pi orbitals (*see* molecular orbitals).

Triple bonds contain six electrons. The first two are considered to form a normal bond and the second two to form a pi orbital (as in the double bond). If the outer shells of the atoms forming the bond each contain another electron (not already forming a bond) in a p orbital, a second pi orbital is formed.

N Symbol for the element nitrogen.

Na Symbol for the element sodium.

naphtha A mixture of hydrocarbons produced from petroleum by fractional distillation. It is the fraction collected between 80–160°C. It is then converted into smaller molecules by cracking.

naphthalene $C_{10}H_8$. An aromatic organic compound formed of two fused carbon rings. It is a white crystalline solid that sublimes at low temperatures; m.p., 80°C; b.p., 218°C. It is used to produces dyes and plastics.

native An element that is found naturally in its free state, uncombined with other elements.

natural gas *See* fossil fuels.

Nb Symbol for the element niobium.

Nd Symbol for the element neodymium.

Ne Symbol for the element neon.

neodymium Element symbol, Nd; rare earth element/lanthanide; soft silvery metal; Z 60; A(r) 144.24; density (at 20°C), 7 g/cm³; m.p.,1,021°C;

pi bond

pi bond

Multiple bonds

Naphthalene

name derived from the Greek words *neo*, "new," and *didymos*, "twin;" discovered 1885; used in glass coloring (violet-purple).

neon Element symbol, Ne; noble gas, group 8; colorless gas; Z 10; A(r) 20.18; density (at 20°C), 0.9 g/l at STP; m.p., −248.7°C; forms no normal chemical compounds; name derived from the Greek *neos*, "new;" discovered 1898; used in red fluorescent tubes.

neptunium Element symbol, Np; actinide; radioactive metal; Z 93; A(r) 237.051; density (at 20°C), 20.45 g/cm^3; m.p., 640°C; named for the planet Neptune; discovered 1940.

neutral a solution whose pH is 7. It is neither acidic nor alkaline.

neutralization The reaction of an acid and a base forming a salt and water. The properties of acids and bases disappear when the reaction is complete, at the end point. The solution is neutral.

neutralizers Substances (such as alkalis and carbonates) added to neutralize acid conditions. Lime is added to acid soil, to lower its pH, and to lakes where the water is becoming too acidic, to support plant and animal life. Indigestion tablets also contain neutralizers to neutralize the excessive stomach acid life that is causing indigestion.

neutral oxides Oxides (such as carbon monoxide and dinitrogen oxide) that have neither the properties of an acid nor a base.

neutron One of the three basic particles in an atom, it is found in the nucleus. With the proton, it is one of the most massive of the subatomic particles. It has zero charge.

neutron number The number of neutrons in the nucleus of an atom. All isotopes of an element have the same atomic number but different neutron numbers.

Ni Symbol for the element nickel.

nichrome A group of nickel chromium alloys that have good resistance to oxidation.

nickel Element symbol, Ni; transition element; silvery white metal, malleable and ductile; Z 28; A(r) 58.71; density (at 20°C), 8.9 g cm^3; m.p., 1,453°C; name derived from the German *Kupfernickel*, "demon's copper;" discovered 1751; used in coins and in steel alloys; used as catalyst in hydrogenation.

niobium Element symbol, Nb; transition element; soft gray-blue metal, ductile; Z 41; A(r) 92.91; density (at 20°C), 8.6 g/cm^3; m.p., 2,468°C; named after Niobe, daughter of Tantalus (Greek mythology); discovered 1801; used in special steels.

niter *See* potassium nitrate.

nitrates Salts of nitric acid. All metallic nitrates are soluble in water. Nitrates, such as sodium nitrate and ammonium nitrate, are important as fertilizers, although overuse can lead to pollution of water (*see* eutrophic).

nitrates, in fertilizers Plant growth requires nitrogen. Different plants require it in different amounts (cereals require more than potatoes), and nitrogen is removed from soil by growing plants. To ensure growth of plants each year, nitrogen should be added. This can be in the form of a synthetic fertilizer that contains nitrogen in the form of nitrates or soluble ionic compounds that dissolve into the soil where the roots of the crop can use them.

nitric acid HNO_3. A colorless, corrosive, poisonous, fuming liquid; r.d., 1.5, m.p., $-42°C$; b.p., $83°C$. It is a strong acid that forms nitrates (soluble salts). Nitric acid is a strong oxidizing agent. It is produced industrially by the Ostwald process. It is used in the manufacture of fertilizers and explosives.

nitrites Salts of nitrous acid. Both sodium and potassium nitrite are formed by heating the corresponding nitrate. They are used in the curing of meat.

nitro-chalk Ammonium nitrate to which powdered chalk has been added to prevent the formation of lumps. It is a fertilizer.

nitrogen Element symbol, N; group 5; colorless gas; Z 7; A(r) 14.01; density (at 20°C), 1.25 g/l at STP; m.p., $-209.9°C$; name derived from the words *niter* ("saltpeter," 18th century) and *genes* ("producing," Greek); discovered 1772; used in Haber process to synthesize ammonia.

nitrogen dioxide NO_2. A poisonous brown gas prepared from the reaction between concentrated nitric acid and copper or by heating dry lead(II) nitrate. It forms a mixture of nitric and nitrous acids in water.

nitrogen fixing The conversion of atmospheric nitrogen into nitrogenous substances. This occurs naturally by the action of certain soil bacteria on the nitrogen in ammonia, and the conversion of atmospheric nitrogen to its oxides by lightning. The Haber process is an industrial process for the fixing of nitrogen.

nitrogen monoxide NO. A colorless, poisonous gas; m.p., $-163.6°C$; b.p., $-151.8°C$. It forms nitrogen dioxide on contact with the oxygen in air.

nitrogen oxides in car exhaust gases In a gasoline engine, the fuel/air mixture is compressed and ignited with a spark. The nitrogen in the air reacts to form nitrogen dioxide, which is emitted and adds to atmospheric pollution because it dissolves in rainwater to increase the problem of acid rain (*see* acid rain).

nitrous acid HNO_2. A weak acid existing only in aqueous solution. It forms salts called nitrites. Nitrous acid decomposes on heating to form nitrogen dioxide and nitric acid.

No Symbol for the element nobelium.

nobelium Element symbol, No; actinide; radioactive metal (most stable isotope 254 has half-life of 55 seconds) Z 102; A(r) 255; named in honor of Alfred Nobel, Swedish inventor and industrialist; discovered 1958.

noble gases *See* group 8 elements.

noble gas structure An atom that has a stable electronic structure. Noble gases have eight electrons that completely fill part of their outer shell, which makes it difficult to form ions.

nonbiodegradable plastics Plastics that do not decay and that therefore last for a number of years.

nonelectrolyte Substances that do not conduct electricity when molten or in solution. (Substances such as mercury that conduct electricity but remain unchanged are also nonelectrolytes.)

nonmetal Generally, nonmetals are electronegative and are poor conductors of heat and electricity. They do not have a luster and are not ductile or malleable. Their oxides are acidic.

nonmetal oxide *See* acidic oxide.

normal salt A salt in which metal ions (or other cations) have replaced all the acidic hydrogen atoms in an acid.

normal solution A solution in which one gram equivalent of the substance is dissolved in one liter of solution.

Np Symbol for the element neptunium.

nuclear reaction A reaction affecting the nucleus of an atom that can split (*see* fission) or decay and emit either a particle or radiation. If a beta particle is emitted, the atomic number of the nucleus increases by one. If an alpha particle is emitted, the atomic number decreases by two and the relative atomic mass decreases by four.

nucleon A proton or neutron.

nucleon number or **mass number** The number of nucleons (protons and neutrons) in the nucleus of an atom.

nucleus The small (about 10^{-14} m diameter) core of an atom. All nuclei contain the positively charged proton, and all but hydrogen contain the zero-charged neutron. The sum of protons and neutrons is the atom's mass number (or nucleon number). The nucleus is surrounded by a cloud of electrons whose number is equal to the number of protons in the nucleus.

Control rod

To steam generator

Coolant out

Fuel element

Coolant in

Shielding

Nuclear reactor

nuclide A particular isotope of an element, identified by the number of protons and neutrons in the nucleus.

nylon A group of polyamides formed by the condensation between an amino group of one molecule and a carboxylic acid group of another. There are three main types of nylon: nylon 6, nylon 6,6, and nylon 6,10. Nylon is very strong, does not rot, and does not absorb water.

O Symbol for the element oxygen.

octane C_8H_{18}. An alkane. A flammable liquid. It has 18 isomers.

octane rating or **octane number** A measure of the quality of gasoline (*see* antiknock). Better fuel contains a higher proportion of molecules with branched chains and has a higher octane rating.

octet A group of eight electrons in the outermost shell of an atom. The noble gases have this structure. In compounds, atoms share (or donate or accept) electrons to form bonds to achieve the octet.

oil–formation *See* fossil fuels.

oil of vitriol Concentrated sulfuric acid.

oil (petroleum), refining *See* fractional distillation of oil.

oils The general name for mixtures of glycerides with a melting point at room temperature.

olefins *See* alkenes.

oleic acid $C_{17}H_{33}COOH$. A liquid unsaturated fatty acid found in many fats and oils. It is one of the fatty acids used in soap manufacture.

oleum $H_2S_2O_7$ (fuming sulfuric acid). A solution of sulfur(VI) oxide (SO_3) in concentrated sulfuric acid.

orbital An area around an atom or molecule where there is a high probability of finding an electron. An orbital has a fixed energy level. There are different types of orbitals with different shapes: s orbitals, p orbitals, d orbitals, f orbitals, etc. Each orbital can hold two electrons. Orbitals are grouped in a series of shells at a gradually increasing distance from the nucleus. *See* electronic structure of atom.

orbit of electrons *See* orbital.

order of reaction A first-order reaction is one in which there is a spontaneous decomposition of one molecule; one that takes place with two molecules is a second-order reaction, and so on.

ore A mineral from which a metal or nonmetal may be profitably extracted.

organic Relates to either living organisms or compounds containing carbon (except carbonates, hydrogen carbonates, and carbon dioxide).

Nylon thread being drawn up

Monomer B solution

Monomer A solution

Nylon

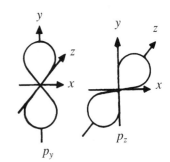

p_y

p_z

P orbitals

Before osmosis

Weak sugar solution   *Strong sugar solution*

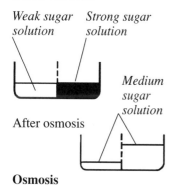

Medium sugar solution

After osmosis

Osmosis

Ammonia + air

Pt/Rh gauze catalyst   *Water*

1,472°F (800°C)

Small glass beads

$NO(g)+O_2(g)$

cooler

$NO_2(g)+O_2(g)$

65% HNO_3

Ostwald process

organic acid A group of acids whose structure includes the carboxyl group. Their general formula is $C_n H_{(2n+1)}$ COOH.

organic compounds Compounds containing carbon but not carbonates or carbon dioxide. (*See also* illustration on page 89.)

Os Symbol for the element osmium.

osmium Element symbol, Os; transition element; blue white metal; Z 76; A(r) 190.2; density (at 20°C), 22.5 g/cm³; m.p., 3,045°C; name derived from the Greek *osme*, "smell;" discovered 1803; used in alloys.

osmosis The movement of solvent molecules through a semipermeable membrane from a dilute solution to a more concentrated solution. There is a tendency for solutions separated in this way to become equal in concentration, and osmosis will stop when equilibrium is reached. Osmosis can also stop if pressure is applied to the stronger solution (*see* osmotic pressure).

osmotic pressure The pressure that must be applied to a solution, when separated from a more dilute solution by a semipermeable membrane, to prevent the inflow of solvent molecules.

Ostwald process The manufacture of nitric acid by the catalytic oxidation of ammonia. In the first step of the process, compressed air and ammonia react (at 1,472°F [800°C] in the presence of a platinum gauze catalyst) to give nitrogen monoxide and water.

$4NH_3 + 5O_2 \rightarrow 4NO + 6H_2O.$

The nitrogen monoxide cools rapidly and reacts with additional oxygen to form nitrogen dioxide $2NO + O_2 \rightarrow 2NO_2$.

The nitrogen dioxide is cooled, mixed with more oxygen, and passed through water, forming nitric acid. $4NO_2 + O_2 + 2H_2O \rightarrow 4HNO_3$.

oxidation A substance is oxidized if it gains oxygen, loses hydrogen, or loses electrons.

oxidation number *See* oxidation state.

oxidation state This gives an indication of the electron control that an atom has in a compound compared with that which it has in a pure element.

It has two parts. One is the sign: if control has increased, it is negative; if it has decreased, positive. The other part is the value, which gives the difference between the number of electrons controlled by the atom in the element and by the atom in a compound.

In oxidation there is an increase in oxidation number. When naming compounds, the oxidation state is given in Roman numerals.

Organic compounds: names (see entry on page 88)

Chain length = first part of name. Functional group = second part of name.

Examples of organic compound names

Molecule	Chain length	Functional group	Name

$$1 \longrightarrow \text{meth-}$$ $$\longrightarrow \text{–ane}$$ **Methane**

$$3 \longrightarrow \text{prop-}$$ $$\longrightarrow \text{–ane}$$ **Propane**

$$3 \longrightarrow \text{prop-}$$ $$C = C \longrightarrow \text{–ene}$$ **Propene**

$$2 \longrightarrow \text{eth-}$$ $$C = C \longrightarrow \text{–ene}$$ **Ethene**

oxide   A compound consisting of oxygen and another element only. They can be either ionic or covalent, and there are four types of oxide— acidic, basic, neutral, and amphoteric.

oxidizing agent A substance that can cause the oxidation of another substance by being reduced itself.

oxonium ion H_3O^+. The hydrated hydrogen ion formed from the combination of a hydrogen ion (single proton) with a water molecule.

oxygen   Element symbol, O; group 6; colorless, odorless gas; Z 8; A(r) 15.9994; density (at 20°C), 1.429 g/l; m.p., –218.4°C; commonly exists as diatomic form (O_2) but also forms the allotrope ozone (O_3); name derived from the Greek words *oxys*, "acid," and *genes*,

Paper chromatography

Peptide bond

"producing;" discovered 1772; used medically in breathing apparatus and has many industrial uses. Also used in rocket fuels.

oxygen, atomicity of *See* atomicity.

ozone One of the two allotropes of oxygen, existing as O_3. It is a bluish gas with a penetrating smell. It is a very strong oxidizing agent.

P Symbol for the element phosphorus.

Pa Symbol for the element protoactinium.

palladium Element symbol, Pd; transition element; soft white ductile metal; Z 46; A(r) 106.42; density (at 20°C), 12.16 g/cm³; m.p., 1,554°C; named after the asteroid Pallas; discovered 1803; used in dental work and as catalyst in hydrogenation.

palmitic acid $C_{15}H_{31}COOH$. A solid saturated fatty acid found in many fats and oils. It is one of the fatty acids used in soap manufacture.

paper chromatography A way in which some substances can be separated and identified. A spot of the mixture being investigated is placed at one edge of a piece of paper suspended in a solvent. The spot separates into its components and the components move up the paper at different rates, depending on their affinity for the paper and for the solvent used. When the paper is removed and dried, the different components appear as a line of spots along the paper and they can be identified by the distance they have traveled in a measured time.

paraffins Former name for alkanes, meaning "little affinity."

partial pressure *See* Dalton's law of partial pressure.

passive A metal that is unreactive because its surface is covered with a layer of oxide.

Pb Symbol for the element lead.

Pd Symbol for the element palladium.

pentane C_5H_{12}. An alkane; m.p., –129.7°C; b.p., 36.1°C.

peptide An organic substance consisting of two or more amino acid units joined by peptide bonds. The bonds are formed by a condensation reaction between the carboxyl group of one amino acid and the amino group of another. A molecule of water is eliminated as a peptide bond is formed.

peptide bond A link joining amino acid units, forming peptides. One end of the link is a carbon atom that has a double bond to an oxygen atom and a single bond to a nitrogen atom. The nitrogen atom forms the other end of the link and also has a single bond to a hydrogen atom.

percentage composition The proportion by mass of the component parts of a compound expressed as a percentage of the mass of the whole compound. When the percentage composition of a substance and the relative atomic mass of each element are known, the empirical formula of the compound can be calculated.

period The horizontal rows of elements in the periodic table.

The first three rows (hydrogen–helium, two elements; lithium–neon, eight elements; sodium– argon, eight elements) are short periods.

The next four rows include the elements known as transition elements (potassium–krypton, 18 elements; rubidium–xenon, 18 elements; cesium–radon, 32 elements; francium and above, 26 elements discovered so far) and are therefore long periods. The cesium–radon period also includes the lanthanides, and the period beginning with francium includes the actinides.

The atoms of the elements in a period have the same number of shells. The number of electrons in the outer shell increases by one for each position moved to the right in the periodic table. There is a change in behavior of the elements in a period from metallic (electropositive) on the left of the periodic table, to nonmetallic (electronegative) at the right of the periodic table.

periodic law Proposed in 1869 by Russian chemist Dmitry Mendeleyev, it is the basis of the modern periodic table of the elements. On arranging the elements known at that time in ascending order of their relative atomic masses, he discovered that elements with similar chemical properties appeared at fixed intervals, or periods. There were gaps in this series of elements, and these led him to predict that elements of a certain relative atomic mass would be discovered to have certain physical and chemical properties.

periodic table A table of elements arranged in ascending order of atomic number. It has eight main groups (*see* group) and seven periods (*see* period). Knowing an element's position in the periodic table enables its physical and chemical properties to be predicted.

permanent hardness Calcium or magnesium sulfates that react with the sodium stearate molecules in soap to form a scum on the surface of the water. *See* soap, hardness in water.

Permutit A compound that can soften water. It does this by exchanging its sodium ions for the calcium and magnesium ions in hard water. It consists of sodium aluminum silicate. It is a zeolite. The sodium ions do not form insoluble salts with soap and therefore do not prevent the formation of a lather. The Permutit can be returned to its original state by soaking in brine.

peroxide A compound that contains the peroxide ion O_2^{2-}. Peroxides are strong oxidizing agents. Hydrogen peroxide H_2O_2 (produced by the

Perspective formula for methane

action of water or dilute acids on sodium peroxide) is used in dilute form as a bleach and disinfectant.

perspective formula Representation of a molecule on paper: a solid line shows a bond in the same plane as the paper; a dotted line, a bond behind the paper; a wedge shape, a bond pointing outwards.

Perspex *See* poly(methylmethacrylate).

petrochemical A chemical made from petroleum.

petrol *See* gasoline.

pH A scale that gives a measure of the acidity of an aqueous solution. The concentration of hydrogen ions is used in the calculations, and the pH value of a solution is given as $\log_{10}(1/H^+)$, where H^+ is the concentration of hydrogen ions. A neutral solution has a pH of 7, while an acidic solution has a lower value and an alkaline solution a higher value. (*See also* illustration on page 93.)

phase Part of a system whose physical properties and chemical composition are consistent and are separated from other parts of the system by a boundary surface. For example, two immiscible liquids form a two-phase liquid system; a vessel containing ice, water, and water vapor is a three-phase system.

phase change The change that occurs when a substance changes its physical state, between being a solid, liquid, or gas or being in solution.

phase diagram A diagram showing the change between states for a substance at different conditions of pressure and temperature.

phenol C_6H_5OH. An aromatic organic compound; m.p., 43°C; b.p., 183°C. It is an acidic, poisonous, corrosive crystalline compound that forms metallic salts. Phenol is colorless, but turns pink on exposure to air and light. It is soluble in water at room temperatures; its solution is called carbolic acid, which is used as a disinfectant. Phenol can be obtained from coal tar, and it is readily halogenated, sulphonated, and nitrated. Phenol is used in the manufacture of phenol/methanal resins, poly(carbonates), epoxy resins, nylon, dyes, and detergents.

phenol/methanal resins Polymers made by a condensation reaction between phenol and methanal. They are dark in color and are good electrical insulators. Bakelite is a phenol/methanal resin.

phenolphthalein An acid-base indicator used in titrations of a weak acid with a strong alkali. Its colorless crystals turn pink when the solution is alkaline.

phenylethene $C_6H_5CH=CH_2$. A liquid aromatic hydrocarbon; m.p., –31°C; b.p., 145°C.

phenyl group The organic group C_6H_5- present in benzene.

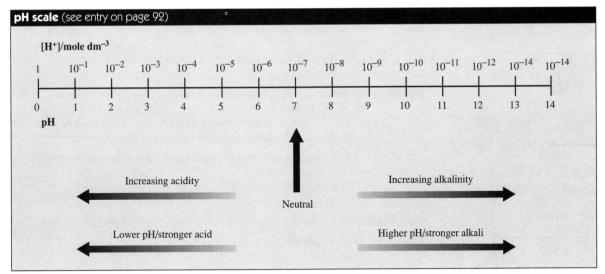

pH scale (see entry on page 92)

[H^+]/mole dm^{-3}

| 1 | 10^{-1} | 10^{-2} | 10^{-3} | 10^{-4} | 10^{-5} | 10^{-6} | 10^{-7} | 10^{-8} | 10^{-9} | 10^{-10} | 10^{-11} | 10^{-12} | 10^{-14} | 10^{-14} |

pH: 0 1 2 3 4 5 6 7 8 9 10 11 12 13 14

Increasing acidity ← → Increasing alkalinity

Neutral

Lower pH/stronger acid   Higher pH/stronger alkali

phosphates Salts of phosphoric acid H_3PO_4. As this is a tribasic acid, three types of phosphate can be formed: the alkaline phosphate (containing the trivalent radical PO_4), the neutral hydrogenphosphate (containing the divalent radical HPO_4), and the acidic dihydrogephosphate (containing the monovalent radical H_2PO_4).

phosphorescence The emission of light by an object, and the persistence of this emission over long periods, following irradiation by light or other forms of radiation. Energy is absorbed by the object and then re-radiated at a longer wavelength than the incident light. White phosphorus, zinc sulfide, and calcium sulfide are phosphorescent substances.

phosphoric(V) acid H_3PO_4 (orthophosphoric acid). A white, very deliquescent crystalline solid; m.p., 42.35°C. It is very soluble in water, forming a weak tribasic acid. It is also soluble in ethanol. Commercially produced from phosphate-containing rocks. *See* phosphates.

phosphorus Element symbol, P; group 5; three main allotropes: white (containing tetrahedral P4 atoms), red (a polymer), and black (structure like graphite); Z 15; A(r) 30.97; density (at 20°C), 1.82 g/cm³ (white); m.p., 44.1°C (white); name derived from the Greek *phosphorus*, "light-bearing;" discovered 1669; used in fertilizers and matches.

phosphorus chlorides PCl_3 (phosphorus(III) chloride, phosphorus trichloride). A colorless fuming liquid, m.p., –112°C; b.p., 75.5°C. It hydrolyzes violently to form phosphonic acid (H_3PO_3), which is used in organic synthesis to replace an –OH group with a chlorine atom.

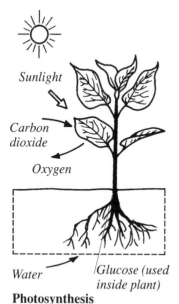

Sunlight

Carbon dioxide

Oxygen

Water | *Glucose (used inside plant)*

Photosynthesis

Safety pipette filler

Graduation mark on pipette

Pipette

PCl$_5$ (phosphorus(V) chloride, phosphorus pentachloride). A yellow-white crystalline solid that fumes in air; m.p., 148°C (under pressure). It sublimes between 160–162°C and decomposes in water to form phosphoric acid and hydrogen chloride. It is also used as a chlorinating agent.

phosphorus oxides P$_2$O$_3$ (phosphorus(III) oxide, phosphorus trioxide). A white, or colorless, waxy solid; m.p., 23.8°C; b.p. 173.8°C; reacts with cold water, forming phosphonic acid (H$_3$PO$_3$). With hot water it reacts to form phosphine gas (PH$_3$) and phosphoric acid.

P$_2$O$_5$ (phosphorus(V) oxide, phosphorus pentoxide); m.p., 580°C under pressure. It sublimes at 360°C and reacts violently with water, forming phosphoric acid. It is used as a drying agent and as a dehydrating agent.

photocatalytic The speeding up or slowing of a chemical reaction by light.

photochemical reaction A chemical reaction that is initiated by a particular wavelength of light.

photolysis The decomposition or disassociation of a compound when exposed to light of a certain wavelength.

photosynthesis This is an important photochemical reaction. It is the process by which green plants make carbohydrates using carbon dioxide and water. Oxygen is also produced.

phototropy The ability of certain substances to change color reversibly on exposure to light of a certain wavelength.

physical change A reversible change, such as a change of state, where no chemical reaction takes place and no new substances are formed. A reversible color change is also a physical change.

physical chemistry The branch of chemistry concerned with the study of the physical properties of elements and compounds, and the relationship between these properties and their chemical structure.

pigment An organic or inorganic chemical that has a characteristic color.

pi orbital *See* molecular orbital.

pipette A glass tube that is used to measure and transfer a fixed volume of liquid. Pipettes are available in a range of volumes. Suction is applied to the top of a pipette to draw a liquid up so that its meniscus is on the marked line on the pipette. When the suction is released, the liquid flows out of the pipette.

planar A molecule whose atoms are in the same plane. (It is flat.)

plaster of Paris *See* calcium sulfate.

plastic A substance that can be shaped by heating and pressure during manufacture to form a stable product.

plasticizer A substance added to polymers and other materials to increase their flexibility.

plastics, burning When plastics burn, they emit poisonous gases. The type of gas depends on the particular plastic, but all plastics will emit carbon monoxide if combustion is incomplete. Polyurethane plastics contain nitrogen, which combines with the carbon and hydrogen that are also in the plastic to form hydrogen cyanide. Hydrogen chloride is produced from the combustion of polychloroethene.

platinum Element symbol, Pt; transition element; soft, shiny silver metal that is malleable and ductile; Z 78; A(r) 195.09; density (at 20°C), 21.4 g/cm^3; m.p., 1,772°C; name derived from the Spanish *plata*, "silver;" discovered before 1700; used in jewelry and electrical contacts; also used as a catalyst in many processes, including the removal of harmful substances from vehicle exhaust gases.

plutonium Element symbol, Pu; actinide; silvery metal, very radioactive; Z 94; A(r) 244; density (at 20°C), 19.8 g/cm^3; m.p., 641°C; 13 isotopes known; named after the planet Pluto; discovered 1940; plutonium-238 is used in nuclear reactors as a power source; plutonium-239 is used in nuclear weapons and some nuclear reactors.

Pm Symbol for the element promethium.

Po Symbol for the element polonium.

poison (1) A substance that causes damage to a living organism.

(2) A substance that destroys the activity of a catalyst.

polar molecule A molecule that has a positive charge at one end and a negative charge at the other. This occurs because the two electrons in covalent bonds are not shared equally between atoms that have different electronegativities. This leads to a separation of charge across the bond. If the effects are not canceled out over the molecule as a whole, the molecule becomes polar. Lone pairs of electrons also cause a molecule to be strongly polar. *See* molecules—shapes of, core charge.

pollution Harmful contamination of the environment caused by, for example, poor disposal of waste products, including exhaust gases, escape of dangerous substances (such as leaks from petrochemical tankers), and excessive amounts of nitrate-containing fertilizers being washed into rivers and lakes.

polonium Element symbol, Po; group 6; radioactive metal; Z 84; A(r) 210; density (at 20°C), 9.4 g/cm^3; m.p., 254°C; name derived from Medieval Latin *Polonia*, "Poland;" discovered 1898.

poly- Prefix meaning "many," used in the naming of chemical compounds.

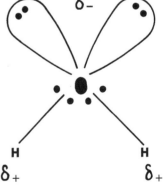

Polar molecule

polyamide A condensation polymer that contains the amide group. Nylon is a polyamide.

polybasic acid An acid that has more than one hydrogen atom that can be replaced to form a salt.

polycarbonates Thermoplastics made by condensation polymerization of carbonyl chloride (phosgene) and dihydroxy organic compounds such as diphenylol propane. Polycarbonates are tough and transparent; they are used for spectacle lenses, babies' bottles, and shatterproof windows.

Polychloroethene

polychloroethene (polyvinyl chloride, PVC) Thermoplastic polymer made by addition polymerization from chloroethene. It is a very tough white solid material and is easy to color. It is resistant to fire, chemicals, and weather, and has many uses. It is used as a floor covering, for artificial leathers, containers, and drainage pipes.

polycondensation *See* condensation polymerization.

polyesters A group of condensation polymers formed from a polybasic carboxylic acid and a polyhydric alcohol. They contain ester groups.

polyethene (**polythene**, **polyethylene**). Thermoplastic polymer made by addition polymerization of ethene. Polyethene is a saturated alkane and is thus very unreactive. Polyethene is a tough white waxy solid that is unaffected by acids, bases, or solvents, or oxidizing or reducing agents. It is flexible and a good insulator. It can be manufactured in one way to produce low-density polyethene or LDPE. This is very flexible and can be manufactured in sheets for packaging. The high-density form (HDPE) can also be made. This is also flexible and can be blow-molded to produce containers. Both types can be used for injection molding to manufacture boxes and bowls, etc.

polymer A material containing very large molecules that are built up from a series of small basic units (monomers). It is a term often applied to plastics. There can be between hundreds and hundreds of thousands of basic units in a polymer. (*See also* illustration on page 97.)

$$n\,C_3H_6 \rightarrow (C_3H_6)n$$

Polymerization of propene

polymerization The formation of a polymer from monomers. There are two types of polymerization reactions: addition and condensation. Polymers formed from a single monomer are called homopolymers. Polymers formed from two or more monomers are called copolymers.

polymethylmethacrylate (**polymethyl 2-methylpropenoate**, Perspex) A transparent thermoplastic addition polymer. Made by polymerizing methyl methacrylate (methyl 2-methylpropenoate), it contains many ester groups and is thus called a polyester. It is lighter and stronger than glass but more easily scratched. It is used for airplane windows and car lights.

polymorphism A substance's potential to exist in more than one form. Allotropy is one form of polymorphism, but polymorphism also covers noncrystalline forms. Each polymorphic form of a substance is stable within a range of physical conditions (temperature, pressure) and will transform to another polymorphic form at a fixed transition temperature.

polypeptide A peptide that contains at least 10 amino acids. Protein molecules usually contain between 100 and 300 amino acids. The particular amino acids present in the structure of the polypeptide and the sequence in which they occur determine its properties. Enzymes are polypeptides.

polyphenylethene (polystyrene) A polymer made by the addition polymerization of phenylethene. Polyphenylethene is resistant to water, acids, alkalis, and solvents. It is similar to polyethene and can be used as a glass substitute. It is often seen in its expanded form—after air or carbon dioxide has been blown into it—when it forms an opaque solid, which has good insulating properties. In this form it is used for cups and packaging material in the fast-food sector.

polypropene (**polypropylene**) Thermoplastic polymer made by addition polymerization of propene. It is similar to polyethene but with greater resistance to heat and organic solvents. It is strong and hard-wearing, is used for carpet, and injection molded for car fenders.

Polymer (see entry on page 96)

Restructuring of propene to make polypropene

polysaccharides *See* carbohydrate.

polystyrene *See* polyphenylethene.

polytetrafluoroethene (PTFE, Teflon, Fluon) Thermosetting polymer formed by the polymerization of polytetrafluoroethene. A very inert substance that is very resistant to chemicals, heat, and wear. It is used to give a nonstick coating to cooking utensils. It has a low coefficient of friction and is used for bearings and in replacement joints in the body.

polythene *See* polyethene.

polyurethanes A wide range of condensation polymers that can be either thermosetting or thermoplastic. They contain the urethane (–NH.CO.O–) group. They are formed from polyhydric alcohols and organic isocyanates. They can be found in adhesives, paints, and plastics. If water is added during manufacture, polyurethanes form into a foam, which can be either rigid or flexible. These foams are used in upholstery, insulation, and carpet backing.

polyvinyl chloride *See* polychloroethene.

p orbital A type of orbital. Three types are possible, each of which can hold two electrons. *See* molecular orbital.

porous Able to allow the passage of water, air, or other fluids.

post-actinide elements *See* transactinide elements.

potassium Element symbol, K; alkali metal, group 1; soft silver-white metal; Z 19; A(r) 39.1; density (at 20°C), 0.87 g/cm^3; m.p., 63.3°C; reacts violently with water; used as reducing agent; name derived from English *potash*; symbol name derived from modern Latin *kalium*; alkali; discovered 1807; used in fertilizers.

potassium bromide KBr. An ionic compound that exists as K$^+$ Br$^-$ (m.p., 750°C). It is nonvolatile and soluble in water. Its aqueous solution is an electrolyte.

potassium carbonate K$_2$CO$_3$. A white deliquescent solid (m.p., 891°C) that is soluble in water, forming an alkaline solution. It is used as a drying agent in the manufacture of soft soap and in the manufacture of hard glass.

potassium chlorate KClO$_3$. A white solid soluble salt (m.p., 360°C) that decomposes above 400°C, giving off oxygen. It is a powerful oxidizing agent. Potassium chlorate is used in matches, fireworks, explosives, weed killers, etc.

potassium chloride KCl. An ionic compound that exists as K$^+$ Cl$^-$ (m.p., 790°C). It is nonvolatile and is soluble in water. Its aqueous solution is an electrolyte.

Lilac flame

Potassium in water

Potassium

potassium hydrogencarbonate $KHCO_3$ (potassium bicarbonate) A white crystalline solid that is soluble in water. It decomposes at about 120°C. It is used in baking, soft drinks, and carbon dioxide fire extinguishers. A solution of potassium hydrogencarbonate makes a good buffer solution.

potassium hydrogensulfate $KHSO_4$ (potassium bisulfate).

potassium hydroxide KOH. A white deliquescent solid (m.p., 306°C; b.p., 1,320°C). It is soluble in water, the aqueous solution is a strong alkali. It is used in the manufacturing of soap and fertilizers, as an electrolyte in batteries, and to absorb acidic gases such as carbon dioxide and sulfur dioxide.

potassium iodide KI. A white crystalline solid; m.p., 686°C; b.p., 1,330°C. It is prepared by adding iodine to a hot concentrated aqueous solution of potassium hydroxide and separating the resulting potassium iodide from the potassium iodate that is also produced. It is soluble in water. Potassium iodide is used medically in the treatment of iodine deficiency diseases.

potassium nitrate KNO_3 (niter, saltpeter) A white crystalline solid that is soluble in water; m.p., 334°C; decomposes at 400°C. It is prepared by the double decomposition of boiling saturated solutions of sodium nitrate and potassium chloride, followed by fractional crystallization (sodium chloride crystallizes out first at the temperature of the reaction). Potassium nitrate is a strong oxidizing agent, and it is used in gunpowder, fertilizer, and fireworks.

potassium silicate K_2SiO_3. It is used, with calcium silicate, in the manufacture of hard glass, which has a higher melting point than ordinary (soda) glass, a mixture of sodium and calcium silicates.

potassium sulfate K_2SO_4. A white crystalline solid; m.p., 1,072°C. It is soluble in water and can be prepared by neutralizing potassium hydroxide with sulfuric acid. It is found as the mineral schonite, and it is used in fertilizers, cements, and glass.

Pr   Symbol for the element praseodymium.

praseodymium Element symbol, Pr; rare earth /lanthanide; soft silvery metal; Z 59; A(r) 140.91; density (at 20 C), 6.77 (white) g/cm³; m.p., 931°C; name derived from the Greek words *prasios*, "green," and *didymos*, "twin;" discovered 1885.

precipitate An insoluble substance formed by a chemical reaction. Precipitation is the process by which a precipitate is formed.

principle of conservation of energy Energy is neither created nor destroyed in a chemical reaction.

producer gas Producer gas is a mixture of one part of carbon monoxide to two

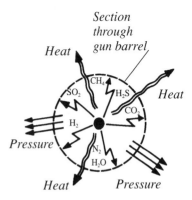

Potassium nitrate acts as an oxidizing agent, producing gases.

Potassium nitrate in gunpowder

parts of nitrogen. It is formed by blowing air through hot coke in a "gas producer." It is much cheaper than coal gas but has a lower calorific value.

$C + O_2 \rightarrow CO_2$ + heat.

$CO_2 + C \rightarrow 2CO$ – heat.

Or $2C + $ air $(O_2 + 4N_2) \rightarrow 2CO + 4N_2$ + heat.

product A substance produced during a chemical reaction. In an equation describing a chemical reaction, the products are shown to the right of the arrow.

promethium Element symbol, Pm; rare earth/lanthanide; soft silvery metal; Z 61; A(r) 145; density (at 20°C), 7.26 g/cm^3; m.p., 1,168°C; named after Promethius, mythical Greek character; discovered 1945; used in luminous paint for watches.

propane C_3H_8. An alkane. It is a colorless flammable gas (m.p., –189°C; b.p., –42°C) that is found in natural gas and petroleum. It is used as a fuel and in the synthesis of organic compounds. When liquefied it is known as liquefied petroleum gas (LPG) and is a clean-burning fuel.

propanone CH_3COOCH_3 (acetone) A ketone; m.p., –95.4°C; b.p., 56.2°C.

propene C_2H_4 (propylene) An alkene. It is a colorless gas (m.p., –81°C; b.p., 48.8°C) that is made by cracking petroleum. It is used in the manufacture of polypropene and other organic chemicals such as propanone and glycerin.

properties The intrinsic features of a substance that can identify it. Physical properties include features such as color, boiling and melting points, crystal form, and solubility. Chemical properties include identifying if the substance is a metal or nonmetal, an oxidizing or reducing agent, its valency, and the result of a reaction with acid.

propyl group The organic group $–C_3H_7$.

proteins Proteins are important in the nutrition, structure, and function of living organisms. They are large polypeptides, and the particular amino acids present in the structure of the protein and the sequence in which they occur determine their properties.

Proteins found in skin, hair, and muscle are fibrous proteins; they are insoluble in water.

Enzymes and protein hormones (such as insulin) are globular proteins, which are soluble in water.

Bond formation in a protein determines its structure. The helical shape of fibrous proteins is caused by hydrogen bonding between N–H and C=O groups.

protoactinium Element symbol, Pa; actinide; Z 91; A(r) 231.04; density (at 20°C), 15.37 g/cm^3; m.p., 1,200°C; name derived from the Greek word *protos*, "first," and *actinium*; discovered 1917.

proton One of the basic particles in the atom, found in the nucleus with the neutron. It is one of the most massive of the subatomic particles, similar in mass to the neutron. It has positive charge. In a neutral atom the number of protons is equal to the number of electrons. Its mass is 1.673×10^{-27} kg.

protonated Containing an additional proton (or hydrogen ion H$^+$). For example, the protonated water molecule is the hydroxonium ion H$_3$O$^+$.

proton number *See* atomic number.

Proust's law *See* law of constant composition.

Pt Symbol for the element platinum.

PTFE *See* polytetrafluoroethene.

Pu Symbol for the element plutonium.

PVC *See* polychloroethene.

pyridine C$_6$H$_5$N. An aromatic heterocyclic compound. It is a very stable colorless liquid with an unpleasant smell. It is used as a solvent.

pyrites A mineral containing metal sulfides such as iron(II) disulfide (FeS$_2$).

pyrolysis The decomposition of a substance by heat. *See* cracking.

quadrivalent (tetravalent) Having a valency of four.

qualitative A statement, or analysis, that gives the composition of an item, not the amounts present.

qualitative analysis The analysis of a sample of an unknown compound to identify its constituent parts. Such analysis is done using chemical and physical tests (for example, flame test).

quantitative A statement, or analysis, that gives the amounts of an item present.

quantitative analysis The analysis of a sample of a compound whose component parts are known in order to estimate the amounts of the component parts present in the sample. Volumetric and gravimetric methods can be used.

quicklime *See* calcium oxide.

Ra Symbol for the element radium.

radical A group of atoms forming part of many molecules. Radicals are very reactive as they have an incomplete electron structure.

Pyridine heterocyclic compound

Initial volume

Volume used

Start

Midway

End

Quantitive analysis

radioactive series There are three naturally occurring radioactive series - the thorium series, the actinium series, and the uranium series. Each series is headed by the named element and radioactive decay of this element proceeds. Alpha and beta particles and gamma radiation are emitted at different stages, creating different nuclides that undergo further decay until a stable nuclide (lead in all three cases) is formed.

radioactive tracers Labeling of non-radioactive material by adding small quantities of a radioactive preparation to study the movement of the material.

radioactivity The spontaneous disintegration of certain isotopes accompanied by the emission of radiation (alpha particles, beta particles, gamma waves).

radiocarbon dating *See* carbon dating.

radium Element symbol, Ra; alkaline earth metal, group 2; radioactive white metal; Z 88; A(r) 226.03; density (at 20°C), 5 g/cm^3; m.p., 700°C; name derived from the Latin *radius*, "ray;" discovered 1898; used in luminous paints, neutron source, and radiotherapy.

radon Element symbol, Rn; noble gas, group 8; colorless radioactive gas; Z 86; A(r) 222; density (at 20°C), 9.96 g/l at STP; m.p., −71°C; name derived from the radium; discovered 1900.

Raoult's law In a solution at a constant temperature, the vapor pressure of the solvent is lowered in proportion to the mole fraction of the solute.

rare earth elements *See* lanthanides.

rate of reaction For a chemical reaction, a measure of either the amount of reactants used or amount of products formed in unit time. It depends on the concentration of the reactants, temperature, catalyst, and pressure.

raw materials Substances used as a starting point in industrial processes. Important raw materials for the chemical industry include air, water, minerals, hydrocarbons, and metallic ores.

rayon An early synthetic fiber made from wood pulp. There are two methods of making rayon: the acetate method and the viscose method. The acetate method uses cellulose ethanoate, which is dissolved in a solvent and extruded into air through very fine nozzles. The solvent evaporates, leaving the filaments of acetate rayon, which can be spun into threads. In the viscose method the wood pulp is dissolved in carbon disulfide and sodium hydroxide. When this liquid is extruded through fine nozzles into a solution of dilute sulfuric acid, cellulose filaments are produced, which can be spun into threads.

Rb Symbol for the element rubidium.

r.d. Abbreviation for relative density.

Re Symbol for the element rhenium.

reactant A substance present at the start of chemical reaction that takes part in the reaction. In an equation describing a chemical reaction, the reactants are shown to the left of the arrow.

reaction A process in which substances react to form new substances. Bonds are broken and reformed in chemical reactions.

reactivity series of metals (activity series of metals) Metallic elements arranged in order of their decreasing chemical reactivity. Hydrogen is included in the series. Metals placed above hydrogen liberate it from water and dilute acids. A metal may displace another metal from the salt of a metal placed below it in the series. Some elements are in different positions in this series from their positions in the electrochemical series.

recycling metals *See* metals recycling.

recycling plastics The collection of waste plastic materials, sorting into different types (labels usually indicate the type of plastic used), and use of the resulting plastics to manufacture new items.

red lead *See* lead oxides.

redox chemistry A process in which one substance is reduced and another is oxidized at the same time.

reducing agent A chemical that can reduce another while being oxidized itself.

reducing sugar A sugar containing an easily oxidized group, such as an aldehyde or ketone group. All monosaccharides and some disaccharides (lactose and maltose) are reducing sugars.

reduction A chemical reaction in which a substance undergoes one of the following changes—a loss of oxygen, a gain of hydrogen, a gain of one or more electrons. It is the reverse of oxidation.

refining The process by which a substance is purified. This can be done by removing impurities, for example, in the extraction of a metal from its ore. It can also describe the separation of a particular substance from a mixture of similar substances, for example, in the production of certain hydrocarbon products by the fractional distillation of petroleum.

reforming The use of a platinum-based catalyst in the conversion of hydrocarbon molecules into other products. It is an important process in the petrochemical industry. The molecule is not changed in size but in structure. The octane rating (the proportion of branched hydrocarbon chains to straight chains) of a fuel is improved by the

Ice

Copper wire

Regelation   *Weights*

reforming process. This process is also used to form aromatic compounds from alkenes.

regelation The melting of ice when subjected to pressure and refreezing on removal of that pressure.

relative atomic mass (A(r)) The ratio of the mass of an average atom of an element to 1/12 of the mass of an atom of the carbon-12 isotope. (Mass of an atom of the carbon-12 isotope is taken as 12.)

relative density (r.d.) The ratio of the density of a substance at 20°C divided by the density of water at 4°C. It is also the ratio of the mass of a volume of the substance to the mass of an equal volume of water (both measure at the same temperature). The relative density of a gas can be given relative to dry air or to hydrogen (all measurements at STP) to that of a reference substance (usually water, for liquids or solids). Formerly called specific gravity.

relative formula mass *See* formula mass.

relative molecular mass (M_r) The ratio of the mass of a molecule of the element or compound to 1/12 of the mass of an atom of the carbon-12 isotope. (Mass of an atom of the carbon-12 isotope is taken as 12.)

repeating unit A group of atoms in the structure of a polymer that is repeated many times.

residue The solid remaining after the completion of a chemical process.

reversible reactions A chemical reaction that can proceed in either direction. It does not reach completion but achieves dynamic equilibrium.

Rf Symbol for the element rutherfordium.

Rh Symbol for the element rhodium.

rhenium Element symbol, Re; transition element; silvery gray metal; Z 75; A(r) 186.2; density (at 20°C), 21.02 g/cm³; m.p., 3,180°C; name derived from the Latin name for the river Rhine (*Rhenus*); discovered 1925; used in alloys, thermocouples, and catalysts.

rhodium Element symbol, Rh; transition element; silvery white metal; Z 45; A(r) 102.91; density (at 20°C), 12.44 g/cm³; m.p., 1,966°C; very inert; name derived from the Greek *rhodon*, "rose;" discovered 1803; used in platinum alloys.

Rn Symbol for the element radon.

rock salt (halite). A mineral form of sodium chloride. It can be extracted by pumping water into underground deposits where it dissolves the rock salt, producing brine that is evaporated to produce the salt. Rock salt is also produced by evaporation of seawater.

roentgenium Element symbol Rg; transition element; Z 111; A(r) 272; named in honor of the German physicist Wilhelm Röntgen. Discovered 1994.

room temperature A temperature in the range 15–25°C.

Ru Symbol for the element ruthenium.

rubber An elastic polymer that is a good insulator. It was originally a natural product formed from the milky sap of rubber trees, but most is now synthetic, derived from butadiene.

rubidium Element symbol, Rb; alkali metal, group 1; silvery white, very reactive metal; Z 37; A(r) 85.47; density (at 20°C), 1.53 g/cm^3; m.p., 38.9°C; very reactive; burns spontaneously in air; name derived from the Latin *rubidus*, "red;" discovered 1861; used as a getter and in photocells.

rusting The way in which iron is attacked by air and water to form rust (hydrated iron oxide) on its surface.

Rusting

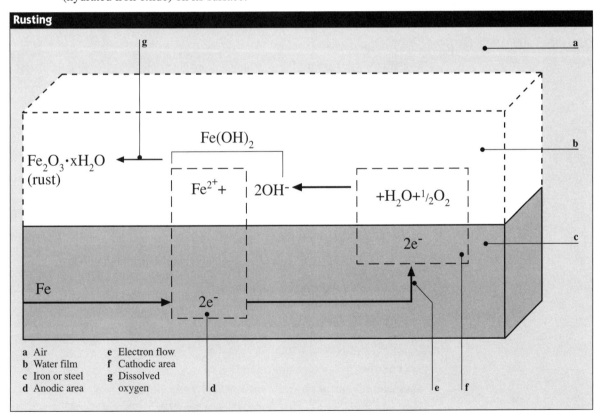

a Air e Electron flow
b Water film f Cathodic area
c Iron or steel g Dissolved
d Anodic area   oxygen

ruthenium Element symbol, Ru; transition element; gray white metal; Z 44; A(r) 101.07; density (at 20°C), 12.36 g/cm^3; m.p., 2,310°C; name derived from the Latin name *Ruthenia* ("Russia"); discovered 1808.

rutherfordium Element symbol, Rf; transition element; Z 104; A(r) 261; named in honor of Lord Rutherford, the New Zealand physicist; discovered 1964. Formerly known as unnilquadium and kurchatovium.

S Symbol for the element sulfur.

sacrificial anode A sacrificial anode is a block of an electropositive metal in contact with an object being protected from corrosion. It relies on the principle that if two metals are in contact, electrons will flow from the more electropositive metal to the less electropositive metal; the more electropositive metal becomes the anode in the cell created. The sacrificial anode is more electropositive than the object being protected so electrons will flow from the sacrificial anode to the object. In this way steel pipes are protected by magnesium filings and iron hulls of ships are protected by zinc blocks. (*See* sacrificial protection.)

sacrificial protection By attaching a more electropositive metal to the metal that requires protection, the protected metal is no longer corroded because the attached metal has become the anode in the corrosion process and is corroded in its place.

sal ammoniac *See* ammonium chloride.

saline A solution containing one or more salts.

salt A compound formed from an acid in which all or part of the hydrogen atoms are replaced by a metal or metal-like group. They are generally crystalline.

saltpeter *See* potassium nitrate.

salts, preparation of Six common methods:
(1) Action of an acid on a metal.
(2) Action of an acid on an insoluble oxide or hydroxide.
(3) Action of an acid on an insoluble carbonate.
(4) Action of an acid on a soluble base (alkali) or on a soluble carbonate.
(5) Precipitation of an insoluble salt.
(6) Synthesis from its elements.

sal volatile *See* ammonium carbonate.

samarium Element symbol, Sm; rare earth element/lanthanide; soft silvery metal; Z 62; A(r) 150.4; density (at 20°C), 7.52 g/cm^3; m.p.,

Steel pipe

Magnesium

Sacrificial anode

1,077°C; neutron absorber; named after Colonel Samarski, Russian mine official; discovered 1879; used to make alloys for nuclear reactor parts; oxide used in permanent magnets.

saponification The treatment of an ester (hydrolysis) with a strong alkaline solution to form a salt of a carboxylic acid and an alcohol. An example is the formation of soap by treating a solution containing esters such as glyceryl stearate with sodium hydroxide to form sodium stearate and the alcohol glycerol.

saturated A solution where there is an equilibrium between the solution and its solute.

saturated hydrocarbon A saturated hydrocarbon that contains only single bonds; it cannot add on extra hydrogen atoms.

saturated solution A solution that can dissolve no more of the solute at a given temperature. There is an equilibrium between the solute and solution.

Sb Symbol for the element antimony.

Sc Symbol for the element scandium.

scandium Element symbol, Sc; transition element; soft, silvery metal; Z 21; A(r) 44.96; density (at 20°C), 2.99 g/cm^3; m.p., 1,541°C; name derived from the Latin *Scandia*, "Scandinavia;" discovered 1879; used in small quantities to strengthen alloys.

Se Symbol for the element selenium.

seaborgium Element symbol, Sg; transition element; Z 106; A(r) 263; named in honor of American nuclear chemist Glenn T. Seaborg; discovered 1974. Formerly known as unnilhexium.

sedimentation The settling out of particles in suspension in a liquid at the bottom of the liquid, because of gravity.

seed crystals A small crystal added to a saturated or supersaturated solution to cause crystallization.

selenium Element symbol, Se; group 6; metalloid; several allotropes: red, gray, and black; Z 34; A(r) 78.96; density (at 20°C), 4.8 g/cm^3 (gray); m.p., 217°C (gray); element is a semiconductor; name derived from the Greek *selene*, "moon;" discovered 1817; used in electronics; gray allotrope is photosensitive and is used in xerography and photo-electric cells.

semi-permeable membrane A substance that allows solvent, but not solute, molecules to pass through.

separation of mixtures The separation method used depends on the physical properties of the components of the mixture. Methods include filtration and fractional distillation.

Selenium cell

Sg Symbol for the element seaborgium.

shell A group of orbitals that are grouped at a similar distance from an atomic nucleus.

$$CH_3CH_3$$

Shortened structural formula

shortened structural formula This gives the sequence of groups of atoms in a molecule, showing which groups of atoms are present, and gives an idea of the molecule's structure, for example, CH_3CH_2OH for ethanol.

SI Abbreviation for *Système International* (d'Unités), which proposed a system of coherent metric units (SI units) for international recognition in 1960 that is now the standard system of units used in science.

Si Symbol for the element silicon.

sigma orbital *See* molecular orbital.

silica *See* silicon(IV) oxide.

silica gel Amorphous form of hydrated silica. It is very hygroscopic and is used to absorb water. When saturated it can be regenerated by heat.

silicon Element symbol, Si; group 4; metalloid; Z 14; A(r) 28.09; density (at 20°C), 2.3 g/cm^3; m.p., 1,410°C; second most abundant element in Earth's crust (SiO_2); name derived from the Latin *silex*, "flint;" discovered 1824; used in transistors.

silicon dioxide *See* silicon(IV) oxide.

silicon(IV) oxide SiO_2 (silicon dioxide, silica) It is a hard crystalline solid (m.p., 1,880°C) occurring naturally as quartz and in sand and flint. In crystals of silicon(IV) oxide, the silicon atoms are bonded tetrahedrally to four oxygen atoms, forming a very rigid structure. Silicon(IV) oxide is used in glass manufacture.

silver Element symbol, Ag; transition element; white shiny ductile metal; Z 47; A(r) 107.87; density (at 20°C), 10.49 g/cm^3; m.p., 961.9°C; name *seolfor* in Old English; element symbol derived from the Latin *argentum*; known since prehistoric times; used in jewelry, electrical components, photography, and as a catalyst.

silver bromide AgBr. An insoluble light yellow salt; m.p., 432°C. Silver bromide dissolves in ammonia solution. On exposure to light it decomposes to form silver and bromine. It is used for photographic emulsions.

silver chloride AgCl. An insoluble white salt, m.p.; 455°C, b.p., 1,550°C. It dissolves in ammonia solution. Silver chloride is sensitive to light, slowly decomposing to form silver and chlorine. It is used for photographic emulsions.

silver iodide AgI. An insoluble yellow solid; m.p., 556°C; b.p., 1,506°C. It does not dissolve in ammonia solution. Silver iodide is sensitive to light, slowly decomposing to form silver and iodine. It is used for photographic emulsions.

silver mirror test Test for the presence of an aldehyde. The sample to be tested is warmed in a test tube with a quantity of Tollen's reagent. If the sample contains an aldehyde, a bright silver mirror is formed on the inside of the test tube as the complex silver ions $[Ag(NH_3)_2]^+$ in the Tollen's reagent are reduced to silver (ketones do not form a silver mirror in this test).

silver nitrate $AgNO_3$. A very soluble white salt; m.p., 212°C. It decomposes to form silver, oxygen, and nitrogen dioxide on heating. It is used for photographic emulsions. Silver nitrate is used in a test for the presence of chloride ions (*see* chlorides). It is also used to test for bromide and iodide ions.

silver sulfide Ag_2S. A very insoluble black salt. It is precipitated when hydrogen sulfide gas is bubbled through a solution containing silver ions. Argentite is a mineral that contains silver sulfide.

simple formula This shows the ratio of ions present in a compound, for example, $CaCl_2$.

single bond A covalent bond formed by a shared pair of electrons (*see* bond).

slag Waste material that collects on the surface of a molten metal during the process of either extraction or refining. It is composed of oxides, phosphates, silicates, and sulfides.

slaked lime *See* calcium hydroxide.

Sm Symbol for the element samarium.

smelting The process of extracting a metal from its ores. It is usually performed by heating the ore with a flux and a reducing agent.

Sn Symbol for the element tin.

soap A substance that will dissolve grease.

Hard soap is a sodium salt of a long chain fatty acid, such as palmitic acid ($C_{15}H_{31}COOH$), oleic acid ($C_{17}H_{33}COOH$), or stearic acid ($C_{17}H_{35}COOH$).

A soft soap is one where sodium is replaced by potassium.

In the manufacture of soap, a hot concentrated solution of sodium hydroxide is added to vegetable oils or animal fats. Vegetable oils and fats contain many different esters, such as glyceryl stearate (formed from an alcohol such as glycerol and a long-chain fatty acid such as stearic acid). Sodium salts of fatty acids (palmitic, stearic, and oleic) form soap, which separates and floats on the surface when

Detergent attacks grease on cloth

Soap

Grease is partly emulsified

Grease is split up into small "soluble" droplets

strong brine is added. Glycerol remains at the bottom of the mixture.

Soap dissolves grease because the –COONa end of the sodium stearate molecule is hydrophilic while the hydrocarbon end is hydrophobic and is soluble in the grease of oils and fats. The grease droplets are surrounded by the hydrocarbon ends of the sodium stearate molecule that emulsifies and then splits up the grease.

Unfortunately, the sodium stearate molecules react with any calcium or magnesium salts in hard water and form calcium and magnesium stearates that are insoluble in water and form a scum on the surface of the water.

soda ash *See* sodium carbonate.

soda-lime A grayish-white granular mixture of sodium hydroxide and calcium hydroxide. It is made by adding sodium hydroxide solution to calcium oxide and drying. It is used to absorb carbon dioxide and as a drying agent.

soda water A solution of carbon dioxide in water.

sodium Element symbol, Na; alkali metal, group 1; soft, white, silvery, metal; Z 11; A(r) 22.99; density (at 20°C), 0.97 g/cm^3; m.p., 97.8°C; reacts quickly with water and oxygen. Name derived from the English *soda*; symbol derived from modern Latin *natrium*; discovered 1807; sodium compounds are very important.

sodium acetate *See* sodium ethanoate.

sodium aluminate $NaAlO_2$. A white solid (m.p., 1,800°C) that is soluble in water, forming a strong alkali. It is used as a mordant, in the manufacture of glass and zeolites, and in cleaning materials.

sodium bromide NaBr. A white crystalline solid; m.p., 747°C; b.p., 1,390°C. It is used medically as a sedative and is also used in analytical chemistry.

sodium carbonate Na_2CO_3. Washing soda ($Na_2CO_3.10H_2O$) is formed on crystallization from an aqueous solution of sodium carbonate. Washing soda is efflorescent; it loses water between 32°C and 34°C to form the monohydrate $Na_2CO_3.H_2O$. This loses water at 109°C. Sodium carbonate is a white solid; m.p., 851°C. It is soluble, forming an alkaline solution. It is manufactured by the Solvay process.

sodium chlorate(I) NaOCl (sodium hypochlorite). Sodium chlorate(I) is soluble, forming an aqueous solution that is used as bleach and as antiseptic.

sodium chlorate(V) $NaClO_3$. A white crystalline solid (m.p., 250°C) that decomposes above 250°C to form oxygen and sodium chloride. It is soluble in water and is a powerful oxidizing agent. Sodium chlorate(V) is used to bleach wood pulp for paper making and is also used as a garden herbicide.

sodium chloride NaCl. (m.p., 803°C) An ionic compound that exists as $Na^+ Cl^-$. It is nonvolatile and is soluble in water. An aqueous solution of sodium chloride is an electrolyte.

sodium ethanoate CH_3COONa. A colorless crystalline solid; m.p., 324°C. It is a salt of a strong base and a weak acid and is therefore useful in buffer solutions.

sodium hydrogencarbonate $NaHCO_3$ (sodium bicarbonate, bicarbonate of soda) A white crystalline solid that decomposes at 270°C to form sodium carbonate, carbon dioxide, and water.
$2NaHCO_3 \rightarrow Na_2CO_3 + CO_2 + H_2O$.
It is soluble in water. It is an acid salt but forms an alkaline solution,

Sodium chloride: formation

A **a** Sodium atom (Na)   **b** Chlorine atom (Cl)   **c** Chlorine ion (Cl^-)   **d** Sodium ion (Na^+)

B Sodium (Na)   Chlorine (Cl)   Sodium chloride (NaCl)

Formation of sodium chloride (NaCl) by ionic bonding

A Sodium atom (**a**) loses the valence electron in its outer shell to a chlorine atom (**b**). This process, called ionic bonding, produces a negatively charged chlorine ion (**c**) and a positively charged sodium ion (**d**), both of them more stable than before.

B The same process shown using the Lewis dot structure.

because HCO_3^- is a stronger base than it is an acid. It is manufactured by the Solvay process. It is used in cooking as baking soda, to neutralize bulk spills of acid, and as an antacid.

sodium hydrogensulfate $NaHSO_4$. A colorless crystalline solid that is soluble in water, forming an acidic solution. It exists in two forms, anhydrous (m.p., above 315°C) and monohydrate, which is deliquescent (m.p., 59°C). Sodium hydrogensulfate decomposes on heating to form sulfur trioxide. It is used in paper and glass manufacture.

sodium hydrogensulfite $NaHSO_3$. A white crystalline solid that turns yellow in aqueous solution. (It is very soluble in water.) It decomposes on heating to form sodium sulfate, sulfur dioxide, and sulfur. It is used in the sterilization of wine casks, as an antiseptic, and as a bleaching agent.

sodium hydroxide $NaOH$ (caustic soda) A white translucent crystalline solid. It is deliquescent and soluble in water, forming a strongly alkaline solution. It is produced by both the Castner-Kellner process and in the diaphragm cell. It is used widely in the laboratory. It is also used in soap manufacture and to absorb acidic gases such as carbon dioxide and sulfur dioxide.

sodium iodide NaI. An ionic compound that exists as $Na^+ I^-$. It is nonvolatile and soluble in water. An aqueous of sodium iodide is an electrolyte.

sodium nitrate $NaNO_3$ (Chile saltpeter) A white soluble deliquescent solid (m.p., 306°C). It decomposes on heating to form sodium nitrite and oxygen; on being strongly heated it forms oxides and peroxides. It is a strong oxidizing agent. Sodium nitrate is used as a fertilizer.

sodium nitrite $NaNO_2$. A yellow hygroscopic crystalline solid; m.p., 271°C; decomposes above 320°C. It is soluble in water. It is used in dyestuffs and to inhibit corrosion.

sodium octadecanoate *See* sodium stearate.

sodium oxide Na_2O (sodium oxide, sodium monoxide) A whiteish gray deliquescent solid that sublimes at 1,275°C. It reacts with water, forming sodium hydroxide solution.

Na_2O_2 (sodium peroxide) A white solid that decomposes at 460°C. It reacts with water, forming sodium hydroxide and hydrogen peroxide. Sodium peroxide can absorb carbon dioxide and liberate oxygen and is thus useful in submarines to regenerate the air supply. It is a strong oxidizing agent and is used as a bleaching agent in the textile and paper industries.

NaO_2 (sodium superoxide) A whiteish yellow solid that reacts with water to form a mixture of sodium hydroxide, oxygen, and hydrogen peroxide; a powerful oxidizing agent.

sodium peroxide *See* sodium oxides.

sodium stearate $C_{12}H_{35}COONa$ (sodium octadecanoate) A component of soap.

sodium sulfate Na_2SO_4. A white crystalline solid; m.p., 888°C. It exists in two hydrated forms: the metastable form $Na_2SO_4.7H_2O$, and $Na_2SO_4.10H_2O$ (Glauber's salt), which loses water at 100°C. It is efflorescent, forming the anhydrous salt. All forms are soluble, forming a neutral solution. Sodium sulfate is used in medicine and glass manufacture.

sodium sulfide Na_2S. It has a variable composition; Na_2S_3 and Na_2S_4 are also present, causing a variety of colors such as yellows and reds. It exists in the anhydrous form (m.p., 1,180°C) and as $Na_2S.9H_2O$. It is deliquescent and soluble in water, forming an alkaline solution. It is a reducing agent and is corrosive.

sodium sulfite Na_2SO_3. A white, solid, soluble salt that oxidizes readily in air to form sodium sulfate and decomposes on heating to form sodium sulfate and sodium sulfide. It is a reducing agent. It is used in the paper industry to remove chlorine after bleaching.

sodium thiosulfate $Na_2S_2O_3$ ("hypo") A white efflorescent solid that is usually found as the pentahydrate $Na_2S_2O_3.5H_2O$. It is soluble in water, forming a solution that is oxidized in the presence of air. In reactions with dilute acids, sulfur and sulfur dioxide are formed. It is used in photography to fix photographs, and in analytical chemistry.

sol A liquid solution or suspension of a colloid.

solder An alloy used to join metals. It contains different metals, depending on the requirements.

solid A state of matter. In a solid, the particles are not free to move but they can vibrate about fixed positions. Solids can be amorphous or crystalline.

solubility A measure of the quantity of a solute that will dissolve in a certain amount of solvent to form a saturated solution under certain conditions of temperature and pressure. It is measured in kilograms per meter cubed or moles per kilogram of solvent, etc.

solubility curve A graphic representation of the changing solubility of a solute in a solvent at different temperatures.

solubility of salts All sodium, potassium, and ammonium salts are soluble.

All nitrates are soluble.

All chlorides are soluble except lead chloride, which is soluble in hot water, and silver chloride.

All sulfates are soluble except those of lead, barium, and calcium (which is slightly soluble).

All carbonates are insoluble except those of sodium, potassium, and ammonia. Soluble salts are prepared by crystallization from an aqueous solution. Insoluble salts are prepared by double decomposition.

soluble   A relative term that describes a substance that can dissolve in a particular solvent. The extent to which this happens is dependent on temperature.

solute   A substance that dissolves in a solvent and thus forms a solution.

solution   A uniform mixture of one or more solutes in a solvent. It usually refers to solids dissolved in liquids but can also refer to gases in liquids, gases in solids, etc.

solvation   The process of interaction between ions of a solute and the molecules of the solvent. This process is known as hydration when the solvent is water.

Solvay process   The production of sodium carbonate from brine (NaCl) and calcium carbonate (limestone) ($CaCO_3$).

As both sodium carbonate and calcium chloride are soluble in water, the process cannot proceed directly. Carbon dioxide is obtained by heating limestone:

$CaCO_3 = CaO + CO_2$.

Ammonia is dissolved in brine and the solution is added to the top of a tower up which carbon dioxide is passed. Ammonium hydrogencarbonate is formed. This reacts to form a precipitate of sodiumhydrogen carbonate, which is sparingly soluble in brine

$NaCl + CO_2 + NH_3 + H_2O = NaHCO_3 + NH_4Cl$. These crystals are collected, purified, and heated to form soda ash (anhydrous sodium carbonate).

$2NaHCO_3 = Na_2CO_3 + CO_2 + H_2O$. The ammonia is recovered from the ammonium chloride produced and is reused.

solvent   A substance, usually a liquid, in which a solute dissolves to form a solution.

s orbital   A type of orbital whose shape is spherical. One type is possible. It can hold two electrons.

specific gravity   *See* relative density.

spectator ions   *See* ionic equation.

Sr   Symbol for the element strontium.

standardization of solutions Hydrochloric, sulfuric, and nitric acids and the hydroxides of sodium and potassium are either volatile or contain an unknown percentage of water. Standard solutions cannot, therefore, be made up from common acids and alkalis. Their molarities are determined by titration against standard solutions of either sodium carbonate or oxalic acid.

standard solution A solution of known concentration.

starch A polysaccharide (*see* carbohydrate) with the formula $(C_6H_{10}O_5)$. It is composed of many molecules of glucose $(C_6H_{12}O_6)$.

states of matter The three states are solid, liquid, and gas.

state symbols (g) gas; (l) liquid; (s) solid; (c) crystal; and (aq) solution in water.

steam H_2O. Invisible gas formed by water above its boiling point. Clouds of "steam," which are seen before water reaches its boiling point, consist of small droplets of water and are not steam.

steam reforming The conversion of methane, at a temperature of 900°C using a nickel catalyst, into a mixture of carbon monoxide and hydrogen (synthesis gas).

$CH_4 + H_2O = CO + 3H_2$.

stearic acid $C_{17}H_{35}COOH$. A solid saturated fatty acid found in many fats and oils. It is one of the fatty acids used in soap manufacture.

steel An alloy of iron. Other elements are added to form steel of different characters. Mild steel is used for car bodies and household appliances. It rusts easily and is galvanized, enameled, or painted to protect the surface. Stainless steel consists of 74% iron, 18% chromium, 8% nickel. It does not rust and has many uses. Steel used for cutting contains tungsten; steels used at high temperature contain molybdenum.

steel manufacture Iron is converted to steel by the Bessemer process or in the basic oxygen furnace.

stereoisomerism Isomers of a compound that have the same formula and functional groups and differ only in the arrangements of groups in space are stereoisomers.

stoichiometry Calculations of the proportions in which elements or compounds (molecules) react with each other.

STP Standard temperature and pressure. 0°C (273.16K), pressure 101 325 Pa (760 mmHg).

strengths of acids and bases Acids and bases are considered to be strong if they are fully dissociated into their component ions in solution.

Stereoisomers

H H
| |
H–C–O–C–H
| |
H H

H H
| |
H–C–C–OH
| |
H H

Structural isomers

(Methane)
CH₃ H + XY= CH₃X+HY

(Ethane)
C₂H₅ H + XY= C₂H₅X+HY

Substitution reactions

strontium Element symbol, Sr; alkali earth metal, group 2; silvery white metal; Z 38; A(r) 87.62; density (at 20°C), 2.6 g/cm³; m.p., 769°C; named after Strontian, a Scottish parish; discovered 1790; element used in some alloys and as a vacuum getter. Compounds used to give a red color to fireworks and military flares.

structural formula *See* perspective formula, full structural formula, shortened structural formula.

structural isomer Molecules that are structural isomers have the same molecular formula but have different molecular structures. They may contain different functional groups.

styrene *See* phenylethene.

subatomic particles *See* elementary particles, fundamental particles.

sublimate The solid substance that forms during sublimation—the reversible process by which a substance in a solid state changes directly to a gas (sublimes). This process can be used to purify a substance.

substitution reaction A typical type of reaction for saturated organic compounds. One or more atoms, or groups of atoms, are replaced by other atoms or groups of atoms.

sucrose $C_{12}H_{22}O_{11}$ (*see* cane sugar) Sucrose is hydrolyzed to form the simple sugars glucose and fructose by the action of dilute acids, or with the enzyme invertase (present in yeast).

$$C_{12}H_{22}O_{11} + H_2O = C_6H_{12}O_6 + C_6H_{12}O_6.$$

sugar (glucose, fructose, sucrose) The general term for members of two groups of sweet-tasting, very soluble carbohydrates—monosaccharides and disaccharides. (*See also* illustration on page 117.)

sulfates Salts and esters of sulfuric acid (H_2SO_4) containing the ion SO_4^{2-}.

sulfites Salts and esters of sulfurous acid (H_2SO_3) containing the trioxosulfate(IV) ion SO_3^{2-}. Sulfites tend to be reducing agents.

sulfur Element symbol, S; group 6; yellow, nonmetallic, has many allotropic forms; Z 16; A(r) 32.06; density (at 20°C), 2.07 g/cm³ (rhombic form), 1.96 g/cm³ (monoclinic form); m.p., 112.8°C (rhombic), 119°C (monoclinic); reactive; name derived from the Latin *sulfur*; known since prehistoric times; used in the manufacture of sulfuric acid and as a plant fungicide.

sulfur dioxide SO_2 (sulfur(IV) oxide) A colorless gas (m.p., –72.7°C; b.p., –10°C) with a pungent odor of burning sulfur. It is very soluble in water, forming a mixture of sulfuric and sulfurous acid. It is a reducing agent. Sulfur dioxide is used in the manufacture of sulfuric acid using the contact process. It is also used as a food preservative and as a bleach.

Sugars: structure (see entry on page 116)

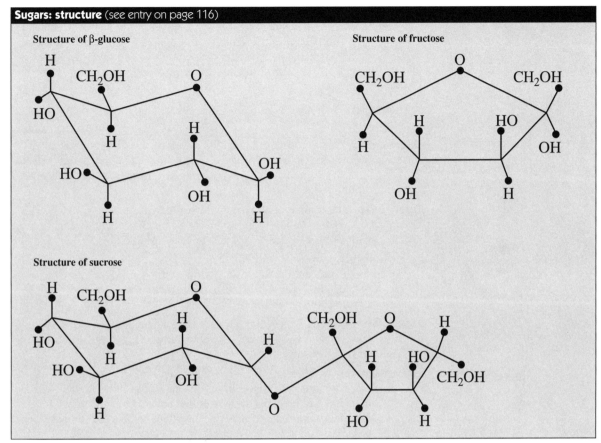

Structure of β-glucose

Structure of fructose

Structure of sucrose

sulfuric acid H_2SO_4 (tetraoxosulfuric acid, oil of vitriol) It is a strong, oily, colorless, odorless dibasic acid; m.p., 10.36°C; b.p., 338°C. Sulfuric acid is usually used as a 96–98% solution. It is manufactured by the contact process, formerly the lead-chamber process. Concentrated sulfuric acid is a powerful drying agent, and concentrated hot sulfuric acid is a strong oxidizing agent. It forms sulfates and hydrogen sulfates. It is used to make superphosphate for fertilizers.

sulfurous acid H_2SO_3 (**sulfuric(IV) acid**, trioxosulfuric(IV) acid) It is a weak dibasic acid found only in solution. It forms sulfites and hydrogensulfites and is a reducing agent.

sulfur trioxide SO_3 (**sulfur(VI) oxide**) A white soluble solid that fumes in moist air. It reacts violently with water to form sulfuric acid. Sulfur trioxide exists in three crystalline forms. It is used in the manufacture of sulfuric acid and oleum.

supercooled vapor A substance that exists as a vapor at a temperature below that at which it should have become liquid.

supercooling The slow cooling of a system, reaching a temperature below that at which a change in phase (liquid to solid or gas to liquid) would normally take place. A supercooled system is in a metastable state.

superheated water Water at a temperature above that of water boiling at one atmosphere.

superheating If a liquid is heated rapidly, its temperature can rise several degrees above the temperature at which it should boil, and it is then said to be superheated. When it does boil, its temperature falls to the boiling point.

superphosphate A mixture of calcium dihydrogen phosphate ($Ca(H_2PO_4)_2$) and calcium sulfate ($CaSO_4$), made by treating calcium(V) phosphate with sulfuric acid and used as a fertilizer as a source of phosphorus.

supersaturated solution A solution that contains a higher concentration of solute than does a saturated solution at that temperature. It is usually obtained by cooling a saturated temperature slowly. A supersaturated solution is metastable.

surface active agent A substance (for example a detergent) added to a liquid that can alter its spreading or wetting characteristics by lowering its surface tension.

surface tension Within a liquid, molecules attract each other equally in all directions. At the surface, however, there is no force attracting them outwards, so the molecules are pulled towards the interior of the liquid. For this reason, liquid surfaces tend to become as small as possible.

Surface tension

surfactant Abbreviation for surface active agent.

suspension A type of dispersion. Small solid particles are dispersed in a liquid or gas.

symbols for elements A letter, or group of letters, used to represent the name that has been given to an element.

synthesis The formation of chemical compounds by constructing them directly from their elements or from other simple compounds.

synthesis gas A mixture of carbon monoxide and hydrogen.

synthetic A material that has been prepared artificially rather than being found naturally.

synthetic fibers Fibers that have been prepared artificially (such as rayon from wood pulp, and nylon and polyesters from petroleum derivatives) rather than being produced naturally (cotton, silk, wool).

Ta   Symbol for the element tantalum.

talc   The white or pale green mineral $Mg_3Si_4O_{10}(OH)_2$. It is soft and greasy and has a hardness of 1 on Mohs' scale. It is often powdered for use in toiletries.

tantalum   Element symbol, Ta; transition element; blue-gray metal; Z 73; A(r) 180.95; density (at 20°C), 16.63 g/cm^3; m.p., 2,996°C; unreactive; named after *Tantalos*, a mythological Greek character; discovered 1802; used to form resistant alloys used in electronic components and surgical appliances.

tar   The heavy thick black liquid that is the residue of the destructive distillation of coal, wood, or petroleum.

tartaric acid   HOOC-$(CHOH)_2$(COOH) 2,3-dihydroxybutanedioic acid. A white soluble crystalline organic acid. Its salts are tartrates, and acid salts are hydrogentartarates (*see* cream of tartar). It is found in many plants and fruits, and it is an ingredient of Fehling's solution. Tartaric acid is used in dyeing and in effervescent powders.

tautomerism   Tautomerism occurs when a compound exists as two different structural isomers that are in dynamic equilibrium with each other.

Tb   Symbol for the element terbium.

Tc   Symbol for the element technetium.

Te   Symbol for the element tellurium.

technetium   Element symbol, Tc; transition element; silvery gray radioactive metal; Z 43; A(r) 98.91; density (at 20°C), 11.5 g/cm^3; m.p., 2,172°C; name derived from the Greek *tekhnetos*, "artificial;" discovered 1925.

tellurium   Element symbol, Te; group 6; silvery metalloid; Z 52; A(r) 127.6; density (at 20°C), 6.25 g/cm^3; m.p., 450°C; name derived from the Latin *tellus*, "earth;" discovered 1783; used in semiconductors.

temperature   A measure of the degree of hotness of a system on a particular scale—Kelvin, degree Celsius, etc.

terbium   Element symbol, Tb; rare earth/lanthanide; silvery metal; Z 65; A(r) 158.93; density (at 20°C), 8.23 g/cm^3; m.p., 1,356°C; named after Ytterby, Swedish town; discovered 1843; used in electronics.

Terylene   *See* Dacron.

test for acid anhydrides   If testing a solid, heat it in a test tube. If testing a solution, boil it to dryness and heat the solid residue. If nitrogen dioxide is produced, the substance is a nitrate, peroxide, or dioxide. If carbon dioxide is produced, the substance is a carbonate or bicarbonate. If sulfur dioxide is produced, the substance is a sulfite or bisulfite.

Test to identify carbonate
rock (carbon tetrachloride)

test for chloride ions *See* chlorides.

test to identify carbonate rock Add a few drops of a dilute acid to a rock sample; bubbles of carbon dioxide will be produced if the rock is a carbonate.

tests   *See* flame test, blue-ring test for thiosulfate; brown-ring test for nitrates; silver mirror test for aldehydes; tests for reducing sugars; tests for gases; carbohydrates, carbonate, chlorides; bromine test for unsaturated hydrocarbons.

tests for gases Carbon dioxide: pass the gas into lime water. If it is carbon dioxide, the solution turns milky white. Hydrogen: apply a burning taper to the gas. If the gas is hydrogen, it will burn with a pop. Oxygen: apply a glowing taper to the gas. If it is oxygen, the taper will re-light.

tests for reducing sugars (**carbohydrates**) *See* Fehling's test or (more sensitive) Benedict's test.

tetrachloromethane CCl_4 (carbon tetrachloride) A colorless, poisonous (can penetrate the skin) heavy liquid; m.p., -23°C; b.p., 76.8°C. It is insoluble in water but soluble in all organic solvents. It is formed by the chlorination of methane. It is used as solvent for fats and oils. It was used in dry cleaning and fire extinguishers but is less used now because of its toxicity.

tetraethyl lead $(C_2H_5)_4Pb$. A colorless insoluble viscous liquid. It is an inhibitor that is added to gasoline to prevent premature ignition (*see* antiknock). Its use is being discontinued to minimize lead pollution.

tetrahedral compound A molecule consisting of five atoms, where one atom is at the center of a tetrahedron and the other four atoms are arranged around it at the corners of a tetrahedron, linked by covalent or coordinate bonds. The angle between the bonds is 109°28'. Carbon compounds form tetrahedral compounds. In methane, a carbon atom is at the center of a tetrahedron and forms covalent bonds to four hydrogen atoms at the corners of a tetrahedron.

Th   Symbol for the element thorium.

thallium Element symbol, Tl; group 3; grayish metal; Z 81; A(r) 204.37; density (at 20°C), 11.85 g/cm^3; m.p., 303.5°C; name derived from the Greek *thallos*, "green shoot;" discovered 1861.

thermal Relating to heat.

thermal conduction The transfer of heat energy through a substance from a region of high to low temperature. Energy is transferred by vibrations of adjacent molecules. The substance itself does not move.

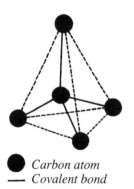

● *Carbon atom*
— *Covalent bond*

Tetrahedral compound

thermal decomposition The breaking down of a chemical compound by heat into smaller components that do not recombine on cooling.

thermal dissociation The breaking down of a chemical compound by heat into smaller components that recombine to form the original compound on cooling.

thermite process This is a reduction process by which liquid iron can be prepared for welding. It can also be used to prepare liquid chromium and titanium. A mixture of aluminum powder and iron oxide is ignited by a magnesium strip, producing iron and aluminum oxide. The reaction is strongly exothermic and causes the iron formed to melt. It can then be used for welding.

thermodynamic temperature *See* absolute temperature.

thermoplastic A substance (particularly a synthetic plastic) that becomes flexible when heated and hardens on cooling with no change in its properties. Thermoplastic polymers have a molecular chain structure.

thermosetting *See* thermosetting polymers, urea/methanal resins.

thermosetting polymers A polymer that has a structure of interlinked chains. Thermosetting polymers cannot be softened by heat but are decomposed by it.

thiosulfate test *See* blue-ring test.

thorium Element symbol, Th; actinide; gray radioactive metal; Z 90; A(r) 232.04; density (at 20°C), 11.73 g/cm^3; m.p., 1,750°C; named after Thor, Scandinavian thunder god; discovered 1829; used as fuel in breeder reactors, used as getter. Oxide used for strengthening nickel and as catalyst.

thorium series One of the naturally occurring radioactive series.

thulium Element symbol, Tm; rare earth/lanthanum; soft gray metal; Z 69; A(r) 168.93; density (at 20°C), 9.32 g/cm^3; m.p.,1,545°C; name derived from the Latin *Thule*, "Northland;" discovered 1879.

Ti Symbol for the element titanium.

tin Element symbol, Sn; group 4; three allotropes—metallic tin, which is a silvery ductile metal, tetragonal, and gray tin; Z 50; A(r) 118.69; density (at 20°C), 7.3 g/cm^3 (white); m.p., 232°C; Old English name *tin*; symbol name derived from Latin *stannum*; known since prehistoric times; used to coat steel and in alloys (solder and bronze). Compounds used as fungicides.

tin cans, corrosion of Steel is coated with tin to make cans that hold food. If the surface of the tin is damaged and the steel becomes exposed, the steel rusts very rapidly. This is because iron (steel) is more electropositive than tin, so electrons flow from the iron to the tin,

Thermosetting polymer

Electrons flow towards tin as iron (steel) corrodes *Water*

e   *e*   *Tin*

Steel

Corrosion of tin cans

causing the steel to corrode more quickly than if the tin coating were not present. *See* sacrificial anode.

titanium Element symbol, Ti; transition element; white metal; Z 22; A(r) 47.9; density (at 20°C), 4.51 g/cm^3; m.p., 1,660°C; named after Titanes, giants in Greek mythology; discovered 1791; is a component of various light, strong alloys used in construction of aircraft, etc. Titanium dioxide is used widely as white pigment in paint.

titration The addition of a solution of known concentration from a burette to a flask containing a known volume of a sample of unknown concentration until the reaction between the two solutions is complete (this point is given by an indicator). The knowledge of the volume of liquid of known concentration added from the burette and the volume of liquid in the flask allows the concentration of the liquid in the flask to be calculated.

Tl Symbol for the element thallium.

Tm Symbol for the element thulium.

Tollen's reagent An aqueous solution containing the complex ion $[Ag(NH_3)_2]^+$. It is prepared by mixing solutions of silver nitrate ($AgNO_3$) and sodium hydroxide (NaOH) to form silver(I) oxide (AgO), which dissolves to form the complex ion $[Ag(NH_3)_2]^+$ when ammonia is added to the solution. This reagent is used in the silver mirror test, which is used to test for the presence of aldehydes.

toluene *See* methylbenzene.

town gas A mixture of coal gas, water gas, and natural gas (a mixture of methane and light gases produced during petroleum refining).

transactinide elements Elements following lawrencium (atomic number 103). This is a transition series; the 6d orbital is being filled. Elements with atomic numbers up to 112 (ununbium, discovered in 1996) have been prepared, and names have been agreed for elements up to 109 (meitnerium, named after Austrian physicist Lise Meitner). Elements 110, 111, and 112 have temporary names. The transactinide elements are unstable and have short half-lives.

transition element Any of the metallic elements with an incomplete inner electron structure.

In the first series of transition elements (scandium to zinc), the elements have two electrons in the s orbital of their fourth shell and d orbitals in their third shell that fill across the row (there can be 10 electrons in d orbitals).

In the second series (yttrium to cadmium), the elements have two electrons in the s orbital of their fifth shell and d orbitals of their fourth shell, which fill across the row.

The third series begins with lanthanum and ends with mercury (it includes the lanthanides). As the atoms increase in size, their structure becomes more complex as the number of types of orbital in each shell becomes greater.

The elements from actinium onwards (the actinides and transactinides) can also be considered as transition elements.

Transition elements have widely differing chemical properties. They can each have several oxidation numbers (oxidation states), and they form colored compounds.

transition metals *See* transition elements.

transition point *See* transition temperature.

transition temperature The temperature at which one allotrope changes to another (one is stable below the transition temperature, the other is stable above it). It can also be the temperature at which a substance changes phase.

transuranic element Any of the elements with higher atomic numbers than uranium. They are all radioactive and are produced artificially.

tribasic acid An acid that has three replaceable hydrogen atoms. A tribasic acid can form three series of salts. *See* basicity of acids.

trichloroethane $CHCl_3$ (chloroform). A heavy, colorless volatile liquid that is toxic, non-flammable, and insoluble in water. It is a substituted alkane; m.p., $-63.5°C$, b.p., $61°C$. It can be made by chlorination of methane, followed by separation of the products. It has been widely used as an anesthetic but can cause liver damage; it has been superseded by other halogenated hydrocarbons.

triple bond *See* bond, multiple bonds.

triple point The conditions of temperature and pressure at which the three phases of a substance—solid, liquid, and gas—are in equilibrium.

tritium An isotope of hydrogen. Its nucleus contains one proton and two neutrons and thus has a relative atomic mass of three.

trivalent Having a valency of three.

tungsten Element symbol, W; transition element; white or gray metal; Z 74; A(r) 183.85; density (at 20°C), 19.3 g/cm³; m.p., 3,410°C; name derived from the Swedish *tung sten*, "heavy stone;" symbol name derived from German *Wolfram*; discovered 1783; used in steel alloys used to make cutting tools, in filaments of lamps and heaters.

U Symbol for the element uranium.

universal indicator A mixture of substances that can be used as an acid-base indicator over a wide range of pH values. Its color changes from red

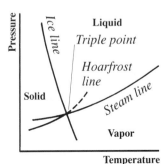

Triple point

(pH values 1–4), orange (pH 5), yellow (pH 6), green (pH 7), blue (pH 8), indigo (pH 9), violet (pH 10–14).

unleaded gasoline Gasoline that does not contain tetraethyl lead to prevent knocking (*see* antiknock). In its place, it contains 15% methyl tertiary butyl ether and 5% methanol.

unsaturated compounds Chemical compounds that contain one or more double or triple bonds in their structure.

Unsaturated hydrocarbons contain double or triple bonds between carbon atoms in their structure. Ethene and ethyne are examples of unsaturated hydrocarbons. Unsaturated hydrocarbons take part in addition reactions when a double bond is converted to a single bond or a triple bond is converted to a double or a single bond.

unsaturated hydrocarbons, test *See* bromine test.

unsaturated solution A solution in which the solvent is able to absorb more solute at a particular temperature.

ununbium Element symbol, Uub; transition element; Z112; A(r) 277; temporary name; discovered 1996.

ununhexium Element symbol, Uuh; transition element; Z 116; A(r) 292; temporary name for element discovered in 1999.

ununpentium Element symbol, Uup; transition element; Z115; A(r)288; temporary name for element discovered in 2004.

ununquadium Element symbol, Uuq; transition element; Z114; A(r)289; temporary name for element discovered in 1998.

ununtrium Element symbol, Uut; transition element; Z113; A(r)284; temporary name for element discovered in 2004.

uranium Element symbol, U; actinide; white radioactive metal; Z 92; A(r) 238.03; density (at 20°C), 19.05 g/cm^3; m.p., 1,132°C; three isotopes, 234, 235, and 238; named after the planet Uranus; discovered 1789; isotope-235 used in nuclear reactors and nuclear weapons.

uranium series One of the naturally occurring radioactive series.

urea (carbamide) NH_2–CO–NH_2. White crystalline soluble solid; m.p., 133°C.

urea/methanal resin Thermosetting polymer made by condensation polymerization between urea and methanal. It is used to form melamine and adhesives.

Uub Symbol for the element ununbium.

Uun Symbol for the element ununnilium.

Urea (carbamide)

Uuu   Symbol for the element unununium.

V   Symbol for the element vanadium.

valency It is the number of electrons an atom needs to form a compound or radical and is related to its electronic structure. Elements tend to lose, gain or share electrons in order to complete their outer electron shell. An ion's valency is equal to its charge. Valency is also seen as the usual number of bonds an atom forms when combining to form a compound.

vanadium Element symbol, V; transition element; silvery white or gray metal; Z 23; A(r) 50.94; density (at 20°C), 6.09 g/cm^3; m.p., 1,890°C; named after Vanadis, Scandinavian goddess; discovered 1801; used as steel additive and in catalysts.

van der Waals forces Weak intermolecular or interatomic forces between neutral molecules or atoms. They are much weaker than chemical bonds.

vapor   Gas that is below the temperature at which it can be liquefied by pressure (the critical temperature).

vapor density The vapor density of a vapor (gas) is the ratio of the mass of a certain volume of the gas to the mass of an equal volume of hydrogen that is at the same temperature and pressure. If the density of hydrogen is taken as one, the vapor density of a gas is half its relative molecular mass.

vaporization The process of change of state of a solid or liquid to a vapor.

vapor pressure The pressure exerted by a vapor given off by a liquid or solid. If this vapor is in equilibrium with the liquid or solid, the vapor pressure is defined as the saturated vapor pressure.

variable A condition, such as temperature, concentration, or pressure, that can be changed in a chemical reaction.

volatile A substance that readily turns into a vapor.

volumetric analysis A method of quantitative analysis such as titration, where the volume of a solution reacting with a measured amount of another solution is determined.

vulcanization The process of making rubber harder and more elastic. Rubber is heated with sulfur (about 5%) at about 150°C. This causes the rubber molecules to become interlinked into a three-dimensional network with the sulfur molecules forming cross-links between adjacent rubber molecules.

W   Symbol for the element tungsten.

washing soda *See* sodium carbonate.

*Vulcanized   Resilient
rubber*

Vulcanization

Water: molecule

Atoms of hydrogen and oxygen   Full shells of a water molecule   Structure of the water molecule

a Hydrogen atoms have one outer-shell electron   c Shared pairs
b Oxygen atom has six outer-shell electrons   d Lone pairs

water H_2O. A colorless, odorless, tasteless liquid; m.p., 0°C, b.p., 100°C. An oxide of hydrogen, it is a covalent compound. The three atoms do not lie in a straight line H-O-H; the position of the two hydrogen atoms is affected by the two lone pairs of electrons in the outer shell of the oxygen atom and, therefore, form an angle of about 105° with the oxygen atom. Water molecules are polar, and there is hydrogen bonding between the molecules. Because of its polar nature, water is an excellent solvent for ionic substances.

water, electrolysis of If slightly acidified, water can be electrolyzed between carbon or platinum electrodes. Gases are evolved above the electrodes. Hydrogen is collected at the cathode (the negative electrode; positive hydrogen ions gain an electron each). Oxygen is collected at the anode (negatively charged hydroxide ions lose an electron, forming oxygen and water).

water gas Water gas is a mixture of approximately equal volumes of hydrogen and carbon monoxide. Formed by passing steam (rather than air, as in producer gas manufacture) through white hot coke, it has a high calorific value.

$$C + H_2O(g) = CO + H_2 - heat.$$

$$CO + H_2O - CO_2 + H_2.$$

Water gas is a cheap source of commercial hydrogen. Methanol is manufactured from water gas and hydrogen. Water gas is added to coal gas to increase its calorific value.

Coke

Water gas

White hot coke

Steam

Ash

Water gas

water ionization A water molecule can split up to form a positively charged hydrogen ion and a negatively charged hydroxide ion.

water of crystallization The exact number of water molecules that are chemically bonded to a molecule of a salt within a hydrated crystalline compound.

water pH Pure water is a neutral liquid (pH = 7). It consists almost entirely of covalent molecules.

water, test for As no two substances have the same freezing points and boiling points, water can be identified as freezing at 0°C and boiling at 100°C.

weak acids and bases Acids and bases are considered to be weak if they do not dissociate into their component ions in solution.

white lead *See* lead(II) carbonate hydroxide.

white vitriol Hydrated zinc sulfate ($ZnSO_4.7H_2O$) or zinc sulfate heptahydrate.

word equation A summary in words of the reactants and products taking part in a chemical reaction.

Xe Symbol for the element xenon.

xenon Element symbol, Xe; noble gas, group 8; colorless gas; Z 54; A(r) 131.3; density (at 20°C), 5.896 g/l at STP; m.p., –111.9°C; name derived from the Greek *xenos*, "strange;" discovered 1898; used in fluorescent lamps and bubble chambers.

Y Symbol for the element yttrium.

Yb Symbol for the element ytterbium.

yield of a reaction Many chemical reactions produce less product than might be predicted from the equation of the reaction. The yield of a reaction is the amount of product produced in a reaction expressed as a percentage of the theoretical yield.

ytterbium Element symbol, Yb; rare earth/lanthanide; silvery metal; Z 70; A(r) 173.04; density (at 20°C), 6.97 g/cm^3; m.p., 819°C; named after Ytterby, a Swedish town; discovered 1878; used in some special steels.

yttrium Element symbol, Y; transition element; silvery gray metal; Z 39; A(r) 88.91; density (at 20°C), 4.47 g/cm^3; m.p., 1,522°C; named after Ytterby, a Swedish town; discovered 1794; alloyed with cobalt to make superconducting alloys and strong permanent magnets. Oxide used in color televisions.

Z Symbol for atomic number.

zeolite A naturally occurring mineral form of sodium aluminum silicate. It has ion-exchange properties.

zeolites Either naturally occurring minerals or synthetic substances that have ion-exchange properties. They can be hydrated silicates of aluminum, sodium, potassium, or calcium. Alternatively, they can be constructed to form molecular sieves because their structures have open pores to trap certain molecules from a mixture passing through them; the molecules are then released by heating the zeolite.

zinc Element symbol, Zn; transition element; hard, brittle bluish white metal; Z 30; A(r) 65.37; density (at 20°C), 7.1 g/cm^3; m.p., 419.6°C; chemically reactive; releases hydrogen from dilute acids; name derived from the German *Zink*; discovered around 1200; used as sacrificial anodes; used in alloys (brass, solder) and to coat steel surfaces (galvanizing).

zinc blende A naturally occurring mineral form of zinc sulfide (ZnS) from which zinc is extracted.

zinc carbonate $ZnCO_3$. A white insoluble crystalline compound that is found in the mineral calamine. Zinc carbonate is used to make zinc ointments.

zinc chloride $ZnCl_2$. A white crystalline soluble compound; m.p., 290°C; b.p., 732°C (it sublimates easily). The anhydrous salt is deliquescent and is used as a dehydrating agent. It is also used as a flux in soldering and as a timber preservative.

zinc oxide ZnO. An insoluble powder that is white when cold and yellow when hot (on heating, it loses a small amount of oxygen, which it reabsorbs on cooling); m.p., 1,975°C. It is found naturally as the ore zincite. It is an amphoteric base. Zinc oxide is used as the white pigment zinc white in the glass and ceramic industries and (it is a mild antiseptic) in antiseptic ointments.

zinc sulfate $ZnSO_4$. A white crystalline water-soluble compound, formerly known as white vitriol in its heptahydrate ($ZnSO_4.7H_2O$) form. It is used as a mordant and to check bleeding (as a styptic).

zinc sulfide ZnS. A yellow-white compound that is phosphorescent when impure. It sublimes at 1,180°C. It is used as a pigment and as a phosphor.

zirconium Element symbol, Zr; transition element; gray white metal; Z 40; A(r) 91.22; density (at 20°C), 6.5 g/cm^3; m.p., 1,852°C; low neutron absorption; name derived from the German *Zirkon*; discovered 1789; alloys used in construction of reactors.

Zn Symbol for the element zinc.

Zr Symbol for the element zirconium.

○ S^{2-}

● ZN^{2+}

Zinc sulphide

SECTION TWO
TWO
BIOGRAPHIES

Abel, Sir Frederick Augustus (1827–1902) English chemist who specialized in the chemistry of explosives. He found a way to make guncotton stable and safe and, in 1889, introduced the new explosive cordite, a mixture of nitroglycerine and guncotton stabilized with camphor. This was used extensively as a propellant in World War I.

Abelson, Philip Hauge (1913–2004) American physical chemist who developed a massive gas diffusion apparatus for the separation of the fissionable uranium-235 isotope from the natural mixture, which was almost all uranium-238. This was an early stage in the production of the first atomic bomb. Abelson also assisted in the creation of the manufactured element neptunium, the first element heavier than uranium. Later he worked with Stanley Miller to try to show in the laboratory how life might have originated on Earth.

Adams, Roger (1889–1971) American chemist who developed a simple way of catalyzing the hydrogenation of unsaturated organic materials, such as vegetable oils (to make margarine and other butter substitutes). He established the molecular structure of various medically active natural substances and isolated tetrahydrocannabinol, the active ingredient in marijuana.

Alder, Kurt (1902–58) German chemist who, in 1928, working with Otto Diels, discovered a relatively easy way to produce a ring (cyclic) compound, starting with a compound containing two double bonds separated by a single bond. This is the Diels-Alder reaction, which became important in organic synthesis and earned Alder a share in the 1950 Nobel Prize in chemistry.

Anaxagoras (ca. 500–ca. 428 BCE) Greek philosopher who was persecuted for believing that the Sun was an incandescent rock. He taught that matter was composed of innumerable tiny particles containing determining qualities.

Anaximenes (ca. 380–ca. 320 BCE) Greek philosopher who believed that the origin of all matter was air and that this could be condensed to make various forms of solid matter or liquids. He believed that the Earth was flat.

Anfinsen, Christian Boehmer (1916–95) American biochemist who assisted in the sequencing of the 128-amino acid enzyme

Christian B. Anfinsen

ribonuclease, an achievement for which he shared the 1972 Nobel Prize in chemistry with Stanford Moore and William H. Stein. Anfinsen went on to study the three-dimensional (secondary and tertiary) structure of this important enzyme.

Archimedes (ca. 287–212 BCE) Greek mathematician and technologist who found formulas for the volume of a wide range of regular solids and for the area of a range of plane figures. His methods were similar to those of the calculus. He originated the science of hydrostatics and discovered that a floating body displaced its own weight of water. He invented the Archimedean screw for raising water and a number of large military weapons. He was the leading figure in rigorous scientific and mathematical thought of the ancient world.

Archimedes

Aristotle (384–322 BCE) Greek philosopher who, through his extensive writings, became historically the most influential figure of the ancient world. He covered every field of contemporary knowledge, but in science wrote on physics, biology, medicine, zoology, taxonomy, and psychology. Much of what he wrote about fundamental science was pure imagination and was wrong. Unfortunately, he was accepted as an almost infallible authority, so for almost 2,000 years, scientific thought was misdirected and real progress hindered.

Arrhenius, Svante August (1859–1927) Swedish physical chemist who, in 1884, was the first to propose that acids, bases, and salts in solution dissociated into ions. His theory of electrolytic dissociation was well before its time and was not scientifically confirmed until the theory of atomic structure was more fully developed. He also worked on reaction rates, and was the first to recognize the greenhouse effect on climate. He was awarded the Nobel Prize in chemistry in 1903.

Aston, Francis William (1877–1945) English atomic physicist who worked with J.J. Thomson at the Cavendish Laboratory, Cambridge. His principal field of study was in elements of equal atomic number but different atomic weight (isotopes). He also invented the mass spectrograph. He was awarded the Nobel Prize in chemistry in 1922.

Avogadro, Amedeo (1776–1856) Italian scientist and physics professor at Turin who in 1811 formulated the hypothesis known as Avogadro's law: equal volumes of gases contain equal numbers of molecules when at the same temperature and pressure.

Axelrod, Julius (1912–2004) U.S. neuropharmacologist who was a member of the research team that discovered the neurotransmitter norepinephrine (noradrenaline). Axelrod was refused entry to several medical schools and decided to study pharmacology. In 1970, he shared the Nobel Prize in physiology or medicine with Sir Bernard Katz and Ulf von Euler.

Bacon, Sir Francis (1561–1626) English philosopher and essayist whose book *The Advancement of Learning* (1605) drew serious attention for the first time to the fact that the real source of scientific knowledge was not the authority of pundits such as Aristotle but was observation, experimentation, direct experience, and careful induction. This was the start of the scientific method that was to prove so fruitful.

Sir Francis Bacon

Bacon, Roger (1220–92) English philosopher who tried to compile an encyclopedia containing all the knowledge of his day. The attempt failed but contained much valuable mathematical information, showed a knowledge of gunpowder, and included some remarkable speculations about mechanical transport, heavier-than-air flying machines, and the possibility of circling the globe.

Baekeland, Leo Hendrik (1863–1944) Belgian-born American industrial chemist who became a millionaire when he sold his Velox photographic paper company to Kodak. He then studied chemistry and investigated phenol-formaldehyde resins and produced a hard material that could be cast and machined and was a good electrical insulator. He called it Bakelite.

Baeyer, Johann Friedrich Wilhelm Adolf von (1835–1917) German chemist who devoted his life to the analysis and synthesis of organic molecules and published more than 300 important papers. He is especially noted for his studies of uric acid and organic dyes. His synthesis of indigo was of great commercial importance, and for this achievement he was awarded the Nobel Prize in chemistry in 1905.

Balard, Antoine-Jérôme (1802–76) French chemist who discovered that iodine produces a blue color in the presence of starch, a finding that produced a sensitive chemical test for iodine that is still in use today.

Balmer, Johann Jakob (1825–98) Swiss mathematician who, in 1885, empirically derived a simple formula for the wavelengths of the spectral lines of hydrogen. This is called the Balmer series, and Balmer could not explain it, but its quantitative element was important in developing atomic theory. Later, better models of the atom accounted for the series.

Baltimore, David (b. 1938) American biochemist who shared the 1975 Nobel Prize in medicine with Howard Temin and Renato Dulbecco for discovering an enzyme, called reverse transcriptase, that could make DNA from RNA. This viral enzyme, present in retroviruses such as HIV, enables these viruses to insert their genome into the DNA of the host cell. Its discovery showed that Francis Crick's fundamental genetic "dogma"—that the sequence is always from DNA to RNA to protein—was wrong.

David Baltimore

Bamberger, Eugen (1857–1932) German chemist who first proposed the term *alicyclic* for unsaturated ring organic compounds. He worked on the synthesis of nitroso compounds and quinols and investigated the structure of naphthalene.

Barger, George (1878–1939) Dutch-born British organic chemist who isolated ergotoxine from ergot and proceeded to study related amines with physiological properties. This eventually had two important effects: it drew attention to the role of neurotransmitters in the function of the nervous system, and it led to the development of a range of valuable drugs.

Bartlett, Neil (b. 1932) English chemist who was the first to find a compound of a noble gas (xenon), one of a class of elements that was previously believed incapable of forming compounds.

Bartlett, Paul Doughty (1907–97) American chemist who worked on the mechanisms of organic reactions such as the actions of free radicals and the way polymer molecules were formed from simple units (monomers).

Barton, Sir Derek Harold Richard (1918–98) English chemist who became noted when he wrote an influential paper on the relationship between the three-dimensional shape of a molecule, resulting from rotation of part of it around a single bond, and its chemical reactivity. This significant and fundamental advance won him the Nobel Prize in chemistry in 1969, which he shared with Odd Hassel.

Beadle, George Wells (1903–89) U.S. biochemist who showed that particular genes code for particular enzymes. The technique used was to cause gene mutations that affected particular biochemical processes, thereby showing the immediate link between the gene and the enzyme. This was a major advance in genetics.

Becher, Johann Joachim (1635–82) German chemist who studied minerals. His *Physica subterranea* (1669) was the first attempt to bring physics and chemistry into close relation.

Becquerel, Antoine-Henri (1852–1908) French physicist who was the first to discover radioactivity. In 1896 he noticed that a uranium salt laid on a totally enclosed photographic plate caused the plate to be exposed. Becquerel concluded that the salt was emitting rays similar to the X-rays that had been discovered by Wilhelm Röntgen the year before. He then studied and described the properties of the natural radioactivity of uranium. For this work, he shared the Nobel Prize in physics with Pierre and Marie Curie in 1903.

Bednorz, Johannes Georg (b. 1950) German physicist who worked with Alexander Müller on the problem of raising the temperature at which superconductivity occurred. Applications of superconductivity were seriously limited because of the energy required to maintain temperatures close to absolute zero. Bednorz and Müller came up with a mixture of lanthanum, barium, and copper oxide that would superconduct at 35K. This was a substantially higher temperature than with any previous material, and it won the two men the 1987 Nobel Prize in physics.

Berg, Paul (b. 1926) American biochemist and molecular biologist who was one of the principal founders of genetic engineering. Berg developed techniques using specific DNA-cleaving enzymes capable of cutting out genes from the DNA of one mammalian species and inserting them into the DNA of another. For this

George W. Beadle

work, he shared the 1980 Nobel Prize in chemistry with Walter Gilbert and Frederick Sanger. Berg also drew up strict rules to govern safe conduct in genetic engineering.

Bergius, Friedrich (1874–1949) German chemist who demonstrated the way in which high pressures and temperatures converted wood into coal. For this work, he shared the 1931 Nobel Prize in chemistry with Carl Bosch.

Bernard, Claude (1813–78) French physiologist, often described as the father of modern physiology. After becoming a doctor, he devoted his life to research in physiology, eventually establishing it as a formal discipline in its own right. Among his many discoveries were that complex food carbohydrates were broken down to simple sugars before absorption; that bile was necessary for the absorption of fats; that the body re-synthesizes the carbohydrate glycogen; and that the bore of arteries was controlled by nerve action. His later research included work on oxygen in the blood and on the opium alkaloids.

Claude Bernard

Bernoulli, Daniel (1700–82) Dutch-born Swiss mathematician often known as the father of mathematical physics. Bernoulli's family produced many celebrated mathematicians, but he was the most famous. He is best known for his work on hydrodynamics and the kinetic theory of gases. His famous treatise *Hydrodynamica* was published in 1738.

Berthollet, Claude-Louis (1748–1822) French physician and inorganic chemist whose ideas on the formation of chemical compounds, although mistaken, led other workers to come nearer to the truth. He made important advances in dye-making, bleaching with chlorine, and steel making. His two major published works were *Researches into the Laws of Chemical Affinity* (1801) and *Essay on Chemical Statics* (1803).

Berzelius, Jöns Jacob (1779–1848) Swedish chemist who was able to work out the atomic weights of more than 45 elements, several of which he discovered, including, cerium, selenium, thorium, and vanadium. He proposed the theories of isomerism and catalysis and was also notable for inventing the present-day symbols for chemical elements and compounds based on abbreviations of the Latin names of the elements.

Jöns Jacob Berzelius

Sir Henry Bessemer

Bessemer, Sir Henry (1813–98) English chemist, inventor, and engineer. In 1855, in response to the need for guns for the Crimean War, he patented the process by which molten pig-iron can be turned directly into steel by blowing air through it in a Bessemer converter. This development of a cheap way to produce steel had enormous economic importance and won him a knighthood in 1879. Bessemer furnaces were enthusiastically exploited by Andrew Carnegie in the United States, who made a fortune from them.

Bevan, Edward John (1856–1921) English industrial chemist who developed the viscous process of rayon (processed cellulose) manufacture. This proved commercially highly profitable until better plastics such as nylon were developed.

Black, Sir James Whyte (b. 1924) Scottish physician and physiologist who studied cell receptors for hormones and drugs and developed two new classes of drugs—the beta blockers (for example, Sectral) and the stomach histamine (H-2) receptor blockers (for example, Zantac). Black, who is remarkable for initiating two entirely new classes of major drugs, shared the 1988 Nobel Prize in physiology or medicine with Gertrude B. Elion and George H. Hutchings.

Black, Joseph (1728–99) Scottish chemist who between 1756 and 1761 evolved the theory of "latent heat" on which his scientific fame chiefly rests. He also showed that the causticity of lime and alkalis is due to the absence of the "fixed air" (carbon dioxide) that is present in limestone and carbonates of alkalis.

Boltwood, Bertram Borden (1870–1927) American nuclear chemist who studied the radioactive breakdown of elements, and first discovered how to apply the ratios of lead to uranium in geological specimens in order to calculate their age. This, and other associated methods, was to bring new standards of accuracy into geology and paleontology. He discovered the radioactive element ionium.

Bonner, James Frederick (1910–96) American molecular biologist who showed that the presence of a protein, histone, shut down gene activity so that only those genes required in a particular situation were operative. Bonner also worked on the artificial synthesis of RNA.

Bosch, Carl (1874–1940) German chemist who invented the first commercially successful method of synthesizing ammonia on an industrial scale. This was of great importance for agriculture and earned him a share of the 1931 Nobel Prize in chemistry. He also worked on the synthesis of methanol and rubber.

Bovet, Daniele (1907–92) Swiss pharmacologist and physiologist who isolated the sulfanilamide part of the red dye prontosil that was being used to treat bacterial infections in mice. This work led to the development of the sulfa drugs, which, until the development of penicillin and other antibiotics, were the most important class of medications.

Boyer, Herbert Wayne (b. 1936) American biochemist and genetic engineering pioneer who showed that, by using an enzyme called an endonuclease, a DNA ring (a plasmid) from a bacterium could be inserted into the DNA of another bacterium or that of a toad. He was then able to clone the hybrid DNA by allowing bacteria containing it to reproduce. Boyer's achievement led to the commercial production of insulin and other valuable proteins.

Boyer, Paul Delos (b. 1918) American chemist who earned a share of the 1997 Nobel Prize in chemistry by his advances in the understanding of the mechanism by which the enzyme ATP synthase (ATPase) catalyzes the synthesis of ATP from ADP and phosphate. Adenosine triphosphate (ATP) is a nucleotide of fundamental importance as the carrier of chemical energy in all living organisms.

Boyle, Robert (1627–91) Irish physicist, chemist, and co-founder of the Royal Society in London whose book *The Sceptical Chymist* (1661) defines the chemical element as the practical limit of chemical analysis. The celebrated Boyle's law (1662) states that, the temperature being kept constant, the pressure and volume of a gas are inversely proportional.

Brand, Hennig (d. 1692) German alchemist who, in 1669 while searching for the philosopher's stone, isolated from urine a solid white substance that glowed in the dark. He called it phosphorus. Brand, whose date of birth is unknown, is the first scientist known to have discovered an element.

Carl Bosch

Daniele Bovet

Robert Boyle

Brandt, Georg (1694–1768) Swedish chemist and assay master of the Swedish mint who discovered cobalt, studied arsenic and established its properties and compounds, and worked to expose fraud in alchemical practice.

Brown, Herbert Charles (1912–2004) American chemist whose work on boron compounds in the synthesis of organic molecules won him the 1979 Nobel Prize in chemistry with Georg Wittig.

Buchner, Eduard (1860–1917) German chemist who researched fermentation and showed that Louis Pasteur was wrong in insisting that alcoholic fermentation required the exclusion of oxygen. For this finding he was awarded the 1907 Nobel Prize in chemistry.

Bunsen, Robert Wilhelm (1811–99) German experimental chemist and inventor. He developed the gas burner that bears his name and the ice calorimeter. Working with the German physicist Gustav Kirchhoff, he developed the important analytical technique of chemical spectroscopy. Bunsen also discovered the elements cesium and rubidium.

Butenandt, Adolf Friedrich Johann (1903–95) German biochemist who isolated the male sex hormone androsterone and, in 1931, a few milligrams of progesterone from the corpus luteum of the ovaries of female pigs. His methods must have been relatively inefficient, as no fewer than 50,000 pigs were required. For his work on hormones he shared the 1939 Nobel Prize in chemistry with Leopold Ružička.

Calvin, Melvin (1911–97) American biochemist who made notable advances in the understanding of photosynthesis—the processes by which sugars and complex carbohydrates such as starches are synthesized by plants from atmospheric carbon dioxide. Calvin used radioactive carbon tracers to follow the movement of carbon through the complex reactions. He also worked on theories of the chemical origin of life and on attempts to utilize carbon dioxide artificially. He was awarded the Nobel Prize in chemistry in 1961 for his work on photosynthesis.

Candolle, Augustin-Pyrame de (1778–1841) Swiss botanist and chemist who introduced the term *taxonomy* for the classification of plants by their morphology, rather than by

Augustin-Pyrame de Candolle

their physiology, as set out in his *Elementary Theory of Botany* (1813). His new edition of *Flore française* appeared in 1805. He accurately described the relationship between plants and soils, a factor that affects geographic plant distribution. He is remembered in the specific names of more than 300 plants, two genera, and one family.

Cannizzaro, Stanislao (1826–1910) Italian chemist who showed that inorganic and organic chemistry were not basically different. He made the important distinction between atomic weights and molecular weights, and produced a table of weights with hydrogen as the unit. He established the use of atomic weights in chemical formulas and calculations.

Cardano, Geronimo (1501–76) Italian mathematician and physician who produced the first printed work on algebra, the *Ars magna* (1545), and described the general method for solving cubic equations. He also published books on medicine, arithmetic, and philosophy and an encyclopedia of inventions and experiments called *De subtilitate rerum* (1550).

Carnap, Rudolf (1891–1970) German philosopher of science who has had considerable influence on scientists. He taught that statements were meaningful only if they can be related to sensory experience and have logical consequences that are verifiable by observation or experience. This idea led to the philosophical school of logical positivism and to the dismissal, by some people, of most or all of the propositions of metaphysics and religion.

Carothers, Wallace Hume (1896–1937) American industrial chemist working for the Du Pont Company at Wilmington, Delaware, who invented nylon after producing the first successful synthetic rubber, neoprene.

Castner, Hamilton Young (1858–98) American chemist who discovered a cheap way to produce metallic sodium from caustic soda so that it could be used to reduce aluminum chloride to the metal. Unfortunately for him, the electrolytic process for aluminum production was, just then, invented. Castner went through a difficult period until the uses of sodium for other purposes increased to the point where he could not produce enough to meet the demand. So he invented an even better process for producing sodium from salt water by electrolysis. He formed a company that became highly successful after his death.

Cavendish, Henry (1731–1810) English chemist and natural philosopher. In 1760, he discovered the extreme levity of inflammable air, and later, at the same time as James Watt, ascertained that water is the result of the union of two gases. He used the gravitational attraction between bodies of known weight to estimate the weight of the Earth.

Caventou, Jean-Bienaimé (1795–1877) French chemist and toxicologist who specialized in alkaloids. Working with Pierre-Joseph Pelletier, he isolated quinine, strychnine, brucine, cinchonine, veratrine, and colchicine, some of which became widely used as drugs.

Cech, Thomas Robert (b. 1947) American biochemist who showed the remarkable fact that a length of protein-free RNA could act as an enzyme for the cleaving and splicing of other RNA. This fact could explain much about the early evolution of organisms. Cech shared the 1989 Nobel Prize in chemistry with Sidney Altman.

Chain, Sir Ernst Boris (1906–79) German-born British biochemist of Russian extraction who isolated and purified penicillin and turned Alexander Fleming's discovery of the antibiotic into one of the greatest successes in the history of medicine. Chain, Howard Florey, and Fleming shared the 1945 Nobel Prize in physiology or medicine.

Sir Ernst Chain

Chance, Britton (b. 1913) American biophysicist who proved that enzymes work by attaching themselves to the substance on which they act (the substrate). He achieved this by a spectroscopic technique using the enzyme peroxidase, which contains iron and absorbs certain light wavelengths strongly. Chance also helped to work out the way cells get their energy from sugar by observing that concentrations of adenosine diphosphate (ADP) were related to the oxidation-reduction states of the proteins in the respiratory chain.

Chargaff, Erwin (1905–2002) Austrian-born American biochemist who, in the mid-1940s, speculated that if DNA was the vehicle of inheritance, its molecule must vary greatly. Using the methods available at the time, however, he found that its composition was constant within a species but that it differed widely between species. In 1950, he established that the number of purine bases (adenine and guanine) was the same as the number of pyrimidine bases (cytosine and thiamine). This was an important fact that James Watson and Francis Crick had to incorporate into their model of the structure of DNA.

Charles, Jacques-Alexandre-César (1746–1823) French physicist and physical chemist who, with Joseph-Louis Gay-Lussac, established a law of the changes in gas volume caused by temperature changes at constant pressure. This is commonly known as Charles' law of pressures.

Jacques Charles

Chevreul, Michel-Eugène (1786–1889) French organic chemist who identified the fatty acids oleic acid, butyric acid, capric acid, and caproic acid and a mixture of stearic and palmitic acids called margaric acid. He found that fats consisted of a glycerol "backbone" to which three fatty acids are attached. He discovered hematoxylin, which became an important stain for tissue microscopy, and investigated how a color image could be formed from large numbers of small spots each of a single color—what we now call *pixels*.

Chittenden, Russell Henry (1856–1943) American physiologist who discovered the glucose polymer glycogen in muscle and who determined the daily protein requirements of a human being, proving that the then estimate of 118 grams was an overestimate and that 50 grams a day was adequate to maintain health. Chittenden helped to establish biochemistry as a discipline in its own right.

Clausius, Rudolf Julius Emanuel (1822–88) German theoretical physicist who greatly advanced the ideas of Sadi Carnot and James Joule, thereby largely establishing thermodynamics. He cleared up previous difficulties by pointing out that heat cannot pass spontaneously from a cold to a hot body, and furthered the understanding of the kinetic theory of gases. He also promoted the concept of entropy.

Rudolf Clausius

Cleve, Per Teodor (1840–1905) Swedish chemist who worked on the rare earths and decided that the "element" didymium, discovered by someone else, was in fact two elements, neodymium and praseodymium. He also discovered holmium and thulium. Ironically, holmium also turned out to be two elements and, in 1886, Paul-Émile Lecoq de Boisbaudran found it was mixed with another new element, dysprosium.

Cohen, Seymour Stanley (b. 1917) American biochemist who in 1946 began to investigate viral infection of cells by tagging viral nucleic acid with radioactive phosphorus. His results strongly suggested that DNA was central to genetics.

Cohen, Stanley Harold (b. 1922) American biochemist who worked on DNA-cutting enzymes. He helped to isolate nerve growth factor, went on to isolate epidermal growth factor and to show how this substance interacted with cells to produce a range of effects. Cohen shared the 1986 Nobel Prize in physiology or medicine with Rita Levi-Montalcini.

Corey, Elias James (b. 1928) American chemist who was one of the pioneers in the use of computers to assist in the analysis of methods of synthesis of organic molecules. This has become an indispensable technique, and it won Corey the 1990 Nobel Prize in chemistry.

Cornforth, Sir John Warcup (b. 1917) Australian-born British chemist who assisted in the synthesis of penicillin and studied the biosynthesis of cholesterol and various steroids. His most important work, however, was in the detailed elucidation of the mode of action of enzymes, in particular the interaction between an enzyme and its substrate. For this work, he shared the 1975 Nobel Prize in chemistry.

Courtois, Bernard (1777–1838) French chemist who, working with Gouton de Morveau, isolated morphine from opium and later accidentally discovered the element iodine.

Cram, Donald James (1919–2001) American chemist who in 1972 described the synthesis of left- and right-hand (chiral) structural forms of the molecules of certain cyclic polyethers (crown ethers) and achieved a method of the separation of left- and right-handed forms (enantiomers) so as to produce enantiometrically pure samples. This is important because enantiomers may have different biological properties. For this work, he shared the 1987 Nobel Prize in chemistry with Jean-Marie Lehn and Charles J. Pedersen.

Crawford, Adair (1748–95) Irish physician and chemist who suggested that animal heat is distributed throughout the body by the arterial blood.

Crick, Francis Harry Compton (1916–2004) English molecular biologist who with James Watson in 1953 built a molecular model of the complex genetic material deoxyribonucleic acid (DNA). Crick was the principal solver of the riddle of the genetic code, showing that different triplets of bases defined different amino acids in the protein sequence. With Watson and Maurice Wilkins, he was awarded the Nobel Prize in physiology or medicine in 1962. Later, Crick turned to neurophysiology and studied the functioning of the brain.

Cronstedt, Axel Frederik (1722–65) Swedish mineralogist who in 1751 was the first to isolate nickel. He then demonstrated its magnetic properties. Cronstedt wrote an influential work, *Essay towards a System of Mineralogy* (1758), in which he suggested that minerals should be classified using their chemical composition.

Crutzen, Paul Josef (b. 1933) Dutch chemist who, working with Sherwood Rowland and Mario Molina, alerted the world to the danger of damage being caused to the ozone layer of the atmosphere, about 9–30 miles up, from artificial nitrogen oxides and chlorofluorocarbon (CFC) gases. For this work, the three men were awarded the 1995 Nobel Prize in chemistry.

Curie, Marie (**née Sklodowska**) (1867–1934) Polish-born French physicist and wife of Pierre Curie, with whom she worked on magnetism and radioactivity, a term she invented in 1898. Her work on radioactivity earned her the Nobel Prize in physics in 1903. She isolated polonium and, in 1910, pure radium. For this work, she was awarded the Nobel Prize in chemistry in 1911. She died from leukemia, a martyr to long exposure to radioactivity.

Marie Curie

Curie, Pierre (1859–1906) French physicist, husband of Marie Curie who, in 1880, discovered piezoelectricity, the property of certain crystals to deform slightly in an electric field and to produce such a field if deformed. Without piezoelectricity, personal computers and ultrasound scanners would have been impossible. He also showed that ferromagnetic materials lose their magnetism at certain temperatures (the Curie point). Curie worked with his wife on radioactivity and showed that emitted particles were either electrically negative (beta particles), positive (alpha particles), or neutral (gamma rays). Pierre shared the 1903 Nobel Prize in physics with his wife.

Curl, Robert Floyd (b. 1933) American chemist who, working with Harold Kroto and Richard Smalley, earned the 1996 Nobel Prize in chemistry for the synthesis of an entirely new molecule consisting only of carbon atoms, which was named a buckminsterfullerene (also known as the buckyball molecule) because of the similarity of its structure to the geodesic domes of the architect Buckminster Fuller. The buckyball is a spherical structure of bonded carbon atoms and has many valuable properties, including acting as an efficient lubricant.

Daguerre, Louis-Jacques-Mandé (1787–1851) French inventor who discovered that silver iodide, freshly prepared in the dark, was sensitive to light and that an image projected onto a surface covered with this compound could be developed chemically and then fixed to form a permanent photograph. This was the daguerreotype process, the first successful and commercially viable photographic method.

Dale, Sir Henry Hallett (1875–1968) British pharmacologist who isolated acetylcholine from the ergot fungus. In 1921, after a hint from Dale, the German pharmacologist Otto Loewi, proved that acetylcholine was the neurotransmitter released at nerve endings in the autonomic nervous system. Dale and Loewi shared the 1936 Nobel Prize in physiology or medicine.

Dalton, John (1766–1844) English chemist and teacher whose atomic theory has become the foundation of modern chemistry. His physical research was chiefly on mixed gases; the law of partial pressures is also known as Dalton's law. In 1794, he first described color blindness, known for a time as Daltonism.

Dam, Carl Peter Henrik (1895–1976) Danish biochemist who discovered vitamin K by showing that a diet deficient in fatty

John Dalton

content led to blood-clotting defects in chicks. He and E.A. Doisy were awarded the 1943 Nobel Prize in physiology or medicine for the discovery of the vitamin. Countless babies have been saved from dangerous bleeding by routine administration of vitamin K.

Dana, James Dwight (1813–95) American mineralogist and geologist who classified minerals, coined the term *geosyncline*, studied coral-rock formation, and theorized about the evolution of the Earth's crust. He wrote the first standard reference books in geology and mineralogy.

Daniell, John Frederic (1790–1845) English chemist and meteorologist who invented a hygrometer (1820), a pyrometer (1830), and the Daniell electric cell, or zinc-copper battery (1836). His *Introduction to Chemical Philosophy* was published in 1839. Daniell also used his hygrometer to investigate atmospheric humidity.

Davy, Sir Humphry (1778–1829) English chemist and science propagandist who, through his experiments, discovered the new elements potassium, sodium, barium, strontium, calcium, and magnesium. In 1815, he invented a safety lamp for use in gas-filled coal mines. Michael Faraday worked under Davy and incurred his jealousy and the contempt of Lady Davy.

Sir Humphry Davy

Debye, Peter Joseph William (Petrus Josephus Wilhelmus) (1884–1966) Dutch-born American physicist and physical chemist who studied molecular structures, the distribution of electric charges in molecules, and the distances between atoms (the turning effect of a force). He studied dielectric constants and developed the theory of dipole moments, showing how these could be applied to understanding the three-dimensional shape of simple molecules, such as those of water. He showed that water molecules were bent and that benzene rings are flat. He received the Nobel Prize in chemistry in 1936 and is remembered in the unit of the dipole moment, the debye.

Peter Debye

Deisenhofer, Johann (b. 1943) German molecular biologist who studied the Y-shaped antibody (immunoglobulin) molecule to discover which sites on the molecule served which particular function. With Robert Huber and Hartmut Michel, he also researched the structure in the purple bacterium *Rhodopseudomonal viridans* in which photosynthesis occurs. This work earned them the 1988 Nobel Prize in chemistry.

Democritus (ca. 460–ca. 370 BCE) Greek philosopher who wrote widely on physics, mathematics, and cosmology. He proposed that all matter consisted of a vast number of tiny particles having a number of basic characteristics, the combinations of which accounted for the variety of objects. This was not a new idea.

Diels, Otto Paul Hermann (1876–1954) German chemist who, working with Kurt Alder, discovered a method of synthesizing new cyclic, or ring organic compounds by heating sterols with selenium to produce steroids. Diels and Kurt Alder were awarded the Nobel Prize in chemistry in 1950.

Domagk, Gerhard (1895–1964) German physician who showed that the red dye prontosil could kill certain bacteria in animals. During his research, his own daughter became gravely ill with a streptococcal infection. In desperation, Domagk injected her with the dye, and she made a full recovery. Domagk's work led to the development of the sulfa drugs. In 1939, he was awarded the Nobel Prize in physiology or medicine.

Dorn, Friedrich Ernst (1848–1916) German chemist who discovered the chemically almost inert, but medically dangerous, radioactive gaseous element radon, a noble gas, and showed that it arose as a decay product of radium.

Du Fay, Charles-François de Cisternay (1698–1739) French chemist whose main contribution to science was in physics. He studied and described the properties of magnetism, showed how magnetic field strength varied with distance, and described natural magnetism. He was also interested in static electricity and was the first to show that an electric charge could be positive or negative, that like charges repelled each other, and that unlike charges were mutually attractive.

Duve, Christian René de (b. 1917) English-born Belgian biochemist who used differential centrifugation to separate biochemical tissue fragments into layers and discovered the cell organelles (little organs), the lysosomes, and the peroxisomes. For this

Gerhard Domagk

work, he shared the 1974 Nobel Prize in physiology or medicine with Albert Claude and George E. Palade.

Edison, Thomas Alva (1847–1931) American inventor and holder of hundreds of patents who invented the phonograph, the tape ticker for notifying stock exchange prices, the carbon granule microphone, the incandescent electric lamp, and the thermionic diode. His example, and that of the economic benefits of technological advance, led to the creation of the modern research laboratory.

Thomas Edison

Ehrlich, Paul (1854–1915) German medical researcher who used aniline dyes for the selective staining of disease organisms and realized that these substances might kill disease germs without killing the patient. He was right, and became the father of chemotherapy. For his studies on immunity he shared the Nobel Prize in medicine or physiology with Ilya Metchnikoff in 1908.

Eigen, Manfred (b. 1927) German physical chemist who carried out research on chemical reactions that occur so quickly that investigation of them is very difficult. Such reactions were previously thought to be instantaneous. He succeeded in developing techniques that allowed the analysis of these reactions and shared with Ronald Norrish and George Porter the 1967 Nobel Prize in chemistry.

Ekeberg, Anders Gustav (1767–1813) Swedish chemist who discovered the metallic element tantalum, so called by him because of the tantalizing difficulty he experienced in persuading its oxide to react with an acid. This makes tantalum useful as a metal.

Elhuyar y de Suvisa, Fausto d' (1755–1833) Spanish mineralogist who discovered the element tungsten.

Elvehjem, Conrad Arnold (1901–62) American biochemist who discovered the cure for the vitamin deficiency disease pellagra. This was the B vitamin nicotinic acid (niacin).

Empedocles (ca. 490–430 BCE) Greek philosopher who wrote a poem *On Nature* in which he claimed that everything was made of the four elements, earth, air, fire, and water, which either combined or repelled each other. This idea was to hold up the advancement of chemistry for 2,000 years. Empedocles is said to have jumped into the crater of the volcano Mount Etna to prove that he was immortal.

Epicurus (341–270 BCE) Greek philosopher who proposed that everything was made from atoms—particles so small that they cannot be subdivided further. The Roman poet Lucretius accepted and described the atomic theory of Epicurus. The Greek word *atom* means "unable to be cut."

Erlenmeyer, Richard August Carl Emil (1825–1909) German chemist who, for his synthetic work, designed the conical Erlenmeyer flask known to all college chemistry students. He synthesized a number of important organic compounds, including guanidine, tyrosine, and isobutyric acid.

Ernst, Richard Robert (b. 1933) Swiss physical chemist whose work on the development and improvement of nuclear magnetic resonance spectroscopy, a powerful technique for determining the molecular structure of organic compounds, won him the Nobel Prize in chemistry in 1991.

Eskola, Pentti Eelis (1883–1964) Finnish geologist who specialized in metamorphic formations—preexisting rock that has been modified by heat, pressure, or chemical action. In 1915, he asserted that in such rock that has reached chemical equilibrium, the mineral composition is controlled only by the chemical composition. Eskola recognized eight types of metamorphic formation.

Euler-Chelpin, Hans Karl August Simon von (1873–1964) Swedish chemist who carried out a great deal of the earliest work on enzymes. He showed their optimum conditions for function, interaction with vitamins, inhibition by metallic ions and other substances, and the distinction between yeast saccharases and those occurring in the intestine. For his work on enzymes he shared the 1929 Nobel Prize in chemistry with Arthur Harden.

Faraday, Michael (1791–1867) English chemist and physicist, the creator of the classical electromagnetic field theory and one of the greatest experimental physicists. He discovered electromagnetic induction (1831), which led to the development of generators, transformers, and electromagnets;

Epicurus

Michael Faraday

proposed the laws of electrolysis (1833); showed the rotation of polarized light by magnetism (1845); and made other fundamental advances.

Feigenbaum, Edward Albert (b. 1936) American computer scientist who has worked on problems of artificial intelligence and expert systems and who has evolved a program that uses mass spectrometer data to identify organic compounds. The program, known as DENDRAL, comes close to achieving a performance as good as that of an expert and knowledgeable chemist.

Fischer, Edmond Henri (b. 1920) American biochemist who, working with Edwin Krebs, showed how glucose molecules—the body's main fuel—are released from the storage form, the glucose polymer glycogen. They showed that the enzyme glycogen phosphorylase, which catalyzes the release, is made operative by receiving a phosphate group from ATP and then made nonoperative by losing this group. Fischer and Krebs shared the 1992 Nobel Prize in physiology or medicine.

Fischer, Ernst Otto (b. 1918) German chemist noted for his elucidation of the structure of the unusual synthetic compound ferrocene, which is a kind of sandwich with carbon rings as the bread and an iron atom as the filling. Thousands of such compounds are now known. For this work, Fischer shared the 1973 Nobel Prize in chemistry with Geoffrey Wilkinson.

Fischer, Hans (1881–1945) German chemist who researched the molecular structure of chlorophyll, determined the structural formulas for biliverdin and bilirubin, synthesized both these bile products, and worked out and synthesized the structure of hemin. For the latter achievement, he was awarded the Nobel Prize in chemistry in 1930.

Fischer, Hermann Emil (1852–1919) German organic chemist who discovered the molecular structures of sugars, including glucose, found the structure of purines, isolated and identified amino acids, and worked on the structure of proteins. He received the Nobel Prize in chemistry in 1902 for his work on sugars and purines.

Fleming, Sir Alexander (1881–1955) Scottish bacteriologist who in 1928 discovered the first antibiotic substance, penicillin, but

Sir Alexander Fleming

without isolating it. He also pioneered the use of salvarsan against syphilis, discovered the antiseptic powers of lysozyme, and was first to use anti-typhoid vaccines on humans. For the discovery of penicillin, he shared the 1945 Nobel Prize in physiology or medicine with Ernst Chain and Howard Florey.

Florey, Howard Walter (Baron Florey) (1898–1968) Australian pathologist who was the first to exploit the full potential of penicillin. In 1939, Florey and Ernst Chain began a research project to purify and test the mold extract that Alexander Fleming had discovered 11 years before. They isolated penicillin, and this led to large-scale production of the world's first antibiotic and saved millions of lives. Fleming, Florey, and Chain were awarded the 1945 Nobel Prize in physiology or medicine.

Flory, Paul John (1910–85) American chemist whose contribution to the understanding of the nature of polymers earned him the 1974 Nobel Prize in chemistry. Polymers are macromolecules consisting of long sequences of repetitions of small chemical groups called monomers. Many natural large molecules are polymers, as are synthetic plastics.

Frankland, Sir Edward (1825–99) English organic chemist who became professor at the Royal Institution, London, in 1863. He propounded the theory of valency and, with Joseph Lockyer, discovered helium in the Sun's atmosphere in 1868.

Franklin, Benjamin (1706–90) American scientist, statesman, and printer who made a number of important contributions to the science of electricity. He is well remembered for flying a kite in a thunderstorm to prove that lightning was electrical in nature. He also showed how buildings could be protected from lightning strikes by metal electrical conductors running down to the ground. In addition, he worked out the course of the Gulf Stream across the Atlantic.

Franklin, Rosalind Elsie (1920–58) English X-ray crystallographer whose work, with Maurice Wilkins, provided James Watson and Francis Crick with the data on which they were able to construct the model of the DNA molecule and achieve scientific immortality. She developed cancer and died in 1958,

Howard Florey

Sir Edward Frankland

four years before she could have shared the Nobel Prize with Wilkins, Watson, and Crick.

Fukui, Kenichi (1918–98) Japanese chemist who demonstrated how chemical reactions were essentially a question of the interaction of only two of the orbital electrons of the interacting atoms. Fukui called these "frontier orbitals" and showed how chemical reactions were partly determined by the symmetry of frontier orbitals. He shared the 1981 Nobel Prize in chemistry with Roald Hoffmann.

Funk, Casimir (1884–1967) Polish-born U.S. biochemist who isolated the first vitamin and suggested, correctly, that others existed. He believed, wrongly, that they all contained an amine ($-NH_2$) group, and suggested they be called "vital amines" or "vitamines." This was later amended to "vitamins."

Gassendi, Pierre (1592–1655) French philosopher and astronomer who studied atomism, acoustics, heat, and thermodynamics, and, in his book on the theory of atoms, *Syntagma philosophicum* (1660), introduced the term *molecule* to indicate the smallest unit of a substance capable of an independent existence.

Gay-Lussac, Joseph-Louis (1778–1850) French chemist and physicist who investigated the expansion of gases with rising temperature and independently formulated the law known as Charles' law of pressures. He investigated the laws of the combination of gases and the properties of many chemical compounds and elements, especially the halogens. He also compiled charts of the solubility of many compounds.

Giauque, William Francis (1895–1982) Canadian-born American chemist who researched the properties of matter at very low temperatures and, by a magnetic process, achieved temperatures within one degree of absolute zero. He also developed a thermometer for measuring very low temperatures. He was awarded the 1949 Nobel Prize in chemistry.

William F. Giauque

Gibbs, Josiah Willard (1839–1903) American physical chemist whose theory of chemical thermodynamics became the foundation of physical chemistry. He also did pioneering work in statistical mechanics, the reports of which were submerged in difficult papers in obscure journals until after they had been independently repeated by scientists of the caliber of Max Planck and Albert Einstein.

Gilbert, Walter (b. 1932) American molecular biologist whose discoveries helped usher in the era of genetic engineering. He developed a method using chemical manipulations to quickly and accurately read the sequence of chemical bases in a segment of DNA. Gilbert shared the 1980 Nobel Prize in chemistry with English biochemist Frederick Sanger and American biochemist Paul Berg.

Gilman, Alfred Goodman (b. 1941) American biochemist who, working with Martin Rodbell, discovered the G protein, a class of chemical messengers that transfer incoming information from receptors in cell membranes to the producers of the second messenger—the hormone that then moves to the effector sites within the cell. G proteins remain inactive until a signal reaches the cell. They then activate. Disease processes can interfere with the G proteins. For this work, Gilman and Martin Rodbell were awarded the 1994 Nobel Prize in physiology or medicine.

Johann Glauber

Glauber, Johann Rudolf (1604–68) German chemist who discovered hydrated sodium sulfate, which was sold as a laxative under the trade name of Glauber's salt. Glauber also designed improved laboratory equipment that contributed to the production of industrial, agricultural, and medical products.

Graham, Thomas (1805–69) Scottish chemist and physicist. He was one of the founders of physical chemistry, and his research on molecular diffusion of gases led him to formulate the law "that the diffusion rate of gases is inversely as the square root of their density." This is known as Graham's law of diffusion.

Thomas Graham

Gregor, William (1761–1817) English chemist, whose interest in analyzing local soils led him to the discovery of the element titanium, which has since become an important metal for its light weight and resistance to corrosion.

Grignard, Victor (1871–1935) French organic chemist who showed how to combine magnesium with reactive organic halogen compounds to make organomagnesium compounds that could be used to produce alcohols. He also synthesized a further and valuable range of organometallic compounds. These compounds, called Grignard reagents, are very useful in organic synthesis and earned him the 1912 Nobel Prize in chemistry.

Haber, Fritz (1868–1934) German chemist who, with brother-in-law Carl Bosch, invented a process for the synthesis of ammonia from hydrogen and atmospheric nitrogen, thus overcoming the shortage of natural nitrate deposits accessible to the German explosives industry in World War I. Haber's development of the process on an industrial scale provided copious quantities of fertilizers and also prompted the development of the chemical industry and chemical engineering. For his work, Haber received the Nobel Prize in chemistry in 1918.

Hahn, Otto (1879–1968) German radiochemist who showed that the radioactive breakdown of certain elements could provide a way of dating some mineral deposits. He is best known, however, for work with slow neutrons, which indicated that it would be possible to initiate and control nuclear fission, nature's most powerful energy source. This led to attempts to harness fission for industrial and military use. He was awarded the Nobel Prize in chemistry in 1944, and it was proposed that element number 108 should be named hahnium in his honor.

Otto Hahn

Hales, Stephen (1677–1761) English botanist and chemist, founder of plant physiology, whose book *Vegetable Staticks* (1727) was the start of our understanding of vegetable physiology. He was one of the first to use instruments to measure the nutrition and movement of liquids within plants. He also invented machines for ventilating, distilling seawater, and preserving meat.

Hall, Charles Martin (1863–1914) American chemist who in 1886 discovered, independently of Paul Héroult, the first economic method of obtaining aluminum from bauxite (electrolytically). He helped to found the Aluminum Company of America and was its vice president from 1890.

Hall, Sir James (1761–1832) Scottish geologist who proved the igneous origin of basalt and dolerite rocks by laboratory tests in which

Sir Arthur Harden

Odd Hassel

he melted and recrystallized minerals. He also showed that molten magma could cause changes in limestone, producing metamorphic rock.

Harden, Sir Arthur (1865–1940) British chemist who shared the 1929 Nobel Prize in chemistry with Hans Euler-Chelpin for their classic work on fermentation enzymes. Harden proved that living organisms were not necessary for fermentation and that the process could be inhibited if a factor was removed by dialysis. This was the enzyme. He also found that during fermentation, inorganic phosphate esterified into organic forms.

Hassel, Odd (1897–1981) Norwegian chemist who used X-ray and electron diffraction methods to determine the molecular structure of the petroleum-derived solvent cyclohexane and related compounds. Cyclohexane is not a flat molecule and can adopt a boat-shaped or a chain conformation. Hassel's work brought to the fore the importance of conformational analysis. He shared the 1969 Nobel Prize in chemistry with Derek Barton.

Hatchett, Charles (1765–1847) English chemist who discovered the metallic element columbium (now niobium,Hatchettine, or hatchettite, a yellowish white semitransparent fossil resin or waxlike hydrocarbon found in South Wales coal, was named for him.

Hauptman, Herbert Aaron (b. 1917) American chemist who, with Jerome Karle in the early 1950s, developed a rapid statistical method of using X-ray crystallography to determine the molecular structure of chemical compounds. Their 1953 paper was largely ignored but the method is now fully established. Hauptman and Karle shared the 1985 Nobel Prize in chemistry.

Haworth, Sir Walter Norman (1883–1950) English chemist who was the first to establish the molecular structure of vitamin C and who named it ascorbic acid. Haworth shared the 1937 Nobel Prize in chemistry with Paul Karrer.

Helmont, Jan Baptista van (1579–1644) Flemish chemist, physician, and physiologist who invented the word *gas*, derived from the Greek word *khaos* (chaos). He distinguished gases other than air; regarded water as a prime element; believed that digestion was due to "ferments" that converted dead food into living flesh; proposed the medical use of alkalis for excess acidity; and believed in alchemy. His works were published by his son.

Henry, William (1774–1836) English chemist who showed that the solubility of a gas in a liquid at a given temperature is proportional to its pressure. This is known as Henry's law. He wrote an influential and often reprinted book called *Elements of Experimental Chemistry* (1801).

Herschbach, Dudley Robert (b. 1932) American physical chemist who shared the 1986 Nobel Prize in chemistry with Yuan Tseh Lee and John Polanyi for his work on the detailed dynamics of chemical reactions. This research was done by a method not previously used in chemistry, in which low-pressure beams of the reacting molecules were made to intersect while sensitive detectors checked for the products.

Herzberg, Gerhard (1904–99) Canadian chemist who used spectroscopic methods to study the energy levels of hydrogen atoms and molecules and of a range of chemical radicals. He was awarded the 1971 Nobel Prize in chemistry.

Hess, Germain Henri (1802–50) Swiss-born Russian chemist who developed thermochemistry and established the law of constant heat summation (Hess's law). This states that the amount of heat evolved in a chemical change is constant whether the reaction occurs in one stage or several.

Hevesy, Georg Karl von (**George de Hevesy**) (1885–1966) Hungarian-born Swedish radiochemist who was the first to suggest the use of radioactive tracers in chemical and biological work. This was to become a technique of great power and value. On Niels Bohr's recommendation, Hevesy also searched for and found a new element, number 72, which he named hafnium. He was awarded the Nobel Prize in chemistry in 1943.

Heyrovský, Jaroslav (1890–1967) Czech chemist who invented the polarograph. This instrument uses a self-cleaning cathode—a narrow tube through which mercury is slowly passed into the solution—and a large nonpolarizable anode. The electrodes are immersed in a dilute solution of the sample and a variable

William Henry

electrical potential is applied to the cell. As each chemical species is reduced at the cathode, the current rises, and the height of each rise is proportional to the concentration of the component. The technique allows detection of trace amounts of metals and investigation of ions interacting with the solvent. Heyrovský was awarded the 1959 Nobel Prize in chemistry.

Higgins, William (1763–1825) Irish chemist who was the first to propose, although without any experimental data, that substances forming chemical compounds do so according to laws of simple and multiple proportions. The principle was later formulated by John Dalton.

Hinshelwood, Sir Cyril Norman (1897–1967) English chemist who, simultaneously with Nikolay Semenov, investigated chemical reaction kinetics in the interwar years, for which they shared the Nobel Prize in chemistry in 1956. He was a linguist and classical scholar, and was president of the Royal Society.

Hisinger, Wilhelm (1766–1852) Swedish mineralogist who discovered the element cerium and published a geological map of southern and central Sweden.

Hjelm, Peter Jacob (1746–1813) Swedish chemist who in 1782 discovered the element molybdenum in a sample of molybdenite sent to him by Carl Scheele, who suspected that a new element might lie therein.

Hodgkin, Dorothy Crowfoot (1910–94) English chemist and crystallographer who used X-ray diffraction to study the structure of the vitamin B_{12} molecule and other complex molecules. In 1949, she became the first chemist to use a computer to determine the structure of an organic chemical, penicillin. She won the Nobel Prize in chemistry in 1964.

Hoffmann, Roald (b. 1937) American chemist who, working with Robert Woodward, worked out the rules for the conservation of orbital symmetry during chemical reactions in which ring compounds are formed from chain structures (cyclization), and bonds break and form simultaneously. With Kenichi Fukui, he was awarded the 1981 Nobel Prize in chemistry for this work, which has proved to be seminal.

Hofmann, August Wilhelm von (1818–92) German chemist who obtained aniline from coal products and discovered many other organic compounds, including formaldehyde (1867). He devoted much labor to the theory of chemical types.

Holmes, Arthur (1890–1965) English geologist and geophysicist who put dates to the geological time scale. He determined the ages of rocks by measuring their radioactive constituents and was an early scientific supporter of Alfred Wegener's theory of continental drift. He was the first to recognize that the Earth's crust formed (solidified) about 4.56 billion years ago. His book *Principles of Physical Geology* (1944) was highly successful.

Hooke, Robert (1635–1703) English physicist, chemist, and architect. One of the most brilliant scientists of his age and one of the most quarrelsome. He formulated Hooke's law of the extension and compression of elastic bodies and effectively invented the quadrant, the microscope, and the first Gregorian telescope. He was curator of experiments at the Royal Society (1662) and later its secretary.

Hopkins, Sir Frederick Gowland (1861–1947) English biochemist who was the first to make a general scientific study of vitamins and to show their importance in the maintenance of health. In 1929, he shared the Nobel Prize in medicine or physiology with Christiaan Eijkmann.

Huber, Robert (b. 1937) German biochemist who helped to determine antibody structure and binding sites; showed that there was a very small structural difference between the active and the inactive form of the enzyme phosphorylase; and, with Hartmut Michel and Johann Deisenhofer, worked out the detailed structure of the membrane-bound region where photosynthesis occurs in the purple bacterium *Rhodopseudomonal viridans*. For this work, he and his colleagues were awarded the 1988 Nobel Prize in chemistry.

Joliot-Curie, Irène (1897–1956) French chemist, daughter of Pierre and Marie Curie, who worked with her husband, Jean-Frédéric Joliot-Curie, on making the first of a series of artificially produced radioactive isotopes by bombarding aluminum with

August Wilhelm von Hofmann

Irène Joliot-Curie

alpha particles. She and her husband were awarded the 1935 Nobel Prize in chemistry. Like her mother, she died from leukemia, presumably as a result of long exposure to radioactivity.

James Joule

Joule, James Prescott (1818–89) English physicist who laid the foundations for the theory of the conservation of energy. He is famous for experiments in heat, which he showed to be a form of energy. He also showed that if a gas expands without performing work, its temperature falls. The Joule, a unit of work or energy, is named after him. With Lord Kelvin, (William Thomson) he devised an absolute scale of temperature.

Karle, Jerome (b. 1918) American chemist whose research advanced the understanding of chemical composition. His research in the use of X-ray crystallography to determine the structure of crystal molecules earned him the 1985 Nobel Prize in chemistry, which he shared with American chemist Herbert A. Hauptman.

Karrer, Paul (1889–1971) Swiss chemist who studied amino acids, proteins, polysaccharides, and plant pigments. He established the molecular structure of carotene and worked on vitamin A and other vitamins. For this work, he shared the 1937 Nobel Prize in chemistry with Walter Haworth.

Kekulé von Stradonitz, Friedrich August (1829–96) German chemist who made a major contribution to organic chemistry by developing structural theories, including the ring (cyclic) structure of benzene. The latter idea, of a ring of six carbon atoms linked by alternate single and double bonds, and each linked to one hydrogen atom, is said to have come to him in a graphic daydream he had while traveling on a London bus. He anticipated the concept of resonance articulated in the early 1930s.

Keller, Andrew (1925–99) Hungarian-born British chemist who specialized in polymer microstructure and in the way these long-chain molecules crystallize to form plastics. He studied how polymers crystallize from solution rather than from melt and, using the electron diffraction technique, showed that polymers crystallize in a regular chain folded pattern.

Kelvin, Baron *see* Thomson, William.

Kendall, Edward Calvin (1886–1972) U.S. biochemist who studied the hormones produced by the outer zone (cortex) of the adrenal gland and, from his findings, synthesized cortisone. This led to the valuable range of corticosteroid drugs. In 1950, Kendall and his colleague, Philip Hench, were awarded the Nobel Prize in physiology or medicine.

Edward C. Kendall

Kendrew, Sir John Cowdery (1917–97) English molecular biologist who established the three-dimensional structure of muscle hemoglobin (myoglobin) by X-ray crystallography in 1959. He shared the 1962 Nobel Prize in chemistry with Max Perutz.

Kirchhoff, Gustav Robert (1824–87) German physicist who, while still a student, derived the laws, now known as Kirchhoff's laws, for determining currents in electrical networks. Working in spectroscopy, he discovered the elements cesium and rubidium, and formulated Kirchhoff's laws of radiation, which stipulate that, for a given wavelength, the ratio of emission to absorption is the same for all bodies at a given temperature.

Klaproth, Martin Heinrich (1743–1817) German chemist who correctly predicted the existence of the elements strontium, titanium, uranium, and zirconium, and confirmed and named tellurium. All these elements were isolated by other chemists. He determined the properties of the minerals yttria and beryllia. Klaproth, who is often considered a founder of analytical chemistry, is noted for his insistence on publishing results that contradicted his own theories.

Klug, Sir Aaron (b. 1926) South African chemist whose work on determining the chemical structure of viruses, including the polio virus, earned him the 1982 Nobel Prize in chemistry. Klug used a variety of techniques, including X-ray diffractions, electron microscopy, and structural modelling.

Kolbe, Adolph Wilhelm Hermann (1818–84) German chemist who was the first to synthesize acetic acid from inorganic material. He discovered the Kolbe reaction in 1859, which allowed large-scale industrial synthesis of salicylic acid. This was important for the production of acetylsalicylic acid (aspirin).

Hermann Kolbe

He also developed a useful electrolytic process for the synthesis of alkanes.

Kosterlitz, Hans Walter (1903–96) German-born Scottish pharmacologist and physiologist who, working with John Hughes, discovered the natural morphine-like body opiates, the enkephalins (endorphins), and showed that they were blocked by the drug naloxone, which antagonizes morphine.

Krebs, Sir Hans Adolf (1900–81) German-born British biochemist who elucidated the cyclical series of biochemical reactions by means of which food is converted into energy for cell function and for the synthesis of biomolecules. This important process is known as the Krebs cycle and is fundamental to cell physiology. Krebs shared the Nobel Prize in physiology or medicine with Fritz Lipmann in 1953.

Kroto, Sir Harold W. (b. 1939) English chemist who, with Richard Smalley and Robert Curl, succeeded in making an entirely new molecule, consisting only of carbon atoms and named a buckminsterfullerene (buckyball) because of the similarity of its structure to the geodesic domes of the architect Buckminster Fuller. The buckyball is a spherical structure of bonded carbon atoms and has many valuable properties. The three men were awarded the 1996 Nobel Prize in chemistry.

Kuhn, Richard (1900–67) German chemist who worked on enzymes and the three-dimensional structure of molecules (stereochemistry) and who made important discoveries in the field of vitamins, especially vitamin A. He was awarded the 1938 Nobel Prize in chemistry.

Langmuir, Irving (1881-1957) American chemist who studied electrical discharges in gases and the chemical forces in solids, liquids, and surface films. He received the Nobel Prize in 1932 for his work on surface chemistry.

Lavoisier, Antoine-Laurent (1743–94) French chemist who has been described as the founder of modern chemistry. He discovered and named oxygen and proved its importance in respiration, combustion, and rusting and as an element that formed many compounds (oxides) with metals. His book *Traité Elémentaire* *de Chimie*, published in 1789, described his experiments. He was guillotined during the Reign of Terror.

Le Châtelier, Henri-Louis (1850–1936) French chemist noted for his rule, known as Le Châtelier's principle, which states that every change in a system in stable chemical equilibrium results in a rearrangement of the system so that the original change is minimized. He devised a railway water brake, an optical pyrometer, and contributed to the field of metallurgy.

Leclanché, Georges (1839–82) French engineer who devised an electric cell using a zinc rod and a porous earthenware pot containing a carbon rod surounded by manganese dioxide and carbon black, all enclosed in a jar filled with a solution of sal ammoniac. This highly successful cell was later converted to a dry form and was used as a portable source of electric energy throughout most of the 20th century.

Lecoq de Boisbaudran, Paul-Émile (1838–1912) French chemist and wine merchant whose main scientific work was in spectroscopic analysis. He found a new element, gallium, and helped in the discovery of five of the 15 rare earth elements (lanthanoids).

Lee, Yuan Tseh (b. 1936) American physical chemist who used molecular beam techniques to study the dynamics of chemical reactions. Lee is credited with a major contribution to the success of developing the molecular beam method and shared the 1986 Nobel Prize in chemistry with John Polanyi and Dudley Herschbach.

Yuan Tseh Lee

Lehn, Jean-Marie (b. 1939) French chemist who demonstrated that sodium and potassium ions can pass across biological membranes in a nonpolar environment by being enclosed within a cavity or channel in a large organic molecule. This discovery opened up a new branch of organic chemistry, called supramolecular chemistry, and it won Lehn a share of the 1987 Nobel Prize in chemistry with Charles Pedersen and Donald Cram.

Leloir, Luis Federico (1906–87) Argentinian biochemist who made a number of biochemical advances important to medicine. He discovered the hormone angiotensin, which raises blood pressure; he showed how the energy-storage polysaccharide glycogen is a polymer built up from units of glucose; and he showed how galactose was converted to glucose. For these findings, he was awarded the 1970 Nobel Prize in chemistry.

Leucippus (fl. 500 BCE) Greek philosopher who is said to have originated the atomistic theory that was taken up by Democritus and the poet Lucretius.

Lewis, Gilbert Newton (1875–1946) American physical chemist who developed theories on chemical thermodynamics, atomic structure, and atomic bonding. He pioneered work on the electronic theory of valency, showing the difference between ionic and covalent bonds. He defined an acid as an electron acceptor and a base as an electron donor.

Libby, Willard Frank (1908–80) American chemist noted for developing the method of radiocarbon dating for determining the age of once living organic material. For this important advance he was awarded the Nobel Prize in chemistry in 1960.

Li, Choh Hao (1913–89) Chinese-born American biochemist who isolated several pituitary hormones and worked out the amino acid sequence of growth hormone and then synthesized it. He also established the sequence in ACTH, the pituitary hormone that prompts the adrenals to produce cortisone.

Liebig, Justus, Freiherr von (1803–73) German chemist and one of the most illustrious chemists of his age, equally great in method and in practical applications. He made his name both in organic and animal chemistry, and in the study of alcohols. He was the founder of agricultural chemistry and the discoverer of chloroform.

Lipmann, Fritz Albert (1899–1986) German-born American biochemist who showed how citric acid is formed from oxaloacetate and acetate and that an unrecognized cofactor, coenzyme A, was required. Lipmann isolated this factor. The formation of citric acid is the first step in the important energy-producing Krebs cycle. Lipmann shared the 1953 Nobel Prize in physiology or medicine with Hans Krebs.

Fritz Lipmann

Lipscomb, William Nunn (b. 1919) American chemist who used ingenious methods to work out the molecular structure of a number of boron compounds, using X-ray crystal diffraction methods at low temperatures. His methods became more generally useful and he was awarded the 1976 Nobel Prize in chemistry.

Loewi, Otto (1873–1961) German pharmacologist who proved that the nerve impulse was transferred from nerve to muscle by a chemical mediator. He distinguished acetylcholine from adrenaline for this function, and the former was later identified by Henry Dale. He shared the Nobel Prize in physiology or medicine with Dale in 1936.

Lomonosov, Mikhail Vasilyevich (1711–65) Russian scientist who set up the country's first chemical laboratory. He seems to have been well ahead of his time and is said to have proposed the law of conservation of mass, the wave theory of light, and the kinetic theory of heat well before these important principles were understood in the West. He believed in popular education.

Lucretius (fl. ca. 100 BCE) Roman poet and philosopher who wrote a long poem called *De rerum natura* ("on the nature of things"), in which he outlined the atomist theory.

McMillan, Edwin Mattison (1907–91) American physicist who, with Philip Abelson, produced the first human-made element, neptunium (atomic number 93). The two men won the Nobel Prize in chemistry in 1951.

Marcus, Rudolph Arthur (b. 1923) Canadian-born American chemist whose work on the theory of electron transfer in chemical reactions, such as oxidation and reduction, changed the way scientists looked at these reactions and provided a clearer understanding of a wide range of chemical processes. This important work earned him the 1992 Nobel Prize in chemistry.

Martin, Archer John Porter (1910–2002) English biochemist who developed methods of partition chromatography, using columns of silica gel, for the separation of amino acids from the mixture produced by hydrolysis of proteins. This method greatly facilitated the work of determining the structure of proteins. He was awarded the 1952 Nobel Prize in chemistry.

Lise Meitner

Meitner, Lise (1878–1968) Austrian nuclear physicist who discovered the radioactive element protoactinium. She made the telling, and correct, suggestion that the presence of radioactive barium in the products of uranium, which had been bombarded with neutrons, was probably due to the fact that some uranium atom nuclei had been split in two. The transuranic element number 108, meitnerium, has been named for her.

Mendeleyev, Dmitry Ivanovich (1834–1907) Russian chemist who arranged the known elements into a table of columns by their chemical properties. This was the periodic table, which was of great importance in the development of chemistry and enabled Mendeleyev to predict the existence of several elements that were subsequently discovered. Element 101 is named mendelevium after him. He also worked on the liquifaction of gases, the expansion of gases, and a theory of solutions.

Merrifield, Robert Bruce (b. 1921) American chemist who developed an ingenious and rapid way of synthesizing proteins by lining up the constituent amino acids in the right order on a polystyrene bead, a process that has now been automated. This work earned him the 1984 Nobel Prize in chemistry.

Meyerhof, Otto Fritz (1884–1951) German-born American biochemist whose work on muscle physiology showed that lactic acid was produced from muscle glycogen during muscle contraction in anaerobic conditions. He also showed that the utilization of glucose as a fuel in living cells involved a cyclic biochemical pathway. For these discoveries, he received the Nobel Prize in physiology or medicine in 1922.

Michel, Hartmut (b. 1948) German biochemist who, working with Robert Huber and Johann Deisenhofer, established the structure of an area of a bacterium in which photosynthesis takes place. He and his colleagues were awarded the 1988 Nobel Prize in chemistry for this work.

Miller, Stanley Lloyd (b. 1930) American chemist who studied the possible origins of life on Earth by using laboratory equipment to simulate supposed early atmospheric gaseous content and electric sparks to simulate lightning. He succeeded in forming amino acids, the units of proteins. Later work on the enzymatic function of RNA added credibility to Miller's ideas.

Mitchell, Peter Dennis (1920–92) English biochemist who revolutionized thought on the process of oxidative phosphorylation in which adenosine triphosphate (ATP) is regenerated from adenosine diphosphate (ADP) and phosphate. Breakdown of ATP to ADP releases large amounts of energy for cell functions from the phosphate bonds. Mitchell proposed that electron transport formed a proton gradient across the mitochondrial membrane that directly brought about the synthesis of ATP from ADP. He was awarded the 1978 Nobel Prize in chemistry.

Mohs, Friedrich (1773–1839) German mineralogist who wrote *The Natural History System of Mineralogy* (1821) and *Treatise on Mineralogy* (1825). He classified minerals on the basis of hardness, and the Mohs' scale of hardness is still in use. This scale, 0–10, is based on the ability of any mineral to scratch another lower down the scale. Talc is 1, diamond is 10.

Moissan, Henri (1852–1907) French chemist who isolated the element fluorine in 1886. He invented an electric arc furnace with which he achieved very high temperatures and synthesized rubies. He was the founder of high-temperature chemistry. He was awarded the 1906 Nobel Prize in chemistry for his work on fluorine.

Molina, Mario (b. 1943) American chemist who, working with Sherwood Rowland and Paul Crutzen, alerted the world to the danger of damage being caused to the ozone layer of the atmosphere from artificially produced nitrogen oxides and chlorofluorocarbon (CFC) gases. The ozone layer protects us against dangerous concentrations of ultraviolet frequencies in sunlight. For this work, the three men were awarded the 1995 Nobel Prize in chemistry.

Monod, Jacques-Lucien (1910–76) French biochemist who worked with François Jacob on messenger RNA. In *Chance and Necessity* (1970) he proposed that humans are the product of chance in the universe.

Moore, Stanford (1913–82) American biochemist who, working with William Stein, invented a chromatography process that could

Stanford Moore

separate from a mass of enzyme-digested protein all the constituent amino acids so that they could be identified and quantified. Moore and Stein also invented an automated method of determining the base sequence in a length of RNA. Moore, Stein, and Christian Anfinsen were awarded the 1972 Nobel Prize in chemistry.

Morley, Edward Williams (1838–1923) American chemist and physicist who, with Albert Michelson, developed a sensitive interferometer with which they showed (1887) that the speed of light is constant, whether measured in the direction of the Earth's movement or perpendicular to that direction (Michelson-Morley experiment).

Moseley, Henry Gwyn Jeffreys (1887–1915) British physicist who used X-rays' scattering by different elements to show that the resulting wavelengths decreased regularly with increase of atomic weight. He concluded, correctly, that each element had a different number of electrons.

Robert S. Mulliken

Mulliken, Robert Sanderson (1896–1986) American chemist who, in the 1930s, helped to develop the molecular orbital theory of molecular structure and chemical bonding. He was awarded the 1966 Nobel Prize in chemistry.

Mullis, Kary Banks (b. 1944) American biochemist who, while driving one evening, conceived the idea of the polymerase chain reaction (PCR) that was to become one of the most important advances in genetic research, engineering, and medicine since Francis Crick and James Watson. PCR provides millions of copies of any DNA fragment. He was awarded the Nobel Prize in chemistry in 1993.

Natta, Giulio (1903–79) Italian chemist who worked on catalysis and developed a scheme for the synthesis of artificial rubber. He used organometallic catalysts to polymerize propene (propylene) to produce a form of the valuable material polypropylene, a synthetic plastic of high melting point and considerable strength. He was awarded the 1963 Nobel Prize in chemistry.

Nernst, Walther Hermann (1864–1941) German chemist who discovered the third law of thermodynamics, that entropy (a measure of the unavailability of a system's energy to do work) increases as temperature approaches absolute zero. He worked on electrical insulators, and the specific heat of solids at low temperature, and explained the chain reaction by which chlorine and hydrogen explode on exposure to light. He was awarded the 1920 Nobel Prize in chemistry.

Newlands, John Alexander Reina (1837–98) British chemist who, like Dmitry Mendeleyev, was one of the first to show that the properties of chemical elements changed in a periodic manner. He arranged the then known 62 elements in order of increasing atomic weight and showed that these could be placed into groups of eight based on similar properties. This was known as the law of octaves.

Nicholson, William (1753–1815) English chemist who showed that water could be broken down into hydrogen and oxygen by inserting two wires into it that were connected to an electric battery. This was the first demonstration of electrolysis. Nicholson, who had had the benefit of publishing his own scientific journal, was able to report some findings with the voltaic pile even before Alessandro Volta.

Nobel, Alfred Bernhard (1833–96) Swedish chemist and engineer who discovered the element nobelium and invented a safer explosive by mixing nitroglycerin with the diatomaceous earth kieselguhr. He called this explosive dynamite. It earned him so much money that he was able to leave more than $9 million for the establishment of the Nobel Prize.

Noddack, Walter (1893–1960) German chemist who, working with his wife, Ida Tacke, discovered the elements rhenium and technetium, and did research on the photopigments of the eye.

Norrish, Ronald George Wreyford (1879–1978) British chemist who was one of the pioneers of photochemistry, and who invented flash photolysis, a technique in which photochemical change caused by a very brief, bright flash of light can immediately be studied by the absorption spectra of the resultant materials. For this advance, he was awarded the 1967 Nobel Prize in chemistry, together with Manfred Eigen and George Porter.

Northrop, John Howard (1891–1987) American chemist who crystallized the protein-digesting enzyme pepsin and showed it to be a protein. He then worked on other large molecules and on the purification of enzymes. He isolated the first virus infecting a bacterium. He was awarded the 1946 Nobel Prize in chemistry.

Ochoa, Severo (1905–93) Spanish-born U.S. biochemist who became a professor at New York University in 1954. A year later, he showed how cells use an enzyme to join DNA fragments. This work led to genetic engineering. For this discovery, Ochoa and a fellow worker on DNA, Arthur Kornberg, shared the 1959 Nobel prize in physiology or medicine.

Olah, George Andrew (b. 1927) American organic chemist who found a way, using powerful acids, of extending the life of fragments of hydrocarbon molecules—compounds that appeared only momentarily as intermediate stages in chemical reactions. This work threw important light on the details of chemical reactions and won Olah the 1994 Nobel Prize in chemistry.

Onsager, Lars (1903–76) Norwegian-born American chemist whose work on the thermodynamics of irreversible processes earned him the 1968 Nobel Prize in chemistry. He also worked on strong electrolytes.

Ostwald, Friedrich Wilhelm (1853–1932) German chemist who was the pioneer of modern physical chemistry and who showed how catalysts work. He was awarded the 1909 Nobel Prize in chemistry.

Pasteur, Louis (1822–95) French chemist and founder of modern bacteriology who proposed the "germ" theory of disease in the late 1860s. This was, perhaps, the greatest single advance in the history of medicine. He also developed pasteurization: rapid, short-term heating to kill harmful bacteria in wine and milk.

Pauling, Linus Carl (1901–94) American chemist noted for his germinal work *The Nature of the Chemical Bond* (1939), which applied quantum theory. He also made major advances in the understanding of protein structures and was awarded the Nobel Prize in chemistry in 1954 for his contributions to the electrochemical theory of valency. His work also covered inorganic complexes, protein structure, antibodies, DNA structure, and the molecular basis of some genetic diseases.

Wilhelm Ostwald

Linus Pauling

His belief in the medical efficacy of vitamin C was condemned during his lifetime but has now been vindicated with the recent understanding of the biological effect of free radicals and the value of vitamin C as a biological antioxidant.

Pedersen, Charles John (1904–89) American chemist who produced a crown-shaped cyclic polyether that was given the name *crown ether*, and discovered that compounds of this kind would bind sodium and potassium ions strongly, making alkali metal salts that were soluble in organic solvents. This work helped to explain how these metallic ions were transported across biological membranes, a matter of great importance in physiology and pharmacology. For this work, he was awarded a share in the 1987 Nobel Prize in chemistry.

Pelletier, Pierre-Joseph (1788–1842) French chemist who named the green leaf pigment chlorophyll, and worked on alkaloids, isolating many, some of which have become important in medicine.

Perkin, Sir William Henry (1838–1907) English chemist who worked as assistant to August Hofmann and, in 1856, discovered a brilliant purple dye. Later named mauveine, his invention became immensely popular, earned him a fortune, and led to the foundation of the modern synthetic dye industry. Some of his work on the synthesis of organic compounds, known as the Perkin synthesis, led to the development of the synthetic perfume industry.

Perutz, Max Ferdinand (1914–2002) Austrian-born British biochemist who, using X-ray diffraction and other methods, achieved the extraordinarily complex task of determining the molecular three-dimensional structure of hemoglobin. For this work, he shared the 1962 Nobel Prize in chemistry.

Polanyi, John Charles (b. 1929) Canadian physical chemist who studied the infra-red light emitted during chemical reactions. This provided information about the distribution of energy in molecules and won him the 1986 Nobel Prize in chemistry.

Porter, George (**Baron Porter of Luddenham**) (1920–2002) British physical chemist who researched photochemistry and, with Ronald Norrish, developed the technique of flash photolysis.

He, Norrish, and Manfred Eigen shared the 1967 Nobel Prize in chemistry.

Porter, Rodney Robert (1917–85) British biochemist who first suggested that antibodies were Y-shaped. In 1962, Porter showed that the gamma globulin antibody could be split by an enzyme into three large fragments. Two of these could bind antigens and were known as "Fab" (fragment antigen binding); the third, a crystalline fragment, could not. Porter showed that this third fragment was common to all antibodies, and that it was the Fab fragments that existed in thousands of different forms that give antibodies their specificity. This important discovery led to his being awarded the 1972 Nobel Prize in physiology or medicine.

Pregl, Fritz (1869–1930) Austrian chemist who developed new techniques of microanalysis to study the tiny quantities of biochemical substances available to him in his work. He developed a weighing balance of unprecedented accuracy and sensitivity and was awarded the 1923 Nobel Prize in chemistry.

Prelog, Vladimir (1906–98) Yugoslavian-born Swiss chemist who synthesized adamantine, a molecule related to diamond. His main work was in the study of molecular shape and, in particular, those molecules that could exist in two shapes, one being the mirror image of the other (chirality). He went on to study the three-dimensional structure of molecules in general and shared the 1975 Nobel Prize in chemistry for his work on the stereochemistry of enzymes.

Joseph Priestley

Priestley, Joseph (1733–1804) English chemist and Presbyterian minister who pioneered the study of the chemistry of gases, and, in 1774, was one of the discoverers of oxygen. He was not the first to identify oxygen, as is often stated, but he earned recognition through publication. The Swedish apothecary Carl Scheele isolated oxygen in 1772.

Prigogine, Ilya (1917–2003) Russian-born Belgian chemist who researched the thermodynamics of irreversible chemical processes and learned how to handle processes far from equilibrium. For this work, he was awarded the 1977 Nobel Prize in chemistry.

Proust, Joseph-Louis (1754–1826) French chemist who studied how elements combined to form molecules and formulated the law of definite proportions, which states that regardless of the way a compound is prepared, it always contains the same elements in the same proportions.

Prusiner, Stanley Ben (b. 1942) American neurologist and biochemist who was the first scientist since the discovery of viruses to detect an entirely new infective agent. Prusiner, as a young neurology resident, was in charge of a patient who died of Creutzfeldt-Jakob disease (CJD). He decided to research the cause. Ten years later, he isolated small protein bodies, which he called prions, and showed that these were the cause of CJD and of the similar bovine spongiform encephalopathy. He was awarded the Nobel Prize in physiology or medicine in 1997.

Joseph-Louis Proust

Ramsay, Sir William (1852–1916) Scottish physical chemist who isolated the five elements argon, neon, krypton, xenon, and radon, constituting the whole class of the noble, or inert, gases in the periodic table. He was also the first to isolate helium, previously believed to exist only in the Sun. His writings include *The Gases of the Atmosphere* and *Elements and Electrons*. He was awarded the Nobel Prize in chemistry in 1904. Radon's atomic weight was determined by Ramsay.

Rāzi, Abū Bakr Muhammad ibn Zakarīyā ar (**Rhazes**) (854–925) Persian physician and alchemist who based his practice on rational grounds, observation, and experience; taught high ethical standards in medical care; and treated poor patients without fees. He recorded all the medical knowledge of his time and wrote 10 medical treatises himself.

Reichstein, Tadeus (1897–1996) Polish-born Swiss biochemist whose work led to the synthesis of vitamin C and an understanding of the chemistry of the natural corticosteroid hormones of the adrenal gland. He was able to isolate 29 natural steroids. This work led to the production of a range of steroid drugs of great medical value that have saved many lives. In 1950, he shared the Nobel Prize in physiology or medicine with Edward Kendall and Philip Hench.

Rhazes see **Rāzi, Abū Bakr Muhammad ibn Zakarīyā ar**

Richards, Theodore William (1868–1928) American chemist who determined with great accuracy the atomic weights of 25 elements. This led to the discovery of natural isotopes of elements, each of which has a slightly different weight because of the different number of neutrons. In 1905, he introduced the adiabatic calorimeter, an instrument that measured the heat rise from combustion without error from loss or gain of heat. He received the Nobel Prize in chemistry in 1914.

Richter, Hieronymus Theodor (1824–98) German chemist who worked with Ferdinand Reich and discovered the metallic element indium.

Robinson, Sir Robert (1886–1975) British chemist who helped to develop penicillin production; conducted research into alkaloids; studied dyes; produced a theory of cyclic benzene-like compounds (aromaticity); and worked on the chemistry of natural products, for which he was awarded the 1947 Nobel Prize in chemistry.

Rodbell, Martin (1925–98) American biochemist who, working with Alfred Gilman, discovered the G protein, a previously unknown class of chemical messengers that, activated by an external hormone (the "first messenger") binding to a cell membrane receptor, effectively turn on the producers of the "second messenger"—the hormone that then moves to the effector sites within the cell and initiates the effect of the external hormone. Disease processes can interfere with the G proteins. For this work, Rodbell and Gilman were awarded the 1994 Nobel Prize in physiology or medicine.

Rose, William Cumming (1887–1984) American biochemist who investigated the individual role of the 20 amino acids in dietary protein and discovered that 10 of them were indispensable to rats but only eight were indispensable to humans. These are known as the "essential" amino acids. The others can be synthesized in the body.

Rowland, Frank Sherwood (b. 1927) American chemist who, working with Paul Crutzen and Mario Molina, alerted the world to the danger of damage being caused to the ozone layer of the atmosphere from artificially produced nitrogen oxides and chlorofluorocarbon (CFC) gases. For this work, they were awarded the 1995 Nobel Prize in chemistry.

Rutherford, Daniel (1749–1819) Scottish chemist who was one of the discoverers of nitrogen gas.

Rutherford, Ernest (1st Baron Rutherford of Nelson) (1871–1937) New Zealand-born British pioneer of subatomic particle physics who proposed the nuclear structure of the atom. He studied the radioactive disintegration of elements and correctly predicted the existence of the neutron. Rutherford won the Nobel Prize in chemistry in 1908.

Ružička, Leopold Stephen (1887–1976) Swiss chemist whose study of perfumes led to a detailed investigation of the unsaturated hydrocarbon essential oils, multi-membered ring structures known as the terpenes. He then discovered their structural relation to the steroids. With Adolf Butenandt, he was awarded the 1939 Nobel Prize in chemistry. His wealth from his discoveries enabled him to set up an art gallery of Dutch and Flemish masters.

Sabatier, Paul (1854–1941) French chemist whose most important work was in the catalyzed hydrogenation of unsaturated organic compounds. This found wide industrial applications, the best known of which is the hydrogenation of vegetable oils to produce margarine and other butter substitutes. He was awarded the 1912 Nobel Prize in chemistry.

Sachs, Julius von (1832–97) German botanist who proved that chlorophyll is critical in the natural synthesis of sugars from carbon dioxide and water and that oxygen was released. He was also the first to find chlorophyll in plant chloroplasts.

Julius von Sachs

Sanger, Frederick (b. 1918) English biochemist who after 12 years of work was able to establish the molecular structure of the protein insulin with its 51 amino acids. He was also able to show the small differences between the insulins of different mammals. Sanger later turned to DNA sequencing and, by laborious methods, was able to determine the base sequence of mitochondrial DNA and of the whole genome of a virus. For his work on insulin, he was awarded the Nobel Prize in chemistry in 1958, and for his achievements in DNA sequencing, he shared the 1980 Nobel Prize in chemistry with Paul Berg and Walter Gilbert.

Scheele, Carl Wilhelm (1742–86) Seriously undervalued Swedish apothecary and chemist who was the actual discoverer of oxygen and nitrogen as well as of the elements arsenic, barium, chlorine, manganese, and molybdenum. He was the victim of scientific neglect by his contemporaries and, for a long time, by scientific historians, but is now being recognized as the chemistry genius that he was. Scheele's life may have been shortened by his habit of tasting every new substance he discovered.

Seaborg, Glenn Theodor (1912–99) American chemist and atomic scientist who discovered many previously unknown isotopes of common elements. He assisted in the production of a number of non-natural, above-uranium (transuranic) elements, including neptunium (93), plutonium (94), americium (95), berkelium (97), einsteinium (99), fermium (100), and nobelium (102). During his lifetime, he was honored by having element 106 named seaborgium. He was also involved in the production of the fissionable isotope plutonium-239, which has formed the basis of atomic weapons ever since. He was awarded the 1951 Nobel Prize in chemistry.

Sefström, Nils Gabriel (1787–1854) Swedish chemist who in 1830 discovered vanadium, the metallic element later alloyed with steel to produce very high-strength, low-corrosion metal for tools and other purposes. Vanadium was actually discovered by Andrés del Rio in 1801, but he let himself be persuaded that the substance he had found was an impure form of chromium.

Semenov, Nikolay Nikolayevich (1896–1986) Russian physical chemist who made notable contributions to chemical kinetics, especially those of chemical chain reactions. He also studied the features of combustion and explosions. For this work, he was awarded the Nobel Prize in chemistry in 1956, the first Soviet citizen to achieve this distinction.

Nikolay Semenov

Skou, Jens Christian (b. 1918) Danish chemist who established that the enzyme sodium, potassium-ATPase was the first enzyme known to promote the transport of ions across a cell membrane. Ionic transport across membranes is fundamental to the transmission of nerve impulses. For this work, Skou was awarded the Nobel Prize in chemistry in 1997.

Smalley, Richard Errett (1943–2005) American chemist who shared the Nobel Prize in chemistry in 1996 with Harold Kroto and Robert Curl for the synthesis of an entirely new molecule, consisting only of carbon atoms, named a buckminsterfullerene (buckyball) because of the similarity of its structure to the geodesic domes of the architect Buckminster Fuller. The buckyball is a spherical structure of bonded carbon atoms and has many valuable properties.

Smith, Michael (1932–2000) British-born Canadian chemist who discovered how to produce deliberate mutations in DNA at precise locations (site-directed mutagenesis), a technique that enabled him to code for new proteins with new properties. He shared the 1993 Nobel Prize in chemistry with Kary Mullis.

Soddy, Frederick (1877–1956) English radio chemist who worked with the physicist Ernest Rutherford on the development of the general theory of the decay of radioactive elements. They showed that this occurred because of the emission of alpha and beta particles and gamma radiation. In 1903, Soddy, working with Sir William Ramsay, discovered that helium was formed during radioactive decay. Alpha particles are helium nuclei and immediately acquire electrons. Soddy also discovered that a radioactive element may have several atomic weights and coined the term *isotope* to indicate that they all occupied the same place in the periodic table. This is because they all have the same number of protons, hence electrons, and hence the same chemical properties. Soddy was awarded the 1921 Nobel Prize in chemistry.

Sørensen, Søren Peter Lauritz (1868–1939) Danish chemist who in 1909, while describing the effect of hydrogen ion concentration on enzyme activity, proposed the use of a negative logarithm of this concentration as a measure of acidity and alkalinity. This became the standard pH scale now in universal use. He also studied amino acids, enzymes, and proteins. He and his wife Magrete were the first to crystallize the egg protein albumin.

Staudinger, Hermann (1881–1965) German chemist who invented an improved way of synthesizing isoprene, the structural unit of natural and synthetic rubber. He insisted, correctly, against opposition, that rubber was a polymer macromolecule and researched biological polymers. His work on polymer chemistry won him the 1953 Nobel Prize in chemistry.

Stein, William Howard (1911–80) American biochemist who worked with Stanford Moore to produce a new method of column chromatography by which they were able to separate and identify amino acids from a mix of material produced by the hydrolysis of proteins. Stein, Moore, and Christian Anfinsen shared the 1972 Nobel Prize in chemistry.

Strohmeyer, Friedrich (1776–1835) German chemist who taught Robert Bunsen and, in 1817, discovered the soft, bluish poisonous metal cadmium, now used in dry batteries, solders, and as a neutron absorber in nuclear reactors.

Sumner, James Batcheller (1887–1955) American biochemist who crystallized the enzyme urease and proved that it was a protein. He then partly determined its mode of function and produced antibodies to it. He proceeded to investigate and purify a considerable range of enzymes active in human biochemistry. He shared the 1946 Nobel Prize in chemistry with Wendell Stanley and John Northrop.

Svedberg, The (Theodor) (1884–1971) Swedish chemist who studied colloidal chemistry, produced synthetic rubber, and developed the ultracentrifuge, which became an important instrument in chemical and biological research. For this, he was awarded the 1926 Nobel Prize in chemistry.

Swan, Sir Joseph Wilson (1828–1914) English chemist and physicist who in 1860 invented the electric lamp 20 years before Thomas Edison. In 1864 he patented the carbon process for photographic printing; in 1871 he invented the dry-plate technique; and in 1879 he produced bromide paper. He was the first to produce a practicable artificial silk.

Synge, Richard Lawrence Millington (1914–94) British chemist who developed partition chromatography using two liquids that

Sir Joseph Swan

would not mix, one being held by the absorbing material (the stationary phase), the other being the moving phase that carries the samples. Synge used powdered cellulose or potato starch as the stationary phase in his columns. He was awarded the 1952 Nobel Prize in chemistry.

Szent-Györgyi Nagyrapolt, Albert von (1893–1986) Hungarian-born American biochemist who found vitamin C in the adrenal gland and in paprika. He studied muscle tissue and action, isolated the two muscle contractile proteins actin and myosin, and investigated the role of the thymus gland. He showed how adenosine triphosphate (ATP) caused these proteins to contract, and he helped to elucidate the metabolic and energetic processes in the muscle cell. He was awarded the 1937 Nobel Prize in physiology or medicine.

Albert von Szent-Györgyi

Takamine, Jokichi (1854–1922) Japanese-born American chemist who in 1901 isolated a substance from adrenal glands that was shown to be epinephrine (adrenaline). This was the first isolation of a pure hormone.

Tartaglia, Niccolò (1499–57) Italian mathematician who found a way of solving equations containing a cube of the unknown. His first book, *Nova scientia* (1537), dealt with ballistics, falling bodies, and projectiles, and showed that a firing angle of 45 degrees should give the maximum range for a gun. He also wrote a three-volume work entitled *Treatise on Numbers and Measurements* (1556–60).

Taube, Henry (1915–2005) Canadian-born American chemist who invented a method for studying the transfer of electrons during chemical reactions. He also showed that metal ions in solution form chemical bonds with water. He was awarded the 1983 Nobel Prize in chemistry.

Henry Taube

Tennant, Smithson (1761–1815) English chemist who proved by burning a diamond that it was a form of carbon and, while studying platinum for commercial purposes, isolated two new elements, iridium and osmium.

Theorell, Axel Hugo Theodor (1903–82) Swedish biochemist who crystallized muscle hemoglobin, investigated enzymes such as peroxidases and dehydrogenases, invented an electrophoresis (electrical attraction) arrangement for separating proteins of different molecular weight, and introduced fluorescence spectrometry. His work earned him the Nobel Prize in medicine or physiology in 1955.

Thomson, William, 1st Baron Kelvin (1824–1907) Irish-born Scottish physicist and mathematician who proposed the absolute, or Kelvin, temperature scale (1848) and, at around the same time as Rudolf Clausius, established the second law of thermodynamics. He also invented a tide predictor and a harmonic analyzer.

Tiselius, Arne Wilhelm Kaurin (1902–71) Swedish chemist who separated the blood proteins into albumins and alpha, beta, and gamma globulins, using an electrophoresis apparatus designed by himself. He showed that antibodies were gamma globulins, and he developed chromatographic methods for the separation and identification of amino acids. In 1948, he was awarded the Nobel Prize in chemistry.

Arne Tiselius

Todd, Sir Alexander Robertus, (Baron Todd of Trumpington) (1907–97) Scottish biochemist who worked on the chemistry of a range of vitamins and other natural products and who showed how the four bases (adenine, guanine, cytosine, and thymine) were attached to sugar and phosphate groups. This is how DNA is formed, and various combinations of these bases, taken three at a time, form the genetic code. For this work, Todd was awarded the 1957 Nobel Prize in chemistry.

Travers, Morris William (1872–1961) English chemist who with Sir William Ramsay discovered krypton, neon, and xenon (1894–1908). Travers isolated these gases from liquid air, a procedure that required very low temperatures, and he developed a way of liquefying hydrogen. He also established the properties of argon and helium and investigated the properties of gases at very high temperatures.

Trembley, Abraham (1710–84) Swiss naturalist who studied the grafting and regeneration of animal tissue but with only limited success.

Urbain, Georges (1872–1938) French chemist who specialized in the study of the rare earth elements. After enormous labor involving hundreds of thousands of fractional crystallizations, he discovered samarium, europium, gadolinium, terbium, holmium, lutetium, and hafnium.

Urey, Harold Clayton (1893–1981) American chemist who discovered deuterium (heavy hydrogen), the isotope of hydrogen that has a neutron and a proton in the nucleus and is thus twice the weight of common hydrogen, which has only a proton. Urey also worked with Stanley Miller to simulate a primitive atmosphere, thought to be similar to Earth's early atmosphere. Urey was awarded the Nobel Prize in chemistry in 1934.

van't Hoff, Jacobus Hendricus (1852–1911) Dutch chemist who pioneered the measurement and study of the rates and mechanisms of chemical reactions under different conditions of temperature, pressure, and so on. He applied thermodynamics to chemical reactions and is considered to be the founder of physical chemistry. He was the first to be awarded the Nobel Prize in chemistry, in 1901.

Vigneaud, Vincent du (1901–78) American biochemist whose principal contribution was in the field of amino acids. He showed how a series of these important protein constituents were synthesized in the body. He also achieved the laboratory synthesis of thiamine and penicillin, and the hormones oxytocin and vasopressin. He was awarded the 1955 Nobel Prize in chemistry.

Virtanen, Artturi Ilmari (1895–1973) Finnish biochemist who discovered the chemical pathways by which bacteria in certain plant root nodules can achieve the fixation of nitrogen into compounds usable by plants. This work earned him the 1945 Nobel Prize in chemistry.

Waals, Johannes Diderik van der (1837–1923) Dutch physical chemist who, aware that real gases did not accurately conform to the simple gas law pV=RT (pressure $\times$ volume = temperature $\times$ the gas constant R), devised a more precise gas law equation that took account of the volume of the gas molecules and the attraction between them. He received the Nobel Prize in physics in 1910.

Johannes van der Waals

Walker, Sir John Ernest (b. 1941) British chemist whose studies on the detailed structure of the enzyme ATP synthase (ATPase) confirmed Paul Boyer's account of the function of this important enzyme and earned him a share, with Boyer, of the 1997 Nobel Prize in chemistry.

Wallach, Otto (1847–1931) German chemist who studied volatile oils and, from this work, established and named the terpene class of compounds. He showed that the terpenes consisted of a variable number of five-carbon units, each of which was called an isoprene unit. He was awarded the 1910 Nobel Prize in chemistry.

Watson, James Dewey (1928–2004) U.S. bird expert (ornithologist) who worked at the Cavendish Laboratory, Cambridge, England, with Francis Crick and, in 1953, made the greatest biological discovery of the 20th century: the structure of DNA. Their joint paper in *Nature* is one of the most important scientific communications ever made, and it revolutionized genetics and molecular biology. Watson shared with Maurice Wilkins and Francis Crick the Nobel Prize in physiology or medicine in 1962, and in 1988 became head of the Human Genome Project to sequence the whole of human DNA.

James D. Watson

Werner, Alfred (1866–1919) Swiss chemist who was the first to point out that isomerism (same molecular formula but different molecular structure) occurred in inorganic as well as in organic chemistry. This was at first rejected by his associates but was later accepted and was highly influential on the progress of chemistry. He also advanced valency theory. For his work, he was awarded the 1913 Nobel Prize in chemistry.

Wieland, Heinrich Otto (1877–1957) German chemist who studied the constitution of bile acids, organic radicals, nitrogen compounds, and contributed to the advancement of organic chemistry. He was awarded the 1927 Nobel Prize in chemistry.

Heinrich O. Wieland

Wilkins, Maurice Hugh Frederick (1916–2004) New Zealand-born British biophysicist who, with Francis Crick, James Watson, and Rosalind Franklin, worked to determine the molecular structure of DNA. Wilkins shared the Nobel Prize in physiology or medicine with Crick and Watson in 1962.

Wilkinson, Sir Geoffrey (1921–96) British chemist whose main work was in the investigation of the organometallic compounds. His study of ferrocene showed that its molecule consisted of an atom of iron sandwiched between two five-sided rings of carbons and hydrogens. Thousands of substances with this kind of structure have since been synthesized and found to be of great chemical importance. He was awarded the 1973 Nobel Prize in chemistry with Ernst Fischer.

Willstätter, Richard Martin (1872–1942) German chemist who carried out extensive investigations into the structure of chlorophyll and other flower pigments. He was awarded the Nobel Prize in chemistry in 1915.

Windaus, Adolf Otto Reinhold (1876–1959) German biochemist who studied the drug digitalis, established the structure of cholesterol, and researched vitamin D and some of the B vitamins. He was awarded the 1928 Nobel Prize in chemistry.

Adolf O.R. Windaus

Winkler, Clemens Alexander (1838–1904) German chemist who discovered germanium, one of the elements predicted by Dmitry Mendeleyev on the basis of the periodic table. Germanium became well known when the physicists William Shockley, Walter Brattain, and John Bardeen used it to make a point contact rectifier and then the first transistor.

Wittig, Georg (1897–1987) German organic chemist who discovered that some organometallic reagents with both negative and positive charges could react readily with aldehydes and ketones to simplify the synthesis of a useful range of organic compounds. He was awarded the 1979 Nobel Prize in chemistry.

Wöhler, Friedrich (1800–82) German chemist whose synthesis of urea from ammonium cyanate in 1828 was the first time a compound of organic origin had been prepared from inorganic material. This achievement revolutionized organic chemistry and showed that living organisms were not fundamentally different in structure from nonliving matter. Wöhler also isolated aluminum in 1827 and beryllium in 1828 and discovered calcium carbide, from which he obtained acetylene.

Wollaston, William Hyde (1766–1828) English chemist who discovered the elements palladium in 1802 and rhodium in

1804 and introduced the methods of powder metallurgy, which he kept secret for commercial reasons. Unusually for a scientist, Wollaston, who made a living by selling platinum, announced his discovery of palladium, not by a paper in a professional journal but by offering it for sale.

Woodward, Robert Burns (1917–79) American chemist who is generally regarded as the greatest synthetic chemist of all time. He achieved the synthesis of a long succession of biochemical substances, including cholesterol, cortisone, chlorophyll, reserpine, strychnine, quinine, the antibiotics cephalosporin and tetracycline, and cyanocobalamin (vitamin B_{12}). For this work, he was awarded the 1965 Nobel Prize in chemistry.

Young, James (1822–93) Scottish chemist and industrialist who showed that low-temperature distillation of shale could yield substantial commercial quantities of paraffin oil and solid paraffin wax. This led to a shale oil industry in Scotland and a fortune for Young, who sold his shale oil business in 1866 for $2 million.

Karl Ziegler

Ziegler, Karl Waldemar (1898–1973) German chemist who made notable advances in the understanding of polymerization. He showed that organometallic compounds brought about polymerization by forming free radicals, and found an effective way of polymerizing ethene monomers to form the now ubiquitous polymer polyethylene (polythene). He was awarded the 1963 Nobel Prize in chemistry.

Zsigmondy, Richard Adolf (1865–1929) Austrian chemist who invented the dark ground illumination method of microscopy and showed that color changes in colloidal solutions were due to particle aggregation. He made many advances in colloidal chemistry for which he was awarded the 1925 Nobel Prize in chemistry.

SECTION THREE
CHRONOLOGY

The elements antimony, carbon, copper, gold, iron, lead, mercury, silver, sulfur, and tin are all known and used in prehistoric times, although their status as elements is not yet realized.

7000–6000 BCE ● Lead and copper production developed in Anatolia, Turkey.

3500 BCE ● Copper and bronze production spreads throughout the Middle East.

2700 BCE ● Evidence of making of iron objects (from meteoric iron).

2500 BCE ● Standardized weights used in Sumeria. Silver sheet-metal working is carried out.

ca. 2500 BCE ● Glass making occurs in Mesopotamia.

2000–1000 BCE ● Hittites develop iron technology.

ca. 1550 BCE ● Glass first made in Egypt.

950–500 BCE ● First Iron Age in Europe. Extraction and working of iron spread gradually across the continent.

ca. 600 BCE ● Tin mining in Cornwall. In China, Lao-tzu explains his philosophy, known as Taoism, in the *Tao Te Ching* (The way of life). The universe is seen in terms of opposites, "yang," the male, positive, hot, and light principle, and "yin," the female, negative, cool, and dark principle. The five elements, earth, water, fire, metal, and wood, are believed to be generated by the struggle between these opposing forces. The Chinese produce gunpowder and are thought to have been able to produce nitric acid. In Greece, the theory that all substances are generated from a single primary matter, a featureless substance, is proposed.

580 BCE ● Early theory of matter proposed by Greek philosopher Thales, suggesting that all things are made from forms of water.

ca. 569 BCE ● Evidence of the use of bellows for metallurgical workings, Anacharsis, Scythia.

ca. 560 BCE ● Matter explained in terms of cold, heat, dryness, and wetness by Greek philosopher Anaximander.

ca. 530 BCE ● Theory that all matter is made of air proposed by Greek philosopher Anaximenes. According to the theory air is condensed under varying conditions to make all known liquids and solids.

ca. 500 BCE ● Chinese use bronze and copper nickel alloys. Steel produced in India.

480–471 BCE ● Greek philosopher Anaxagoras suggests materials are made up of large numbers of "seeds," particles that determine qualities.

450 BCE ● Greek philosopher Empedocles introduces the four-element theory of matter (fire, air, water, earth). According to this theory, water (moist and cold), air (moist and hot), fire (dry and hot), and earth (dry and cold) combine in various ways and proportions to generate all of the materials found in the universe.

ca. 445 BCE ● Atomic theory of matter introduced by Greek philosopher Leucippus.

430–421 BCE ● Greek philosopher Democritus expands concept of atoms.

350–341 BCE ● Greek philosopher Aristotle defines chemical elements as constituents of bodies that cannot be decomposed into other constituents.

310–301 BCE ● Greek philosopher Epicurus founds philosophical school based on a theory of atoms, particles so small that they cannot be subdivided further.

150 BCE ● Use of bellows in metallurgic furnaces.

60 BCE ● Roman poet and philosopher Lucretius writes on Greek atomic theory.

105 CE ● Chinese court official Ts'ai Lun makes paper from vegetable fibers.

ca. 185 ● Earliest known work on alchemy, forerunner of chemistry, compiled in Egypt.

200 ● Practice of casting iron established in China.

ca. 185
Drawing of stills and furnaces, as used in alchemy.

400–409 ● Alexandrian scholars use the term *chemistry* for first time to describe the activity of changing matter.

789 ● Standard units of weight and measure introduced by Charlemagne, Frankish king, later emperor of the West.

880 ● Persian physician and alchemist Rhazes produces the text *Secret of Secrets*. This work describes various laboratory procedures basic to the study of chemistry—purification, separation, mixing, removal of water, and solidification—and describes many items of laboratory equipment recognizable today. It also classifies substances into animal, vegetable, mineral, and derivative. Substances are further classified as metals, vitriols, boraxes, salts, and stones. He prepares sal ammoniac by distilling hair with salt and urine.

1140 ● Iron industry established in Europe.

ca. 1250 ● German scientist Albertus Magnus describes and manufactures the element arsenic.

ca. 1300 ● Alum discovered at Roccha, Syria. Sulfuric acid described.

ca. 1340 ● Blast furnaces being used in Europe.

1500 ● Paracelsus (Philippus Aureolus Theophrastus Bombast von Hohenheim) develops new study of iatrochemistry, use of chemistry in medicine. He introduces the doctrine of the *tria prima*: medical substances are made up of the four Aristotelian elements.

1540 ● German scientist Valerius Cordus discovers ether.

1592 ● Italian scientist Galileo Galilei invents an early thermometer.

1595 ● German scientist Andreas Libau describes how to produce sulfuric acid.

1597 ● Andreas Libau publishes *Alchemia*, said to be the first chemistry textbook. It includes classification and standardization of laboratory techniques and substances used in the study of chemistry.

1597
Title page of Andreas Libau's Alchemia, *the first chemistry textbook.*

ca. 1600 ● Belgian scientist Jan Baptista van Helmont proposes two elements, air (a physical medium) and water (the material from which all substances are formed). He says that fire is the agent of change. He conducts an experiment to grow a willow tree in controlled environment, and deduces that any weight gain in the plant is solely caused by water. He also suggests the existence of a universal solvent (alcahest) that others try to isolate without success. He defines gas as "This spirit, hitherto unknown, which can neither be retained in vessels or reduced to a visible body… I call by the new name *gas*."

1611 ● German scientist Andreas Libau prepares hydrochloric acid.

1637 ● French philosopher René Descartes proposes the philosophical study of scientific method. He also publishes a theory of refraction.

1649 ● French philosopher Pierre Gassendi revives the atomic theory of matter in his book *Syntagma Philosophicum* in which he introduces the term *molecule* for the smallest unit of a substance capable of an independent existence.

1654 ● German phycisist Otto von Guericke invents the air pump. He demonstrates how air can be pumped out of a copper globe to leave a vacuum. He finds that the atmosphere exerts a tremendous compressing force on the globe (demonstrated in 1657 in the Magdeburg experiment where two metal hemispheres placed together and then evacuated with a pump could not be pulled apart by a team of 16 horses).

1660 ● Irish chemist Robert Boyle publishes *New Experiments Physico-Mechanical touching the Spring of the Air and its Effects*. Boyle also formulates concepts of elements, acids, and alkalis.

1661 ● Irish chemist Robert Boyle publishes *The Sceptical Chymist*, his greatest work and regarded today as the founding text of modern analytical chemistry. In it he defines the chemical element as the practical limit of chemical analysis.

1657
Otto von Guericke demonstrates the force of atmosphere on a globe.

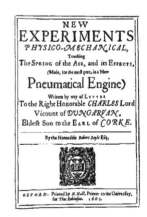

1660
Robert Boyle publishes his New Experiments Physico-Mechanical.

1662 ● Irish chemist Robert Boyle formulates Boyle's law, which states that the pressure and volume of a gas are inversely proportionate.

1669 ● German chemist Hennig Brand discovers the element phosphorus. Johann Joachim Becher publishes *Physica Subterranea*, the first attempt to relate observations and concepts in physics and chemistry.

1670 ● English biologist John Ray discovers formic acid.

1676 ● English chemist Robert Hooke formulates Hooke's law relating to elastic bodies.

1692 ● English physicist Sir Isaac Newton writes *De natura acidorium*. In this and other writings he suggests that there are exceedingly strong attractive powers between the particles of bodies that extend for a short range and vary in strength between chemical species. This leads to the idea of "elective affinities" concerning the replacement of one metal by another in acid solutions. He makes a list giving the replacement order of six common metals in nitric acid.

1695 ● English botanist Nehemiah Grew isolates Epsom salts (magnesium sulfate) from spring water.

1702 ● German chemist Wilhelm Homberg discovers boracic or boric acid.

1714 ● First practical mercury thermometer invented by German physicist Daniel Gabriel Fahrenheit, who also devises the Fahrenheit scale.

1718 ● French chemist Étienne Geoffroy produces the first table of affinities (following Sir Isaac Newton's work on elective affinities). German chemist Georg Stahl proposes the phlogiston theory. Phlogiston is described as a substance present in all materials that can be burned and that is released on burning. Stahl also believes that vitriolic acid (sulfuric acid) is the universal solvent.

1723 ● French chemist M.A. Capeller publishes the first-known treatise on crystallography.

1714
Gabriel Fahrenheit's original thermometer.

1727 ● English chemist Stephen Hales establishes that air takes part in chemical reactions.

1729 ● English physicist Stephen Gray finds that electricity travels through conductors.

1730 ● French physicist René-Antoine Ferchault de Réaumur develops the alcohol thermometer.

1735 ● Swedish chemist Georg Brandt discovers the element cobalt.

1736 ● French engineer and agriculturalist Henri-Louis Duhamel du Monceau distinguishes between sodium and potassium salts.

1742 ● Swedish astronomer Anders Celsius devises the Celsius (centigrade) temperature scale, with the boiling point at zero and the freezing point at 100 degrees. French metallurgist Paul-Jacques Malouin invents the technique of galvanizing.

1744 ● Russian scientist Mikhail Lomonosov describes heat as a form of motion.

1745 ● Dutch physicist Pieter van Musschenbroek and German physicist Ewald Georg von Kleist independently invent the Leyden jar (for the storage of static electricity). It is the ancestor of the modern capacitor.

1746 ● English chemist John Roebuck of Birmingham designs a large-scale process for manufacturing sulfuric acid using large lead-lined wooden boxes (the lead-chamber method).

1747 ● German scientist Andreas Marggraf produces sugar from raw beetroot.

1748 ● French physicist Jean-Antoine Nollet discovers osmotic pressure (relating to solutions).

ca. 1750 ● French chemist Guillaume-François Rouelle proposes a theory classifying salts by their crystalline shape and by the acids and bases from which they are produced. He uses the term *water of crystallization*.

1751 ● Swedish mineralogist Axel Fredrik Cronstedt discovers

1742
Swedish postage stamp commemorating Anders Celsius and his temperature scale.

the element nickel. He also demonstrates its magnetic properties.

1754 ● Scottish chemist Joseph Black discovers carbon dioxide.

1755 ● Scottish chemist Joseph Black recognizes magnesium as an element. Black shows that carbon dioxide (carbonic acid gas) is different from ordinary air. He demonstrates that magnesium carbonate contains a gas (carbon dioxide) that is different from atmospheric air; it turns limewater milky and does not support burning.

1756 ● Scottish chemist Joseph Black publishes *Experiments upon magnesia, quicklime, and other alkaline substances,* the first detailed examination of chemical action. It is the first work in quantitative chemistry and sounds the death knell for the phlogiston theory.

1758 ● Swedish mineralogist Axel F. Cronstedt publishes *Essay on the new mineralogy,* in which he classifies minerals by chemical structure.

1761 ● In his study of calorimetry, Joseph Black establishes the concepts of latent heat and specific heat capacity.

1762 ● John Roebuck develops iron smelting with coal rather than charcoal at the Carron Ironworks in Scotland.

1766 ● English chemist Henry Cavendish discovers the element hydrogen.

1767 ● English chemist Joseph Priestley publishes *The history and present state of electricity*. In it he explains what later becomes known as the Priestley rings (the rings formed by an electric discharge on a metal) and describes American scientist Benjamin Franklin's kite experiment (flying a kite in a thunderstorm to prove that lightning is electrical).

1770 ● Swedish chemist Carl Wilhelm Scheele discovers tartaric acid.

1771 ● Swedish chemist Carl Wilhelm Scheele discovers the element fluorine. British chemist Peter Woulfe discovers picric acid.

1772 ● Scottish chemist Daniel Rutherford and English chemist Joseph Priestley independently discover the element nitrogen. French scientist Jean Rome de Lisle describes the process of crystallization. Priestley discovers laughing gas (nitrous oxide) and describes how to make seltzer. Swedish chemist Carl Wilhelm Scheele produces oxygen. French chemist Louis-Bernard Guyton de Morveau demonstrates that metals gain weight on calcination. French chemist Antoine Lavoisier proves that when sulfur and phosphorus burn they gain weight as a result of combining with atmospheric air. He also proves that diamonds can burn.

1773 ● French chemist Antoine Lavoisier publishes *The Analytic Spirit*, suggesting the existence of three distinct states of matter—solid, fluid, and the state of expansion of vapors. The same body can exist in each of the forms, depending on the quantity of the matter of fire combined with it.

1774 ● Swedish mineralogist Johan Gottlieb Gahn discovers the element manganese. English chemist Joseph Priestley measures the composition of the atmosphere. Chlorine used for bleaching in Sweden. French chemist Antoine Lavoisier provides the first scientific description of combustion. Swedish chemist Carl Wilhelm Scheele discovers formic acid.

1775 ● English chemist Joseph Priestley discovers the gaseous form of hydrochloric acid.

1776 ● Swedish chemists Carl Wilhelm Scheele and Torbern Bergman independently discover uric acid.

ca. 1778 ● French chemist Antoine Lavoisier proves that matter cannot be destroyed.

1778 ● French chemist Antoine Lavoisier determines that air is a mixture primarily of oxygen and nitrogen. Swedish chemist Torbern Bergman gives the first comprehensive analysis of mineral waters.

1779 ● Swedish chemist Carl Wilhelm Scheele discovers glycerin. French chemist Antoine Lavoisier suggests the

1774
Joseph Priestley discovers hydrochloric and sulfuric acids.

term *oxygen* for that part of air that is responsible for combustion.

1780 ● French chemists Pierre-Simon de Laplace and Antoine Lavoisier develop the calorimeter. German chemist Johann Wolfgang Döbereiner discovers that platinum can act as a catalyst. Swedish chemist Carl Wilhelm Scheele discovers lactic acid.

1781 ● English chemist Joseph Priestley sparks "inflammable air" (hydrogen) with air using an electrostatic machine. He discovers that water is produced. Swedish chemist Peter Jacob Hjelm discovers the element molybdenum.

1782 ● Artificial ice made chemically by English chemist John Walker. Austrian mineralogist Franz Joseph Müller discovers the element tellurium.

1783 ● Spanish scientists José and Fausto d'Elhuyar y de Suvisa discover the element tungsten.

1784 ● English chemist Henry Cavendish describes how he discovered that water could be synthesized from hydrogen and oxygen by putting a mixture of hydrogen and oxygen into a narrow glass tube and introducing an electric spark. French physicist Gaspard Monge becomes the first person to liquefy a substance normally a gas when he liquefies sulfur dioxide. Swedish chemist Carl Wilhelm Scheele discovers citric acid.

1785 ● Antoine Lavoisier attacks the phlogiston theory as being a "veritable Proteus that changes its form every instant!" (in order to explain various apparently contradictory phenomena). French chemist Claude-Louis Berthollet determines the composition of ammonia. English chemist Henry Cavendish discovers the composition of the atmosphere.

1787 ● French physicist Jacques Charles propounds Charles' law (connecting the expansion of gas with its rise in temperature). French chemists Louis-Bernard Guyton de Morveau, Antoine Lavoisier, Claude Berthollet, and Antoine Fourcroy publish *Méthode de nomenclature chimique*. Substances have one fixed name: the name reflects composition and names are chosen from Greek and Latin roots. Lavoisier establishes the first version of the law of conservation of matter (total weight does not change in chemical reactions.)

1789 ● French chemist Nicholas Leblanc devises a process for the manufacture of soda. French chemist Antoine Lavoisier publishes *Traité élémentaire de chimie*, in which he defines a chemical element as a substance that cannot be analyzed by chemical means. He makes a list of 33 elements and divides them into five classes. German chemist Martin H. Klaproth discovers a compound of uranium and the element zirconium.

1790–99 ● A committee of seven Frenchmen devise the metric system to regulate scientific measurements.

1790 ● Introduction of Nicholas Leblanc's process for soda manufacture. Scottish physician Adair Crawford discovers the element strontium.

1791 ● English chemist William Gregor discovers the element titanium.

1792 ● German chemist Jeremias Richter studies the mass ratios of substances combining together, which leads to the Law of Reciprocal Proportions and to the subject of stoichiometry (a branch of chemistry concerned with the proportions in which elements are combined in compounds).

1798 ● Louis-Nicolas Vauquelin discovers the elements beryllium and chromium.

1799 ● Benjamin Thompson (Count Rumford) founds the Royal Institution in London. The aim of the institution is to publicize ways in which science can be used to improve the quality of life. French chemist Joseph-Louis Proust articulates Proust's law: the elements in a compound always combine in definite proportions by mass.

1800 ● English chemists William Nicholson and Anthony Carlisle use electricity to produce chemical change. Italian physicist Alessandro Volta invents the electric cell.

1789
Antoine Lavoisier publishes Traité élémentaire de chimie.

The electric cell, "voltaic pile," is made from alternating zinc and silver disks and is regarded as the first battery. This early battery can decompose water into hydrogen and oxygen at the different poles of the battery.

1801 ● English chemist Charles Hatchett discovers the element niobium. English chemist John Dalton formulates his law on gas pressure (partial pressures in a mixture of gases) in his paper "New theory of the constitution of mixed aeriform fluids and particularly of the atmosphere." English chemist and physicist William Henry formulates Henry's law (that the amount of gas absorbed by a liquid varies directly with the pressure). Spanish mineralogist Andrés del Rio discovers the element vanadium. He names it *erythronium*. Swedish chemist Nils Sefström, who discovers it independently in 1830, later names it *vanadium*.

1802 ● Swedish chemist Anders Gustav Ekeberg discovers the element tantalum. English chemist John Dalton makes atomic weight tables. Danish physicist Hans Ørsted discovers electromagnetism. French chemist Joseph-Louis Gay-Lussac discovers that at a given pressure all gases increase by the same percentage in volume when subjected to the same increase in temperature.

1803 ● French chemist Claude-Louis Berthollet suggests that mass (concentration), temperature, and pressure have an effect on chemical reactions. English chemist William H. Wollaston discovers the elements palladium and rhodium. Swedish chemist Jöns Jakob Berzelius, Swedish mineralogist Wilhelm Hisinger, and German chemist Martin Heinrich Klaproth discover the element cerium. English chemist John Dalton publishes his "Table of the relative weights of the ultimate particles of gaseous and other bodies." This is the first table of atomic weights. English chemist Smithson Tennant discovers the elements iridium and osmium.

1804 ● Studying electrolysis, both Humphry Davy and Jöns Jakob Berzelius (with Wilhelm Hisinger) conclude that "combustible bodies and bases" are released at the negative pole; oxygen and oxidized bodies are released at the positive pole.

1806 ● French chemists Louis-Nicholas Vauquelin and Pierre-Jean Robiquet isolate asparagines, the first amino acid to be discovered.

1807 ● English chemist Humphry Davy discovers the elements sodium and potassium. English physicist Thomas Young is the first to use the word *energy* with a meaning close to its modern sense. Jöns Jakob Berzelius classifies chemicals as organic or inorganic.

1808 ● English chemist Humphry Davy discovers the elements barium and calcium. French chemist Joseph-Louis Gay-Lussac proposes Gay-Lussac's law: gases combine among themselves in very simple proportions. English chemist John Dalton publishes *A New System of Chemical Philosophy*, in which he formulates the atomic weight theory. Davy, Gay-Lussac, and French chemist Louis-Jacques Thénard isolate the element boron. Polish chemist Jedrzej Sniadecki discovers the element ruthenium.

1810 ● English chemist Humphry Davy proves chlorine to be an element and names it. Davy also proves that oxygen is not a constituent of hydrochloric acid.

1811 ● Italian chemist Amedeo Avogadro proposes Avogadro's hypothesis: equal volumes of gas contain the same number of molecules (defined as stable multi-atomed particles). French chemist Bernard Courtois discovers the element iodine while studying the liquor obtained in leaching the ashes of burnt kelp.

1812 ● Swedish chemist Jöns Jakob Berzelius publishes *Versuch über die Theorie der chemischen Proportionen und über die chemische Wirkung der Elektrizität,* in which he proposes that all atoms have electrical charges.

1813 ● Swedish chemist Jöns Jakob Berzelius devises chemical symbols. As a result of his experiments on the electrolysis of various solutions, Berzelius devises Latin

1808
John Dalton's symbols for elements in A New System of Chemical Philosophy.

1808
Dalton explains atomic theory.

classification of substances based on electrochemical phenomena. Substances are divided into two types, electropositive and electronegative. He defines electropositive substances as those attracted to the negative pole and introduces some basic terms in the study of electromagnetic phenomena.

1815 ● English chemist William Prout calculates the specific gravities of elements using air as the standard and then comparing the result with that of hydrogen (assumed to have a specific gravity of one). His calculations produce whole numbers, and he suggests that hydrogen could be the basis of all matter ("Prout's hypothesis").

1817 ● Swedish chemist Johan August Arfvedson discovers the element lithium. German chemist Friedrich Strohmeyer discovers the element cadmium. Swedish chemist Jöns Jakob Berzelius discovers the element selenium.

1818 ● French chemists Pierre-Louis Dulong and Alexis Thérèse Petit formulate the Dulong-Petit law: in solid elements the product of the specific heat and the atomic mass is a constant. French chemist Louis-Nicholas Vauquelin isolates cyanic acid.

1819 ● British chemist John Kidd derives naphthalene. German chemist Eilhardt Mitscherlich discovers the phenomenon of isomorphism and develops the law that chemical composition is related to crystalline form.

1821 ● Austrian chemist Johann Joseph Loschmidt introduces the practice of using a single line for single bonds, a double line for double bonds, etc. into organic chemistry.

1822 ● German metallurgist Friedrich Mohs proposes the Mohs' scale for mineral hardness.

1823 ● English chemist Humphry Davy liquefies gases.

1824 ● Swedish chemist Jöns Jakob Berzelius discovers the element silicon. French chemist Joseph-Louis Gay-Lussac discovers isomers.

1825 ● English chemist and physicist Michael Faraday isolates

1815
Humphry Davy invents his safety lamp for use in mines.

benzene (benzol) from compressed oil gas. Danish chemist Hans Christian Ørsted produces aluminum.

1826 ● French chemist Antoine-Jérôme Balard discovers the element bromine. German chemist Otto Unverdorben discovers aniline by distilling indigo. Scottish scientist Thomas Drummond invents limelight (when heated, calcium oxide or lime becomes incandescent). French chemist Henri Dutroche finds that the osmotic pressure is proportional to the degree of concentration.

1827 ● English scientist John Walker invents the friction match.

1828 ● Swedish chemist Jöns Jakob Berzelius discovers the element thorium. Friedrich Wöhler synthesizes urea from ammonium cyanate. This is the first time a compound of organic origin has been prepared from inorganic material. Scottish metallurgist James Neilson discovers the value of using a hot-blast (precursor of the blast furnace) in iron smelting. Finnish scientist Johan Gadolin discovers the element yttrium.

1829 ● Döbereiner's triads: German chemist Johann Döbereiner shows the existence of groups of three chemically similar elements, or triads. The atomic weight of the central element in each triad is the arithmetic mean of the other two. Scottish chemist Thomas Graham propounds Graham's law relating to the diffusion rate of gases.

1830 ● Swedish chemist Jöns Jakob Berzelius identifies the phenomenon of isomerism (compounds of identical chemical composition but different structure and properties). German chemist Karl Ludwig Reichenbach discovers paraffin. French chemist Pierre-Louis Dulong perfects his incineration method for determining the percentage of hydrogen and carbon in organic compounds.

1831 ● English chemist and physicist Michael Faraday discovers electromagnetic induction. French chemist Eugène Soubeiran and German chemist Justus von Liebig simultaneously discover chloroform.

1831
Structure of chloroform discovered by Soubeiran and Liebig.

1832 ● English chemist and physicist Michael Faraday proposes the laws of electrolysis. German chemist Eilhardt Mitscherlich prepares nitrobenzene. French chemists Jean-Baptiste-André Dumas and Augustin Laurent discover anthracite in coal tar.

1833 ● German chemist Karl Ludwig Reichenbach discovers creosote. English physicists Michael Faraday and William Whewell coin the terms *electrode*, *cathode*, *anode*, *ion*, *cation*, *anion*, *electrolyte*, and *electrolysis*. Swedish chemist Jöns Jakob Berzelius coins the word *polymer*. French chemist Anselme Payen discovers the first enzyme (diastase from barley).

1834 ● German scientist Friedlieb Ferdinand Runge discovers carbolic acid in coal tar. He pioneers the field of chromatography.

1835 ● French chemists Jean-Baptiste-André Dumas and Eugène-Melchior Péligot prepare methyl alcohol.

1836 ● German physiologist Theodor Schwann discovers the first animal enzyme (pepsin). Welsh electrochemist Sir William Robert Grove invents the fuel cell.

1837 ● German chemist Justus von Liebig introduces the convention of using subscripts to denote numbers of atoms of an element in a compound (for example H_2O). British metallurgist Thomas Spencer invents electroplating.

1839 ● Swedish chemist Carl Gustaf Mosander discovers the element lanthanum. American inventor Charles Goodyear discovers the effects of heating rubber with sulfur (vulcanization). German chemist Christian Friedrich Schönbein discovers ozone.

1840 ● Russian chemist Germain Henri Hess articulates Hess's law: the total heat change during a complete chemical reaction is dependent on the substances, not the reactions involved.

1841 ● French chemist Augustin Laurent isolates phenol in his study of coal tar derivatives. Swedish chemist Jöns Jakob Berzelius discovers allotropy in carbon.

1842 ● American physician Crawford Long first uses ether as an anesthetic. English agricultural scientist Sir John Bennett Lawes develops the artificial fertilizer superphosphate,

1842–45 ● French chemist Charles-Frédéric Gerhardt formulates the idea of homologous series.

1843 ● English agricultural scientist Sir John Bennett Lawes patents the process of manufacturing superphosphate. Swedish chemist Carl Gustaf Mosander identifies the elements erbium and terbium.

1845 ● Establishment of the Royal College of Chemistry.

1847 ● German mathematician and physicist Julius Plücker discovers cathode rays. German physicist Hermann Ludwig Ferdinand von Helmholtz and English physicist James Joule state the first law of thermodynamics. Italian chemist Ascanio Sobrero discovers nitroglycerin.

1848 ● Foundation of the American Association for the Advancement of Science. French scientist Louis Pasteur founds the science of stereochemistry (the study of the spatial arrangement of atoms in molecules and the effect of these arrangements on chemical properties). Scottish physician Sir James Simpson first uses chloroform as an anesthetic during experiments. English chemist Sir Edward Frankland and German chemist Adolph Kolbe discover ethane. Scottish physicist William Thomson, later Baron Kelvin, formulates the concept of absolute zero.

1848
Louis Pasteur discovers anerobic organisms.

1849 ● English chemist Charles Mansfield introduces fractional distillation. Scottish physicist William Thomson, later Baron Kelvin, introduces the term *thermodynamics*.

1850 ● German physicist Rudolf Julius Emmanuel Clausius formulates the second law of thermodynamics. German chemist Robert Bunsen invents the Bunsen burner. English chemist and physicist Michael Faraday discovers the regelation of ice. Scottish chemist Thomas Graham founds the field of colloidal chemistry.

1850
Robert Bunsen's laboratory burner.

1852 ● Irish physicist George Stokes coins the term *fluorescence*. English chemist Edward Franklin describes the phenomenon later called valence. Canadian geologist Abraham Gesner discovers kerosene.

1854 ● English chemist Alexander William Williamson is the first to explain how a catalyst works.

1855 ● French chemist Charles-Adolphe Wurtz develops a method for synthesizing long-chain hydrocarbons.

1856 ● British chemist Sir William Perkin synthesizes the first artificial dye, a brilliant mauve dye marketed as "aniline purple" or "mauveine." Anglo-German metallurgist Sir Charles William Siemens designs the regenerative furnace. French chemist Charles-Adolphe Wurtz prepares the first dihydroxy alcohol, ethylene glycol.

1858 ● Italian chemist Stanislao Cannizzaro shows the validity of Avogadro's number. German chemist Friedrich Kekulé von Stradonitz and Scottish chemist Archibald Cooper suggest the modern system of showing graphically how elements in compounds are attached to each other.

1859 ● Robert Bunsen and Gustav Kirchhoff develop the spectroscope (an instrument for recording a spectrum of electromagnetic radiation by dispersal). This enables the identification of new elements. Scottish physicist James Clerk Maxwell develops the kinetic theory of gases.

1860 ● English metallurgist Sir Henry Bessemer invents the Bessemer converter for steel manufacture. German chemists Robert Bunsen and Gustav Kirchhoff discover the element cesium. Scottish physicist James Clerk Maxwell and Austrian physicist Ludwig Eduard Boltzmann independently develop statistics for analyzing the behavior of molecules in a gas. Robert Bunsen invents the magnesium light. Italian chemist Stanislao Cannizzaro convinces an international conference of chemists to use the value of atomic weights determined by Swedish chemist Jöns Jakob Berzelius to standardize chemical formulas.

Molten iron

Slag

Air in

Tuyères (air channels)

1860

Bessemer converter converts molten iron into steel.

1861 ● Belgian chemist Ernest Solvay designs the Solvay tower for the production of soda. Carbon dioxide is forced up a tower down which flows ammoniated salt. The process uses brine and ammonia as raw materials. German chemists Robert Bunsen and Gustav Kirchhoff discover the element rubidium. English physicist William Crookes discovers the element thallium.

1862 ● British scientist Alexander Parkes prepare the first plastic (Parkesine). Nitrocellulose is mixed with wood naphtha (a mixture of methanol, acetone, acetic acid, and methyl acetate formed during the distillation of wood) to produce a malleable solid. It is marketed, with little success, as a sculpting material. German chemist Friedrich Wöhler first makes calcium carbide, from which he later obtains acetylene.

1863 ● German mineralogists Ferdinand Reich and Theodor Richter discover the element indium. German chemist Joseph Wilbrand discovers TNT (trinitrotoluene). Production of aminoazobenzene (aniline yellow), the first yellow azo dye. German chemist Adolf von Baeyer develops the first barbiturate.

1864 ● English chemist John Newlands arranges elements in order of ascending atomic weight and discovers that "the difference between the number of the lowest member of a group and that immediately above it is seven; in other words, the eighth element starting from a given one is a kind of repetition of the first, like the eight notes of an octave of music." He calls this the Law of Octaves. He is the first to assign a number to an element, leaving spaces for elements that are as yet undiscovered. German-born British electrical engineer Sir Charles William Siemens and Pierre-Émile Martin, a Frenchman, invent open-hearth steel production. Norwegian chemists Cato Guldberg and Peter Waage publish the law of mass action: a reaction is dependent on both the volume and mass of the constituents.

1865 ● English surgeon and medical scientist Joseph Lister pioneers antiseptic surgery (using phenol). German scientist Friedrich Kekulé von Stradonitz suggests that

1865
Joseph Lister's carbolic acid sprayer.

benzene consists of a cyclic arrangement of six tetravalent carbon atoms with alternating single and double bonds between the carbon atoms. Belgian chemist Jean-Servais Stas produces the first modern table of atomic weights.

1867
The Nobel Prize struck in gold awarded for physics and for chemistry in memory of Alfred Nobel.

1867 ● Swedish inventor, manufacturer, and philanthropist Alfred Nobel invents dynamite. This stable and safe explosive for industrial use makes him a fortune. French chemist Charles-Adolphe Wurtz synthesizes phenol.

1868 ● German organic chemist Adolf von Baeyer demonstrates that complex organic molecules can be split into simpler compounds using heat and a zinc catalyst. French astronomer Pierre-Jules-César Janssen and English astronomer Joseph Norman Lockyer discover the element helium in the solar spectrum. French engineer Georges Leclanché invents the zinc-carbon battery. British chemist Sir William Perkin invents coal tar perfumes. Russian scientist Vladimir Markovnikov discovers that in the hydrohalogenation of unsymmetrical unsaturated compounds, addition of the hydrogen takes place on the carbon with the most attached hydrogen, the halide added to the carbon with the least number of hydrogen atoms.

1869 ● Meyer's atomic volume curve: German chemist Julius Meyer plots the atomic volume (atomic weight divided by density) of each element against its atomic weight and shows that elements whose chemical properties are similar appear in similar positions on the waves of the curve. Russian chemist Dmitry Mendeleyev publishes the first periodic table for chemical elements. He writes, "The properties of the elements are in periodic dependence upon their atomic weight." His table shows how the elements are related to each other and how increasing atomic weight affects their chemical reactivities. Gaps in the table indicate elements yet to be discovered and predict their properties. Mendeleyev coins the term *transition element*. British chemist Sir William Perkin develops synthetic alizarin for manufacture from the madder plant.

1871 ● German chemist Max Bodenstein develops the concept of chain reactions.

1872 ● Scottish chemist James Dewar develops the Dewar flask, a container for storing liquid gas.

1875 ● French chemist Paul-Émile Lecoq de Boisbaudran discovers the element gallium. The German industrial chemist Rudolph Messel perfects the "contact" process for sulfuric acid manufacture.

1876 ● German physicist Eugen Goldstein discovers cathode rays.

1877 ● French chemist Charles Friedel and American chemist James Mason Crafts discover that an aluminum chloride catalyst transforms organic chlorides into hydrocarbons and acid halides into ketones. This becomes known as the Friedel-Crafts reaction and is important in chemical synthesis. French physicist Louis-Paul Cailletet and Swiss physicist Raoul Pictet liquefy oxygen.

1878 ● Swiss scientists Jacques-Louis Soret and Marc Delafontaine discover the element holmium, which also is independently discovered by Swedish chemist Per Theodor Cleve. Swiss chemist Jean-Charles de Marignac discovers the element ytterbium.

1879 ● Swedish chemist Lars Nilson discovers the element scandium. French chemist Paul-Émile Lecoq de Boisbaudran discovers the element samarium. Swedish chemist Per Theodor Cleve discovers the element thulium.

1880 ● Swiss chemist Jean-Charles de Marignac discovers the element gadolinium. French chemist Pierre Curie discovers piezoelectricity.

1881 ● English physicist Sir Joseph John Thomson introduces the concept of electromagnetic mass.

1882 ● German chemist Viktor Meyer discovers thiophene.

1883 ● British inventor Sir Joseph Swan makes artificial silk.

1884 ● Swedish physical chemist Svante Arrhenius proposes in his doctoral thesis the theory of electrolytic dissociation

1881
Sir Joseph John Thomson who devised the concept of electromagnetic mass.

or ionization (acids, bases, and salts in solution dissociate into ions). French chemist Louis Chardonnet develops rayon, the first artificial fiber in common use.

1885 ● Austrian chemist Carl Auer discovers the elements neodymium and praseodymium. Peter Laar describes and names the phenomenon of *tautomerism*. Swedish physician Magnus Gustav Blix suggests the idea of the centrifuge. Dutch chemist Jacobus van't Hoff develops his formula for osmotic pressure.

1886 ● German chemist Clemens Winkler discovers the element germanium. French chemist Paul-Émile Lecoq de Boisbaudran discovers the element dysprosium. American scientist Charles Hall and French metallurgist Paul Héroult independently achieve the extraction of aluminum by electrolysis of aluminum oxide. French chemist Henri Moissan isolates the element fluorine. French chemist Eugène Turpin invents melinite. Americans Constantin Fahlberg and Ira Remsen invent saccharine.

1887 ● American chemist Arthur Michael discovers the "Michael condensation" reaction—the transformation of an unsaturated compound into a saturated compound with an additional carbon atom. German physical chemist Friedrich Wilhelm Ostwald formulates Ostwald's dilution law. German physicist Heinrich Rudolf Hertz discovers the photoelectric effect. American chemist Herman Frasch develops a process for removing sulfur from crude oils.

1889 ● English chemist Sir Frederick Augustus Abel develops cordite, a "smokeless" propellant that is safe to handle.

1891 ● American chemist Edward Goodrich Acheson discovers a process for making carborundum, a material that is almost as hard as diamond.

1892 ● American chemist Hamilton Young Castner develops an electrolytic cell for the formation of sodium hydroxide. This is later improved by Austrian engineer Karl Kellner, who devises a mercury cathode. German organic chemist Adolf von Baeyer introduces cis-trans terminology to the study of isomers. British chemical technologist Charles Cross invents the viscose rayon production process.

1894 ● Scottish chemist William Ramsay and English physicist Lord Rayleigh (John William Strutt) discover the element argon.

1895 ● Scottish physicist Charles Thomson Rees Wilson develops the cloud chamber, an instrument for studying high-energy particles by detecting their tracks through an enclosed medium. Scottish chemist William Ramsay is first to discover element helium on Earth from the mineral clevite. German physicist Wilhelm Conrad Röntgen discovers X-rays.

1896 ● Dutch physicist Pieter Zeeman discovers the Zeeman effect, involving the splitting of spectral lines in a magnetic field. Swedish physical chemist Svante Arrhenius makes the link between global temperature and atmospheric carbon dioxide. French physicist Antoine-Henri Becquerel discovers radioactivity.

1897 ● American chemist Hamilton Castner and Austrian paper pulper Karl Kellner introduce the Castner-Kellner process for sodium hydroxide manufacture. English physicist Sir Joseph John Thomson discovers the electron and calculates its mass.

1898 ● French chemist Pierre Curie and French physicist Marie Curie discover the elements radium and polonium. Marie Curie coins the term *radioactivity* after her study of these elements. Scottish chemist William Ramsay and English chemist Morris William Travers discover the elements krypton, neon, and xenon. Scottish chemist Sir James Dewar produces liquid hydrogen.

1899 ● British nuclear physicist Ernest Rutherford (later Lord Rutherford of Nelson, New Zealand) distinguishes two types of radioactivity, alpha and beta rays (later known as alpha and beta particles). French chemist André-Louis Debierne discovers the element actinium. German organic chemist Emil Fischer develops the "lock and key" hypothesis for enzymes.

1895
Wilhelm Röntgen discovers X-rays.

$$E = hf$$

1900
Formula for Max Planck's law of electromagnetic radiation, or quantum theory.

1900 ● English physicist Sir Owen Willans Richardson discovers that heated metals tend to emit electrons (thermionic emission). German physicist Max Ernst Ludwig Planck states Planck's radiation law to explain the spectral-energy distribution of radiation emitted by a blackbody. German physicist Friedrich Ernst Dorn discovers the element radon.

1901 ● French chemist Eugène-Anatole Demarçay discovers the element europium. Japanese chemist Jokichi Takamine isolates adrenaline.

1902 ● Czech scientist Bohuslav Brauner suggests that rare earth elements should be placed together in one space of the periodic table between lanthanum and tantalum.

1903 ● Hardening of fats by hydrogenation discovered. Industrial production of viscose begins.

ca. 1905 ● German chemist Friedrich Wilhelm Ostwald devises the Ostwald process for the commercial production of nitric acid.

1905 ● German-born physicist Albert Einstein devises the special theory of relativity, including the formula $E = mc^2$. German chemist Richard Willstätter discovers the structure of chlorophyll.

1906 ● German physical chemist Walther Hermann Nernst formulates the third law of thermodynamics (entropy as a measure of disorder is a function of temperature). Russian scientist Mikhail Tsvett discovers chromatographic analysis as a means of separating dyes.

1907 ● French chemist Georges Urbain discovers the element lutetium. German chemist Emil Hermann Fischer synthesizes a polypeptide from amino acids.

1908 ● German physicist Louis Paschen discovers the Paschen series of lines in the infrared spectrum. German chemist Adolf Windaus synthesizes histamine. German chemist Fritz Haber develops the Haber process for synthesizing ammonia by extracting nitrogen from the air.

1909 ● Danish biochemist Søren Peter Lauritz Sørensen describes the effect of hydrogen ion concentration on enzyme activity and proposes the use of a negative logarithm of this concentration as a measure of acidity and alkalinity. A book about hydrogen ion concentration by German medical chemist Leonor Michaelis makes the pH scale more widely known. American (formerly Russian) biochemist Phoebus Levene discovers DNA and RNA. German scientist Karl Hoffman invents the first synthetic rubber. German chemist Alfred Stock synthesizes boron hydrides.

1910 ● English physicist Sir Joseph John Thomson confirms the existence of isotopes. German founder of chemotherapy, Paul Ehrlich, discovers the first specific antibacterial agent (salvarsan, for treatment of syphilis). Production of Bakelite, a phenol-formaldehyde resin. This had been discovered by Belgian-American chemist Leo Hendrik Baekeland and was widely used in industry.

1911 ● British nuclear physicist Ernest Rutherford (later Lord Rutherford of Nelson) proposes the nuclear structure of the atom.

1912 ● German theoretical physicist Max von Laue discovers X-ray crystallography technique.

1913 ● British scientist Henry Moseley confirms the existence of exactly 14 rare earth elements. German physicist Johannes Stark discovers the Stark effect, concerning the splitting of spectrum lines. English chemist Frederick Soddy coins the term *isotope*. Danish physicist Niels Bohr proposes quantum theory and the Bohr atomic model. French physicist Charles Fabry discovers the ozone layer in the Earth's atmosphere. American scientist Elmer McCollum isolates vitamin A. Trial industrial plant for ammonia synthesis is built at Ludwigshafen, Germany. Hungarian chemist Georg von Hevesy develops use of radioactive isotopes as tracers. German chemist Leonor Michaelis develops the Michaelis-Menton equation, describing the rate at which enzymes catalyze reactions.

1914 ● British nuclear physicist Sir Ernest Rutherford (Lord Rutherford of Nelson) gives the name *proton* to the positively charged nucleus of the hydrogen atom.

1915 ● German-born physicist Albert Einstein conceives the general theory of relativity.

1916 ● American chemist Gilbert N. Lewis introduces the concept of the shared pair of electrons in a chemical bond. Russian-Israeli chemist Chaim Weizmann discovers a method for mass-producing acetone, an essential ingredient for cordite, used in World War I.

1917 ● Austrian organic chemist Fritz Pregl develops techniques for analyzing tiny amounts of organic chemicals. British chemists Frederick Soddy and John Cranston discover the element protactinium.

1919 ● British nuclear physicist Sir Ernest Rutherford (Lord Rutherford of Nelson) achieves the first artificial atomic fission. English chemist Francis William Aston invents the mass spectrograph.

1920 ● German chemist Hermann Staudinger establishes that polymers consist of long-chain molecules.

1921 ● Danish physicist Niels Bohr produces a detailed picture of the distribution of electronic shells.

1922 ● American chemist Roger Adams discovers the use of brown platinum oxide as a catalyst in hydrogenation.

1923 ● American physicist Arthur Holly Compton coins the word *photon*. Dutch physicist Dirk Coster and Hungarian chemist Georg von Hevesy discover the element hafnium. American chemist Gilbert N. Lewis publishes *Valence and Structure of the Atom*, a pioneering work on the electronic theory of valency.

1924 ● French physicist Louis-Victor de Broglie discovers the wave nature of electrons.

1925 ● German chemists Walter Noddack, Ida Tacke, and Otto C. Berg discover the elements rhenium and technetium. French physicist Pierre-Victor Auger discovers the Auger effect, the spontaneous process in which an atom with an electron vacancy in the innermost shell readjusts itself to a more stable state by ejecting one or more electrons instead of radiating a single X-ray photon. Austrian-born Swiss physicist Wolfgang Pauli propounds the Pauli "exclusion principle" (no two electrons can be in the same energy state). German physicist Friedrich Hund establishes Hund's Rule: the electronic configuration in degenerate orbitals will have the minimum number of paired electrons.

1926 ● Irish physicist John Desmond Bernal invents the Bernal chart to assist with the analysis of crystal structures. American biochemist James Sumner isolates urease. German philosopher and physicist Werner Heisenberg develops "new quantum mechanics." Austrian physicist Erwin Schrödinger puts forward the hypothesis of wave mechanics to study electrons in an atom.

1927 ● American physicist Clinton Joseph Davisson and English physicist George Paget Thomson independently discover the electron diffraction of crystals.

1927–28 ● German chemist Friedrich Hund and American chemist Robert S. Mulliken propose the Hund-Mulliken interpretation of molecular spectra, which gives a description of the molecular orbital theory of bonding.

1928 ● By this date quantum physicists show that the orbital closest to the nucleus (s orbital) is spherical. The next three electron energy shells (p orbitals) are seen as having the shape of dumbbells along the three coordinate axes. Polymethyl methacrylate (Perspex) invented. German organic chemists Otto Diels and Kurt Alder develop an addition reaction in which double-bonded dienes (compounds containing two double bonds separated by a single bond) are transformed into cyclic compounds. This is known as the "Diels-Alder reaction" and it is important for the synthesis of a range of natural products. Hungarian-American physicist Eugene Paul Wigner develops the concept of parity of atomic states. Scottish biochemist Sir Alexander Fleming discovers penicillin as a result of the chance exposure of a culture of

1927
Clinton J. Davisson, one of the discoverers of electron diffraction in crystals.

staphylococci. American scientists Charles Glen King and Albert von Szent-Györgyi (Hungarian-born) discover vitamin C.

1929 ● German-born physicist Albert Einstein develops a unified field theory.

1930 ● French chemical engineer Eugène Houdry develops the Houdry petroleum cracking process. (Houdry moved to the United States to obtain finance and later became a U.S. citizen.) German corporation I.G. Farberindustrie develops polystyrene. Scientists at the American corporation B.F. Goodrich invent polyvinyl chloride. English physical biochemist William Thomas Astbury begins using X-ray diffraction to study the three-dimensional structure of proteins. American chemist Thomas Midgeley invents Freon, which becomes widely used in refrigerating freezers and air conditioners. In the late 20th century scientists discover that Freon is one of chemicals destroying the ozone layer that protects Earth from ultraviolet radiation.

1931 ● American chemist Wallace H. Carothers formulates nylon, the first all-synthesized fiber (marketed by Du Pont in 1938) Carothers also studies the mechanism of polymerization and shows that it principally takes place by either addition or condensation reactions. Swiss chemist Albert Hofmann synthesizes lysergic acid diethylamide (LSD). German scientists Ernst Ruska and Max Knoll invent the electron microscope. Russian-born Swiss organic chemist Paul Karrer identifies the structure of vitamin A. German phyicist and physical chemist Erich Hückel suggests that the stability of the benzene ring is caused by six sigma bonds in the plane of the ring and six pi electrons in orbits above and below the plane. American chemist Julius Arthur Nieuwland develops neoprene, a synthetic rubber.

1932 ● English physicist Sir John Cockcroft and Irish physicist Ernest Walton achieve the first nuclear reaction to result from the bombardment of an element by artificially accelerated particles. English physicist Sir James Chadwick discovers the neutron. American physicist Carl David Anderson discovers the positron. Anglo-German biochemist Hans Krebs discovers the urea cycle. Bactericidal properties of the red dye "Prontosil" (sulfamido chrysoidine) are recognized. German chemist Adolf Windaus establishes the structure of cholesterol. American engineer Edwin Land develops a synthetic substance that will polarize light. American biochemist John Northrop crystallizes the enzyme trypsin. American chemist Harold Urey discovers deuterium, an isotope of hydrogen that has a nucleus of one proton and one neutron.

1932
James Chadwick's neutron.

1933 ● German-American physicist Otto Stern demonstrates the magnetic characteristics and wave aspects of molecular beams. American chemist Gilbert N. Lewis obtains heavy water (deuterium oxide).

1934 ● English physicist Sir James Chadwick and Austrian-American physicist Maurice Goldhaber determine the mass of a neutron. French physicists Irene and Jean-Frédéric Joliot-Curie achieve artificial radioactivity. Italian-American physicist Enrico Fermi splits the nucleus of the atom. English chemist Walter Norman Haworth synthesizes ascorbic acid (vitamin C).

1935 ● American biochemist John Northrop crystallizes the enzyme chymotrypin.

1936 ● Swedish biochemist Arne Wilhelm Tiselius develops electrophoresis, a method for separating proteins in suspension using electric current.

1937 ● American physicist Carl David Anderson discovers the "muon" particle. American chemist Michael Sveda discovers cyclamate.

1938 ● PTFE (polytetraflouroethylene) invented in the United States. German chemist Otto Hahn and Austrian physicist Lise Meitner discover chain reaction nuclear fission. American physicist Isidor Isaac Rabi develops the technique of magnetic resonance. German chemist

THE GEORGE FISHER BAKER
NON-RESIDENT LECTURESHIP IN CHEMISTRY
AT CORNELL UNIVERSITY

THE NATURE
OF THE CHEMICAL BOND
AND THE STRUCTURE OF MOLECULES
AND CRYSTALS

An Introduction to Modern Structural Chemistry

BY

LINUS PAULING
*Professor of Chemistry in the
California Institute of Technology*

SECOND EDITION

ITHACA, NEW YORK
CORNELL UNIVERSITY PRESS
LONDON: HUMPHREY MILFORD
OXFORD UNIVERSITY PRESS
1940

1939
Linus Pauling publishes The
Nature of the Chemical Bond.

Richard Kuhn isolates vitamin B_6. The first form of Teflon® discovered by American chemist Roy Plunkett.

1939 ● American physical organic chemist Linus Pauling publishes *The Nature of the Chemical Bond*. American physicist Felix Bloch calculates the magnetic movement of a neutron. French physicist Marguerite Perey discovers the element francium.

1939–41 ● English biochemists Archer John Porter Martin and Richard Synge invent partition chromatography.

1940 ● American physicists Emilio Segrè, Dale Corson, and K.R. Mackenzie discover the element astatine. American physicists Glenn T. Seaborg, Arthur Wahl, and Joseph Kennedy discover the element plutonium. American physicists Edwin M. McMillan and Philip H. Abelson discover the element neptunium. Swiss scientist Paul Müller invents DDT. American biochemist Vincent Du Vigneaud identifies biotin. American biochemist Martin David Kamen discovers carbon-14, a radioactive isotope later used to date ancient materials.

1941 ● English chemists John Whinfield and James T. Dickson invent the synthetic fiber Terylene. German industrial giant I.G. Farberindustrie begins producing polyurethanes.

1942 ● Italian-American physicist Enrico Fermi creates the first controlled chain reaction in a uranium and graphite pile. American chemist Louis Fieser develops napalm. American chemist Frank Harold Spedding produces large quantities of extremely pure uranium for use in developing the atomic bomb.

1943 ● American industrial corporation Dow Corning begins manufacturing the first silicones. Swiss chemist Albert Hofmann discovers that lysergic acid diethylamide (LSD) is hallucinogenic.

1944 ● American physicists Glenn T. Seaborg, Ralph James, Leon Morgan, and Albert Ghiorso discover the elements americium and curium. English biochemists Archer John Porter Martin and Richard Synge invent paper chromatography, a technique for separating and identifying individual amino acids in a mixture.

1945 ● American chemists Jacob A. Marinsky, Lawrence E. Glendenin, and Charles D. Coryell discover the element promethium.

1947 ● English physicist Cecil Frank Powell discovers the first true meson (pi-meson or pion) by investigating cosmic radiation at high altitudes.

1948 ● Shell model of atomic nucleus advanced by American physicist Maria Goeppert-Mayer and German physicist Johannes Hans Daniel, who independently introduce the concept of magic numbers. (These are the numbers 2, 8, 20, 28, 50, 82, or 126. If a nucleus has a magic number of either protons or neutrons, it is more than usually stable.) American physicists Richard Feynman and Seymour Schwinger, and Japanese physicist Shin'ichiro Tomonaga invent quantum electrodynamics.

1949 ● American physicists Glenn Seaborg, Stanley Thompson, and Albert Ghiorso discover the element berkelium. English biochemist Dorothy Crowfoot Hodgkin is the first chemist to use a computer to determine the structure of an organic chemical, penicillin.

1950s ● Two main classes of elementary particles are identified: hadrons (including nucleons, mesons, and hyperons) and leptons (including electrons, neutrinos, and muons).

1950 ● American physicists Glenn Seaborg, Albert Ghiorso, Stanley Thompson, and Kenneth Street discover the element californium. Acrylic fiber invented. Artificial sweetener cyclamate is marketed. It is later discovered to cause cancer and is banned in the United States in 1970.

1952 ● Polish physicists Marian Danysz and Jerzy Pniewski discover the K meson (or kaon) and lambda particle. American physicists Albert Ghiorso, Stanley Thompson, Gregory Choppin, and Glenn Seaborg discover the element einsteinium. They also discover the element fermium in the remains of the first thermonuclear explosion.

1953
Francis Crick and James Watson receive the Nobel Prize for discovering the structure of DNA.

1953 ● American physicist Donald Arthur Glaser invents the bubble chamber for detecting ionizing radiation. American physicists Frederick Reines and Clyde Lorrain Cowan discover antineutrinos. American physicist Charles Townes produces the maser, forerunner of the laser. English molecular biologist Francis Crick and American molecular biologist James Watson discover the double-helix structure of DNA. German chemist Karl Ziegler develops the first catalyst that combines monomers into a polymer in a regular fashion, producing stronger polyethylene. Italian chemist Giulio Natta develops the first isotactic polymers.

1954 ● The Bevatron particle accelerator is completed at the Lawrence Berkeley Laboratory in California. It can accelerate uranium atoms to 6.5 billion electron volts.

1955 ● American physicist Erwin Wilhelm Müller invents the field ion microscope, the first device to yield images of individual atoms. Two types of K mesons are detected with differing modes of decay. American physicists Albert Ghiorso, Bernard Harvey, Gregory Choppin, Stanley Thompson, and Glenn Seaborg discover the element mendelevium. American physicists Owen Chamberlain and Emilio Segrè discover antiprotons, negatively charged particles that have the mass of protons. English chemist Dorothy Crowfoot Hodgkin identifies the composition of vitamin B_{12}.

1956 ● American biochemist Choh Hao Li and his colleagues determine the composition of adrenocorticotrophic hormone (ACTH) and isolate human growth hormone.

1957 ● American biochemist John Sheenan synthesizes penicillin.

1958 ● American physicists Albert Ghiorso, Torbjørn Sikkeland, John Walton, and Glenn T. Seaborg discover the element nobelium.

1959 ● Japanese physicists Saburo Fukui and Shotaro Miyamoto invent the spark chamber to detect ionizing particles selectively.

1960s ● Advent of high-resolution mass spectrometers and nuclear magnetic resonance (NMR) spectroscopy.

1960 ● South African molecular biologist Sydney Brenner and French molecular biologist François Jacob discover messenger RNA. American chemist Lyman Creighton Craig purifies the hormone parathormone.

1961 ● Record set by Russian military scientists for largest nuclear explosion when they test a 58-megaton weapon. American physicist Murray Gell-Mann classifies elementary particles called hadrons in a system he calls the Eightfold Way. American physicists Albert Ghiorso, Torbjørn Sikkeland, Almon Larsh, and Robert Latimer discover the element lawrencium.

1962 ● British physicist Heinz London develops a technique for inducing very low temperatures with a mixture of helium-3 and helium-4. Canadian chemist Neil Bartlett combines noble gas xenon with platinum fluoride to produce xenon fluoroplatinate, the first-known case of a noble gas bonding with another element to form a compound. British-born American inorganic chemist Herbert Charles Brown works out the process of hydroboration.

1963 ● American physicists Murray Gell-Mann and George Zweigus suggest the subatomic particle, the quark. English scientist Leslie Phillips invents carbon fiber.

1964 ● Soviet physicist Georgy Flerov and his colleagues at the Joint Institute for Nuclear Research in Dubna, USSR, report the discovery of element 104, which they name *kurchatovium* (after the head of the Soviet nuclear research program). American physicists, led by Albert Ghiorso at the Lawrence Radiation Laboratory in California, dispute the claim.

1965 ● American chemist James M. Schlatter discovers aspartame.

1967 ● Soviet scientist Georgy Flerov and his colleagues at the Joint Institute for Nuclear Research in Dubna, USSR, announce the discovery of the element dubnium. American physicists, led by Albert Ghiorso at the Lawrence Radiation Laboratory in California dispute the claim. German chemist Manfred Eigen, and British chemists Ronald Norrish and George Porter develop the technique of flash photolysis. American physical organic chemist Linus Pauling, in *The Chemical Bond: A Brief Introduction to Modern Structural Chemistry*, includes the principles of the molecular orbital theory while stating that, for introductory teaching and the consideration of the ground states of molecules, the valence bond theory is still preferable.

1969 ● American physicist Albert Ghiorso and his colleagues at the Lawrence Berkeley National Laboratory in California discover the element rutherfordium (element 104). English chemist Dorothy Crowfoot Hodgkin discovers the structure of insulin.

1970 ● American biochemist Choh Hao Li synthesizes human growth hormone. American physicist Albert Ghiorso and his colleagues at the Lawrence Radiation Laboratory in California claim to have produced the element dubnium.

1971 ● Protein is obtained from hydrocarbons.

1974 ● Soviet physicists Georgy Flerov, Yuri Oganessian, and their colleagues at the Joint Institute for Nuclear Research in Dubna, USSR, report synthesizing the element seaborgium. The result, however, could not be confirmed.

1976 ● Two unmanned NASA probes, *Viking 1* and *Viking 2*, touch down on the surface of the planet Mars and conduct the first chemical analysis of the surface of that planet. The prime mission objective for the landing craft is to determine if life is or ever has been present on the planet, using chemical analysis of the soil and atmosphere. Probe telemetry reports high concentrations of iron in the soil but no sign of life. Recombinant DNA technique identified by American scientists Stanley Cohen and Herbert Boyer. Yuri Oganessian and his colleagues at the Joint Institute for Nuclear Research in Dubna, USSR, claim to have discovered the element bohrium.

1969
Dorothy Hodgkin discovers the structure of insulin.

1980 • Development of scanning tunneling microscope, which can produce images of individual atoms on the surface of a material.

1981 • Physicists at the Gesellschaft für Schwerionenforschung in Darmstadt, Germany, confirm the existence of the element bohrium, after Russian scientists originally report its discovery in 1976.

1982 • Unmanned Russian spacecraft *Venera 13* dispatches a landing craft to the surface of the planet Venus, which conducts the first successful chemical analysis of the surface of this hostile environment. Analysis of a surface sample by the lander's X-ray fluorescence spectrometer classifies the material as melanocratic alkaline gabbroids. Peter Armbruster, Gottfried Münzenberg, and their colleagues at the Gesellschaft für Schwerionenforschung in Darmstadt, Germany, discover the element meitnerium.

1984 • American scientist Dan Schechtman discovers the first quasi-crystal. Peter Armbruster, Gottfried Münzenberg and their colleagues at the Gesellschaft für Schwerionenforschung in Darmstadt, Germany, discover the element hassium.

1985 • American researchers discover lanxides, substances with the properties of both metal and ceramics. British chemists Harold Kroto and David Walton discover fullerenes.

1991 • American chemist Joel Hawkins corroborates existence of the buckyball molecule (or buckminsterfullerene), a form of pure carbon.

1994 • Peter Armbruster and his colleagues at the Gesellschaft für Schwerionenforschung in Darmstadt, Germany, discover the elements darmstadtium and roentgenium.

1995 • American physicist David H. White and his colleagues at Los Alamos National Laboratory deduce that neutrinos, previously thought to be massless, have a mass. This is later contested.

1996 ● Peter Armbruster, Sigurd Hofmann and their colleagues at the Gesellschaft für Schwerionenforschung in Darmstadt, Germany, discover the element ununbium. This is a temporary name.

1998 ● Russian physicists Yuri Oganessian, Vladimir Utyonkov and their colleagues at the Joint Institute for Nuclear Research in Dubna, Russia, discover the element ununquadium. This is a temporary name.

1999 ● American scientists Kenneth Gregorich, Victor Ninov, and their colleagues at the Lawrence Berkeley National Laboratory in California discover the element ununhexium. This is a temporary name. They also announce that they have discovered ununoctium but later retract that claim.

2001 ● Scientists at Brookhaven National Laboratory in New York announce that they have used a particle accelerator to create the highest density matter ever seen on Earth. By smashing gold nuclei at nearly the speed of light, the scientists produced densities more than 20 times greater than those found in the nuclei of ordinary matter.

2002 ● Scientists create molecules consisting of four nitrogen atoms (nitrogen molecules in air have only two atoms).

2003 ● Scientists develop threads composed of carbon nanotubes that are tougher than any other natural or artificial materials.

2004 ● Scientists from the Lawrence Livermore National Laboratory in California and the Joint Institute for Nuclear Research in Dubna, Russia, announce that they have discovered two new chemical elements: ununtrium (113) and ununpentium (115).

2005 ● Japanese and American chemists synthesize nickel gallium sulfide, which may behave as a "liquid" magnetic material at temperatures near absolute zero. Theoreticians first proposed the state in 1975.

SECTION FOUR
FOUR
KEY ADVANCES

Analytical chemistry
Title page of Boyle's The Sceptical Chymist *(1690 edition shown).*

Battery
Alessandro Volta uses "piles" of alternating zinc and silver disks in his Voltaic pile, the first battery.

acetic acid Adolph W.H. Kolbe (Germany) makes acetic acid, becoming the first to synthesize an organic compound from inorganic materials. [1845]

acid Svante Arrhenius (Sweden) and Friedrich W. Ostwald (Germany) separately propose the definition of an acid. [1884]

air composition Antoine Lavoisier (France) determines that air is a mixture primarily of oxygen and nitrogen. [1778]

alpha particles Sir Ernest Rutherford (U.K.) distinguishes two types of radiation: alpha rays and beta rays (later known as alpha and beta particles). [1899]

ammonia Claude-Louis Berthollet (France) determines the chemical constituents of ammonia. [1785]

analytical chemistry Robert Boyle (Ireland) publishes *The Sceptical Chymist*, the founding text of modern analytical chemistry. [1661]

atomic theory Leucippus (Greece) introduces an atomic theory of matter. [ca. 445 BCE]
(1) John Dalton (U.K.) proposes that all materials are composed of tiny, indivisible particles. [1803]
(2) Sir Ernest Rutherford (U.K.) theorizes that the atom has a positive nucleus surrounded by electrons. [1911]

atomic weight (1) John Dalton (U.K.) publishes the first table of atomic weights. [1803]
(2) John Dalton (U.K.) formulates atomic weight theory. [1808]

Avogadro's number (1) Amedeo Avogadro (Italy) proposes what eventually becomes known as Avogadro's number. [1811]
(2) Stanislao Cannizzaro (Italy) shows the validity of Avogadro's number. [1858]

base Svante Arrhenius (Sweden) proposes a measure of the strength of bases. [1884]

battery Alessandro Volta (Italy) devises the voltaic pile for storing electricity (the first battery). [1800]

benzene Michael Faraday (U.K.) first isolates benzene. [1825]

beta particles (1) Sir Ernest Rutherford (U.K.) distinguishes two types of radiation: alpha rays and beta rays (later known as alpha and beta particles). [1899]
(2) Rutherford names *beta rays*. [1900]

boric acid Wilhelm Homberg (Germany) discovers boric acid. [1702]

Boyle's Law Robert Boyle (Ireland) formulates Boyle's law: the pressure and volume of a gas are inversely proportioned. [1662]

Bunsen burner Robert Bunsen (Germany) invents the Bunsen burner. [1850]

calorimeter Pierre-Simon de Laplace (France) and Antoine Lavoisier (France) develop the calorimeter. [1780]

carbolic acid Friedlieb Ferdinand Runge (Germany) discovers carbolic acid. [1834]

carbon dioxide Joseph Black (U.K.) discovers carbon dioxide. [1754]

centrifuge Magnus Gustav Blix (Sweden) suggests the idea of the centrifuge. [1885]

Charles' law Jacques Charles (France) proposes Charles' law connecting the expansion of gas with its rise in temperature. [1787]

chemical elements (1) Philosopher Aristotle (Greece) defines chemical elements as constituents of bodies that cannot be decomposed into other constituents. [350–341 BCE]
(2) Belgian scientist Jan Baptista van Helmont proposes two elements, air (a physical medium) and water (the material from which all substances are formed). [ca. 1600]
(3) Robert Boyle (Ireland) states that a chemical element is a substance that cannot be further broken down into smaller substances. [1661]
(4) Antoine Lavoisier defines a chemical element as a substance that cannot be analyzed by chemical means. [1789]
(5) John Dalton (U.K.) states that elements compound together in fixed proportions by weight. [1808]

chemical formulas Stanislao Cannizzaro (Italy) convinces chemists to use the value of atomic weights as determined by Jöns Jakob Berzelius (Sweden) to standardize chemical formulas. [1860]

Bunsen burner
The adjustable gas burner invented in 1850 and used in laboratories worldwide.

MÉTHODE
DE
NOMENCLATURE
CHIMIQUE,

Propofée par MM. DE MORVEAU, LAVOISIER, BERTHOLET, & DE FOURCROY.

ON Y A JOINT

Un nouveau Syftême de Caractères Chimiques, adaptés à cette Nomenclature, par MM. HASSENFRATZ & ADET.

A PARIS,

Chez CUCHET, Libraire, rue & hôtel Serpente.

M. DCC. LXXXVII.

Sous le Privilège de l'Académie des Sciences.

Chemical structure
Title page of Lavoisier's Méthode de Nomenclature Chimique.

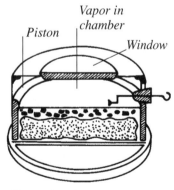

Vapor in chamber

Piston

Window

Cloud chamber
An early device for detecting subatomic particles as they pass through supersaturated water vapor.

chemical nomenclature (1) Antoine Lavoisier (France) standardizes the language of chemistry in *Méthode de Nomenclature Chimique.* [1787]
(2) Justus von Liebig (Germany) introduces the convention of using subscripts to denote number of atoms of an element in a compound. [1837]

chemical structure Friedrich Kekulé von Stradonitz (Germany) and Archibald Cooper (U.K.) suggest the modern system of showing graphically how elements in a compound are attached to each other. [ca. 1858]

chemical symbols Jöns Jakob Berzelius (Sweden) proposes that element be referred to by one or two letter abbreviations of their Latin names. [1811]

chirality Louis Pasteur (France) discovers the property of handedness in molecules. [1848]

chromatography (1) Mikhail Tsvett (Russia) discovers chromatographic analysis. [1906]
(2) Archer J.P. Martin (U.K.) and Richard Synge (U.K.) invent partition chromatography. [1939–41]
(3) Archer J.P. Martin (U.K.) and Richard Synge (U.K.) invent liquid chromatography. [ca. 1940]
(4) Archer J.P. Martin (U.K.) and A.T. James (U.K.) discover gas chromatography. [[1942–53]
(5) Archer J.P. Martin (U.K.) and Richard Synge (U.K.) invent paper chromatography. [1944]
(6) Arne Tiselius (Sweden) discovers adsorption chromatography. [1948]
(7) Elbert A. Peterson (U.S.) and Herbert A. Sober (U.S.) perfect ion-exchange chromatography. [1956]

chloroform Eugène Soubeiran (France) and Justus von Liebig (Germany) simultaneously discover chloroform. [1831]

cloud chamber Charles T.R. Wilson (U.K.) develops the cloud chamber. [1895]

colloid Thomas Graham (U.K.) distinguishes the class of substances now known as colloids. [1850]

combustion Antoine Lavoisier (France) provides the first scientific description of combustion. [1774]

conservation of mass Antoine Lavoisier (France) proves that matter cannot be destroyed. [ca. 1778]

creosote Karl Ludwig Reichenbach (Germany) discovers creosote. [ca. 1833]

crystallization Jean Rome de Lisle (France) describes the process of crystallization. [1772]

Dewar flask Sir James Dewar (U.K.) develops a container for storing liquid gases. [1872]

Diels-Alder reaction Otto Diels (Germany) and Kurt Alder (Germany) develop the Diels-Alder reaction in which double-bonded dienes are transformed into cyclic compounds. [1928]

diffusion Thomas Graham (U.K.) shows that the rate of diffusion of a gas is inversely proportional to the square root of its molecular weight. [1831]

Döbereiner's triads Johann Döbereiner shows the existence of groups of three chemically similar elements, or triads. [1829]

electrolysis Michael Faraday (U.K.) proposes the laws of electrolysis. [1832]

electromagnetic induction Michael Faraday (U.K.) discovers electromagnetic induction. [1831]

electron Sir Joseph John Thomson discovers and calculates the mass of the electron. [1897]

electron microscope (1) Ernst Ruska (Germany) and Max Knoll (Germany) develop the forerunner of the modern electron microscope. [1931]
(2) Albert V. Crewe (U.S.) develops the first practical electron microscope. [1970s]

electrophoresis Arne Tiselius (Sweden) invents a device that permits the separation of charged molecules. [1936]

formic acid John Ray (England) discovers formic acid. [1670]

Vacuum

Dewar flask
A vacuum flask for storing gases in liquid form.

Friedel-Crafts reaction Charles Friedel (France) and James Mason Crafts (U.S.) discover the Friedel-Crafts reaction, in which an aluminum chloride catalyst transforms organic chlorides into hydrocarbons and acid halides into ketones. [1877]

fullerenes Harold Kroto (U.K.), Robert Curl Jr., (U.S.), and Richard E. Smalley (U.S.) discover fullerenes. [1985]

gas laws (1) Robert Boyle (Ireland) discovers an inverse relationship between the volume and the pressure of gases at a constant temperature. [1662]
(2) Jacques Charles (France) discovers the law of gases. [1787]

gas, liquefaction of Humphry Davy (U.K.) achieves the liquefaction of gas. [1823]

Gay-Lussac's law Joseph-Louis Gay-Lussac (France) proposes that gases combine among themselves in very simple proportions. [1808]

Graham's law Thomas Graham (U.K.) formulates the law on the diffusion rate of gases. [1829]

gunpowder (1) The Chinese produce gunpowder. [ca. 600 BCE]
(2) Gunpowder rendered obsolete by invention by Paul Vieille (France) of a smokeless propellant called *Poudre B*.

heat (1) Joseph Black (U.K.) establishes the concepts of latent heat and specific heat capacity. [1761]
(2) James Joule (U.K.) shows that heat is a form of energy. [1847]

Henry's law William Henry (U.K.) formulates Henry's law: the amount of gas absorbed by a liquid varies directly with the pressure. [1801]

Hooke's law Robert Hooke (England) formulates Hooke's law relating to elastic bodies. [1676]

hydroboration Herbert Charles Brown (U.S.) works out the process of hydroboration. [1962]

hydrochloric acid Andreas Libau (Germany) prepares hydrochloric acid. [1611]

Pressure increases

Volume increases

Gas laws
Diagram illustrating Boyle's law of pressure and volume.

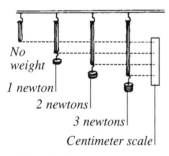

No weight
1 newton
2 newtons
3 newtons
Centimeter scale

Hooke's law

insulin Dorothy Crowfoot Hodgkin (U.K.) discovers the structure of insulin. [1969]

ion Svante Arrhenius (Sweden) proposes that ions are atoms bearing electric charges. [1884]

isomer Joseph-Louis Gay-Lussac (France) discovers that two or more compounds can have the same chemical formula yet have different structures and properties. [1824]

isotope (1) Sir Joseph John Thomson (U.K.) confirms the existence of isotopes. [1910]
(2) Frederick Soddy (U.K.) uses the term *isotope* to describe the different atoms of elements that vary in atomic weight but not in chemical properties. [1913]

kinetic theory of gases James Clerk Maxwell (U.K.) and Ludwig Boltzmann (Austria) devise the kinetic theory of gases. [1859]

Leyden jar Pieter van Musschenbroek (the Netherlands) and Ewald Georg von Kleist independently invent the Leyden jar, the ancestor of the modern capacitor. [1745]

lysergic acid diethylamide (LSD) Albert Hofmann (Switzerland) synthesizes lysergic acid diethylamide (LSD). [1938]

Leyden jar

mass spectrometer Francis William Aston (U.K.) develops the mass spectrometer. [1919]

Michael condensation reaction Arthur Michael (U.S.) discovers the Michael condensation reaction, the transformation of an unsaturated compound into a saturated compound with an additional carbon atom. [1887]

microscope (1) Zacharias Janssen (the Netherlands) devises the first compound microscope. [1590]
(2) Ernst Ruska (Germany) and Max Knoll (Germany) develop the forerunner of the modern electron microscope. [1931]
(3) Erwin Wilhelm Müller (Germany and U.S.) invents the field ion microscope. [1955]

molecule Pierre Gassendi (France) introduces the term *molecule* to indicate the smallest unit of a substance capable of an independent existence. [1649]

Matter
Anaximander, the Greek philosopher.

matter (1) Philosopher Thales (Greece) proposes an early theory of matter: all things are made from forms of water. [580 BCE]
(2) Philosopher Anaximander (Greece) explains matter in terms of cold, heat, dryness, and wetness. [ca. 560 BCE]
(3) Philosopher Anaxagoras (Greece) suggests materials are made up of large numbers of "seeds," particles that determine qualities. [480–471 BCE]
(4) Philosopher Empedocles (Greece) introduces the four-element theory of matter (fire, air, water, earth). [450 BCE]
(5) Philosopher Epicurus (Greece) founds philosophical school based on a theory of atoms, particles so small that they cannot be subdivided further. [310–301 BCE]
(6) Philosopher Pierre Gassendi (France) revives the atomic theory of matter. [1649]
(7) Antoine Lavoisier (France) proposes that matter exists in three states: solid, fluid, and gas. [1773]
(8) John Dalton (U.K.) proposes that matter is composed of many homogeneous atoms and that each element's atoms differ slightly in mass. [1808]

Mohs' scale Friedrich Mohs (Germany) proposes a scale of mineral hardness. [1822]

neutron (1) Sir James Chadwick (U.K.) discovers the neutron. [1932]
(2) Sir James Chadwick (U.K.) and Maurice Goldhaber (U.S.) determine the mass of a neutron. [1934]

nitric acid Friedrich W. Ostwald (Germany) devises the process for the commercial production of nitric acid. [ca. 1905]

nitroglycerin Chemist Ascanio Sobrero (Italy) produces the unstable and powerful explosive nitroglycerine. [1846]

nitrous oxide Joseph Priestley (U.K.) discovers nitrous oxide (laughing gas). [1772]

nylon Wallace Carothers (U.S.) formulates nylon. [1931]

organic compound synthesis Friedrich Wöhler (Germany) accidentally produces an organic compound (urea) from inorganic substances. [1828]

osmosis Jean-Antoine Nollet (France) discovers osmosis. [1748]

Ostwald's dilution law Friedrich Wilhelm Ostwald (Germany) formulates Ostwald's dilution law. [1887]

paraffin Karl Ludwig Reichenbach (Germany) discovers paraffin. [1830]

periodic table Dmitry Mendeleyev (Russia) constructs the periodic table. [1869]

phenol Auguste Laurent (France) isolates phenol. [1841]

picric acid Peter Woulfe (U.K.) discovers picric acid. [1771]

Planck's radiation law Max Ernst Ludwig Planck (Germany) states Planck's radiation law. [1900]

polymer (1) Jöns Jakob Berzelius (Sweden) coins the word *polymer*. [1833]
(2) Hermann Staudinger (Germany) establishes that polymers consist of long-chain molecules. [1920]

photoelectric effect Heinrich Rudolf Hertz (Germany) discovers the photoelectric effect. [1887]

radioactivity (1) Antoine-Henri Becquerel (France) discovers radioactivity. [1896]
(2) Marie Curie coins the term *radioactivity*. [1898].

scientific method (1) Physician Hippocrates (Greece) first uses the scientific method in treating disease. [ca. 400 BCE]
(2) Sir Francis Bacon (England) emphasizes the importance of the scientific method in *The Advancement of Learning*. [1605]
(3) Philosopher René Descartes (France) proposes the philosophical study of scientific method. [1637]

specific gravity William Prout (U.K.) calculates the specific gravities of elements. [1815]

spectroscope Robert Bunsen (Germany) and Gustav Kirchhoff (Germany) invent the spectroscope. [1859]

sulfuric acid (1) Andreas Libau (Germany) describes how to produce sulfuric acid. [1595]
(2) John Roebuck (U.K.) designs a large-scale process for manufacturing sulfuric acid. [1746]

OH

Phenol

Radioactivity
Stamp commemorating Henri Becquerel, who discovered radioactivity.

tartaric acid Carl Wilhelm Scheele (Sweden) discovers tartaric acid. [1770]

Teflon® Roy J. Plunkett (U.S.) discovers Teflon®. [1938]

temperature scale (1) Daniel Gabriel Fahrenheit devises the Fahrenheit scale. [1714]
(2) Anders Celsius (Sweden) devises the Celsius (centigrade) temperature scale. [1742]

thermionic emission Sir Owen Richardson (U.K.) discovers that heated metals tend to emit electrons. [1900]

thermodynamics (1) James Joule (U.K.) and Hermann von Helmholtz (Germany) state the first law of thermodynamics. [1847]
(2) William Thomson (U.K.), later Lord Kelvin, introduces the term *thermodynamics*. [1849]
(3) Rudolph Clausius (Germany) enunciates the second law of thermodynamics. [1850]
(4) Walther Hermann Nernst (Germany) formulates the third law of thermodynamics. [1906]

thermometer (1) Galileo Galilei (Italy) invents an early thermometer. [1592]
(2) Daniel Gabriel Fahrenheit (Germany) invents the first practical mercury thermometer. [1714]
(3) René-Antoine Ferchault de Réaumur (France) develops the alcohol thermometer. [1730]

transition element Dmitry Mendeleyev (Russia) coins the term *transition element*. [1869]

urea cycle Hans Krebs (Germany) discovers the urea cycle. [1932]

valence Sir Edward Frankland (U.K.) describes the phenomenon later called *valence*. [1852]

water (1) Henry Cavendish (U.K.) discovers that water consists of hydrogen and oxygen. [1784]
(2) Joseph-Louis Gay-Lussac (France) establishes the composition of water. [1805]

X-rays Wilhelm Conrad Röntgen discovers X-rays. [1895]

Zeeman effect Pieter Zeeman discovers the Zeeman effect. [1896]

RÉPUBLIQUE DE GUINÉE
OFFICE DE LA POSTE GUINÉENNE
750F
1928-9
OWEN RICHARDSON

Thermionic emission
Stamp commemorating Sir Owen Richardson.

SECTION FIVE
NOBEL PRIZE WINNERS

1901 ● **Jacobus Henricus van't Hoff** (1852–1911), the Netherlands, "in recognition of the extraordinary services he has rendered by the discovery of the laws of chemical dynamics and osmotic pressure in solutions."

1902 ● **Hermann Emil Fischer** (1852–1919), Germany, "in recognition of the extraordinary service he has rendered by his work on sugar and purine syntheses."

1902
Emil Fischer

1903 ● **Svante August Arrhenius** (1859–1927), Sweden, "in recognition of the extraordinary services he has rendered to the advancement of chemistry by his electrolytic theory of dissociation."

1904 ● **Sir William Ramsay** (1852–1916), United Kingdom, "in recognition of his services in the discovery of the inert gaseous elements in air, and his determination of their place in the periodic system."

1905 ● **Johann Friedrich Wilhelm Adolf von Baeyer** (1835–1917), Germany, "in recognition of his services in the advancement of organic chemistry and the chemical industry, through his work in organic dyes and hydroaromatic compounds."

1906 ● **Henri Moissan** (1852–1907), France, "in recognition of the great services rendered by him in his investigation and isolation of the element fluorine, and for the adaptation in the service of science of the electric furnace called after him."

1907 ● **Eduard Buchner** (1860–1917), Germany, "for his biochemical researches and his discovery of cell-free fermentation."

1908 ● **Ernest Rutherford** (1871–1937), United Kingdom and New Zealand, "for his investigations into the disintegration of the elements, and the chemistry of radioactive substances."

1909 ● **Wilhelm Ostwald** (1853–1932), Germany, "in recognition of his work on catalysis and for his investigations into the fundamental principles governing chemical equilibria and rates of reaction."

1910 ● **Otto Wallach** (1847–1931), Germany, "in recognition of his services to organic chemistry and the chemical industry by his pioneer work in the field of alicyclic compounds."

1911 ● **Marie Curie** (1867–1934), France, "in recognition of her services to the advancment of chemistry by the discovery of the elements radium and polonium, by the isolation of radium and the study of the nature and compounds of this remarkable element."

1912 ● **Victor Grignard** (1871–1935), France, "for the discovery of the so-called Grignard reagent, which in recent years has greatly advanced the progress of organic chemistry;" **Paul Sabatier** (1854–1941), France, "for his method of hydrogenating organic compounds in the presence of finely disintegrated metals whereby the progress of organic chemistry has been greatly advanced in recent years."

1913 ● **Alfred Werner** (1866–1919), Switzerland, "in recognition of his work on the linkage of atoms in molecules by which he has thrown new light on earlier investigations and opened up new fields of research especially in inorganic chemistry."

1914 ● **Theodore William Richards** (1868–1928), U.S., "in recognition of his accurate determination of the atomic weight of a large number of chemical elements."

1915 ● **Richard Martin Willstätter** (1872–1942), Germany, "for his researches on plant pigments, especially chlorophyll."

1916–17 ● No prize given.

1918 ● **Fritz Haber** (1868–1934), Germany, "for the synthesis of ammonia from its elements."

1919 ● No prize given.

1920 ● **Walther Hermann Nernst** (1864–1941), Germany, "in recognition of his work in thermochemistry."

1913
Alfred Werner

1915
Richard Willstätter

1920
Walter Nernst

1921
Frederick Soddy

1921 ● **Frederick Soddy** (1877–1956), United Kingdom, "for his contributions to our knowledge of the chemistry of radioactive substances, and his investigations into the origin and nature of isotopes."

1922 ● **Francis William Aston** (1877–1945), United Kingdom, "for his discovery by means of his mass spectrograph, of isotopes, in a large number of non-radioactive elements, and for his enunciation of the whole-number rule."

1923 ● **Fritz Pregl** (1869–1930), Austria, "for his invention of the method of micro-analysis of organic substances."

1924 ● No prize given.

1925 ● **Richard Adolf Zsigmondy** (1865–1929), Germany, "for his demonstration of the heterogeneous nature of colloid solutions and for the methods he used, which have since become fundamental in modern colloid chemistry."

1926 ● **The** (**Theodor**) **Svedberg** (1884–1971), Sweden, "for his work on dispersed systems."

1927 ● **Heinrich Otto Wieland** (1877–1957), Germany, "for his investigation of the constitution of the bile acids and related substances."

1928 ● **Adolf Otto Reinhold Windaus** (1876–1959), Germany, "for the services rendered through his research into the constitution of the sterols and their connection with the vitamins."

1929 ● **Arthur Harden** (1865–1940), United Kingdom; **Hans von Euler-Chelpin** (1873–1964), Sweden, "for their investigations on the fermentation of sugar and fermentative enzymes."

1930 ● **Hans Fischer** (1881–1945), Germany, "for his researches into the constitution of hemin and chlorophyll and especially for his synthesis of hemin."

1931 ● **Carl Bosch** (1874–1940), Germany; **Friedrich Bergius** (1884–1949), Germany, "in recognition of their contributions to the invention and development of chemical high pressure methods."

1932 • **Irving Langmuir** (1881–1957), U.S., "for his discoveries and investigations in surface chemistry."

1933 • No prize given.

1934 • **Harold Clayton Urey** (1893–1981), U.S., "for his discovery of heavy hydrogen."

1935 • **Frédéric Joliot** (1900–58), France; **Irène Joliot-Curie** (1897–1956), France, "in recognition of their synthesis of new radioactive elements."

1936 • **Petrus (Peter) Josephus Wilhelmus Debye** (1884–1966), the Netherlands, "for his contributions to our knowledge of molecular structure through his investigations on dipole moments and on the diffraction of X-rays and electrons in gases."

1937 • **Walter Norman Haworth** (1883–1950), United Kingdom, "for his investigations on carbohydrates and vitamin C;" **Paul Karrer** (1889–1971), Switzerland, "for his investigations on carotenoids, flavins, and vitamin A and B_2."

1938 • **Richard Kuhn** (1900–67), Germany, "for his work on carotenoids and vitamins."

1939 • **Adolf Friedrich Johann Butenandt** (1903–95), Germany, "for his work on sex hormones;" **Leopold Ružička** (1887–1976), Swizerland, "for his work on polymethylenes and higher terpenes."

1940–42 • No prize given.

1943 • **George de Hevesy** (1885–1966), Hungary, "for his work on the use of isotopes as traces in the study of chemical processes."

1944 • **Otto Hahn** (1879–1968), Germany, "for his discovery of the fission of heavy nuclei."

1936
Peter Debye

1945 ● **Artturi Ilmari Virtanen** (1895–1973), Finland, "for his research and inventions in agricultural and nutrition chemistry, especially for his fodder preservation method."

1946 ● **James Batcheller Sumner** (1887–1955), U.S., "for his discovery that enzymes can be crystallized;" **John Howard Northrop** (1891–1987), U.S.; **Wendell Meredith Stanley** (1904–71), U.S., "for their preparation of enzymes and virus proteins in a pure form."

1947 ● **Sir Robert Robinson** (1886–1975), United Kingdom, "for his investigations on plant products of biological importance, especially the alkaloids."

1948 ● **Arne Wilhelm Kaurin Tiselius** (1902–71), Sweden, "for his research on electrophoresis and adsorption analysis, especially for his discoveries concerning the complex nature of the serum proteins."

1949 ● **William Francis Giauque** (1895–1982), U.S., "for his contributions in the field of chemical thermodynamics, particularly concerning the behavior of substances at extremely low temperatures."

1950 ● **Otto Paul Hermann Diels** (1876–1954), Federal Republic of Germany; **Kurt Alder** (1902–58), Federal Republic of Germany, "for their discovery and development of the diene synthesis."

1950
Otto Diels

1951 ● **Edwin Mattison McMillan** (1907–91), U.S.; **Glenn Theodore Seaborg** (1912–99), U.S., "for their discoveries in the chemistry of the transuranium elements."

1952 ● **Archer John Porter Martin** (1910–2002), United Kingdom; **Richard Laurence Millington Synge** (1914–94), United Kingdom, "for their invention of partition chromatography."

1953 ● **Hermann Staudinger** (1881–1965), Federal Republic of Germany, "for his discoveries in the field of macromolecular chemistry."

1954 ● **Linus Carl Pauling** (1901–94), U.S., "for his research into the nature of the chemical bond and its application to the elucidation of the structure of complex substances."

1955 ● **Vincent du Vigneaud** (1901–78), U.S., "for his work on biochemically important sulfur compounds, especially for the first synthesis of a polypeptide hormone."

1956 ● **Sir Cyril Norman Hinshelwood** (1897–1967), United Kingdom; **Nikolay Nikolaevich Semenov** (1896–1986), USSR, "for their researches into the mechanism of chemical reactions."

1957 ● **Lord** (**Alexander Robertus**) **Todd** (1907–97), United Kingdom, "for his work on nucleotides and nucleotide co-enzymes."

1958 ● **Frederick Sanger** (b. 1918) United Kingdom, "for his work on the structure of proteins, especially that of insulin."

1959 ● **Jaroslav Heyrovský** (1890–1967), Czechoslovakia, "for his discovery and development of the polarographic methods of analysis."

1960 ● **Willard Frank Libby** (1908–80), U.S., "for his method to use carbon-14 for age determination in archaeology, geology, geophysics, and other branches of science."

1961 ● **Melvin Calvin** (1911–97), U.S., "for his research on the carbon dioxide assimilation in plants."

1962 ● **Max Ferdinand Perutz** (1914–2002), United Kingdom; **John Cowdery Kendrew** (1917–97), United Kingdom, "for their studies of the structures of globular proteins."

1963 ● **Karl Ziegler** (1898–1973), Federal Republic of Germany; **Giulio Natta** (1903–79), Italy, "for their discoveries in the field of the chemistry and technology of high polymers."

1964 ● **Dorothy Crowfoot Hodgkin** (1910–94), United Kingdom, "for her determinations by X-ray techniques of the structures of important biochemical substances."

1964
Dorothy Hodgkin

1965 • **Robert Burns Woodward** (1917–79), U.S., "for his outstanding achievements in the art of organic synthesis."

1966 • **Robert Sanderson Mulliken** (1896–1986), U.S., "for his fundamental work concerning chemical bonds and the electronic structure of molecules by molecular orbital method."

1967 • **Manfred Eigen** (b. 1927), Federal Republic of Germany; **Ronald George Wreyford Norrish** (1897–1978), United Kingdom; **George Porter** (1920–2002), United Kingdom, "for their studies of extremely fast chemical reactions, effected by disturbing the equilibrium by means of very short pulses of energy."

1968 • **Lars Onsager** (1903–76), U.S., "for the discovery of the reciprocal relations bearing his name, which are fundamental for the thermodynamics of irreversible processes."

1969 • **Derek H.R. Barton** (1918–98), United Kingdom; **Odd Hassel** (1897–1981), Norway, "for their contributions to the development of the concept of conformation and its application in chemistry."

1970 • **Luis F. Leloir** (1906–87), Argentina, "for his discovery of sugar nucleotides and their role in the biosynthesis of carbohydrates."

1971 • **Gerhard Herzberg** (1904–99), Canada, "for his contributions to the knowledge of electronic structure and geometry of molecules, particularly free radicals."

1972 • **Christian B. Anfinsen** (1916–95), U.S., "for his work on ribonuclease, especially concerning the connection between the amino acid sequence and the biologically active conformation;" **Stanford Moore** (1913–82), U.S.; **William H. Stein** (1911–80), U.S., "for their contribution to the understanding of the connection between chemical structure and catalytic activity of the active center of the ribonuclease molecule."

1972
Christian B. Anfinsen

1973 ● **Ernst Otto Fischer** (b. 1918), Federal Republic of Germany; **Geoffrey Wilkinson** (1921–96), United Kingdom, "for their pioneering work, performed independently, on the chemistry of organometallic, so-called sandwich compounds."

1974 ● **Paul J. Flory** (1910–85), U.S., "for his fundamental achievements, both theoretical and experimental, in the physical chemistry of the macromolecules."

1975 ● **John Warcup Cornforth** (b. 1917), Australia and United Kingdom, "for his work in the stereochemistry of enzyme-catalyzed reactions;" **Vladimir Prelog** (1906–98), Switzerland, "for his research into the stereochemistry of organic molecules and reactions."

1976 ● **William N. Lipscomb** (b. 1919), U.S., "for his studies on the structure of boranes illuminating problems of chemical bonding."

1977 ● **Ilya Prigogine** (1917–2003), Belgium, "for his contributions to non-equilibrium thermodynamics, particularly the theory of dissipative structures."

1977
Ilya Prigogine

1978 ● **Peter D. Mitchell** (1920–92), United Kingdom, "for his contribution to the understanding of biological energy transfer through the formulation of the chemiosmotic theory."

1979 ● **Herbert C. Brown** (1912–2004), U.S.; **Georg Wittig** (1897–1987), Federal Republic of Germany, "for their development of the use of boron- and phosphorus-containing compounds, respectively, into important reagents in organic synthesis."

1980 ● **Paul Berg** (b. 1926), U.S., "for his fundamental studies of the biochemistry of nucleic acids, with particular regard to recombinant-DNA;" **Walter Gilbert** (b. 1932), U.S.; **Frederick Sanger** (b. 1918), United Kingdom, "for their contributions concerning the determination of base sequences in nucleic acids."

1981 ● **Kenichi Fukui** (1918–98), Japan; **Roald Hoffmann** (b. 1937), U.S., "for their theories, developed independently, concerning the course of chemical reactions."

1982 ● **Aaron Klug** (b. 1926), United Kingdom, "for his development of crystallographic electron microscopy and his structural elucidation of biologically important nucleic acid-protein complexes."

1983 ● **Henry Taube** (1915–2005), U.S., "for his work on the mechanisms of electron transfer reactions, especially in metal complexes."

1983
Henry Taube

1984 ● **Robert Bruce Merrifield** (b. 1921), U.S., "for his development of methodology for chemical synthesis on a solid matrix."

1985 ● **Herbert A. Hauptman** (b. 1917), U.S.; **Jerome Karle** (b. 1918), U.S., "for their outstanding achievements in the development of direct methods for the determination of crystal structures."

1986 ● **Dudley R. Herschbach** (b. 1932), U.S.; **Yuan T. Lee** (b. 1936), U.S.; **John Charles Polanyi** (b. 1929), Canada, "for their contributions concerning the dynamics of chemical elementary processes."

1987 ● **Donald J. Cram** (1919–2001), U.S.; **Jean-Marie Lehn** (b. 1939), France; **Charles J. Pedersen** (1904–1989), U.S., "for their development and use of molecules with structure-specific interactions of high selectivity."

1988 ● **Johann Deisenhofer** (b. 1943), Federal Republic of Germany; **Robert Huber** (b. 1937), Federal Republic of Germany; **Hartmut Michel** (b. 1948), Federal Republic of Germany, "for the determination of the three-dimensional structure of a photosynthetic reaction center."

1989 ● **Sidney Altman** (b. 1939), Canada and U.S.; **Thomas R. Cech** (b. 1947), U.S., "for their discovery of catalytic properties of RNA."

1990 ● **Elias James Corey** (b. 1928), U.S., "for his development of the theory and methodology of organic synthesis."

1991 ● **Richard R. Ernst** (b. 1933), Switzerland, "for his contributions to the development of the methodology of high resolution nuclear magnetic resonance (NMR) spectroscopy."

1992 ● **Rudolph A. Marcus** (b. 1923), U.S., "for his contributions to the theory of electron transfer reactions in chemical systems."

1993 ● **Kary B. Mullis** (b. 1944), U.S., "for his invention of the polymerase chain reaction (PCR) method;" **Michael Smith** (1932–2000), Canada, "for his fundamental contributions to the establishment of oligonucleotide-based, site-directed mutagenesis and its development for protein studies."

1994 ● **George A. Olah** (b. 1927), U.S., "for his contribution to carbocation chemistry."

1995 ● **Paul J. Crutzen** (b. 1933), the Netherlands; **Mario J. Molina** (b. 1943), U.S.; **F. Sherwood Rowland** (b. 1927), U.S., "for their work in atmospheric chemistry, particularly concerning the formation and decomposition of ozone."

1996 ● **Robert F. Curl, Jr.** (b. 1933), U.S.; **Sir Harold W. Kroto** (b. 1939), Great Britain; **Richard E. Smalley** (1943–2005), U.S., "for their discovery of fullerenes."

1997 ● **Paul D. Boyer** (b. 1918) U.S.; **John E. Walker** (b. 1941), United Kingdom; "for their elucidation of the enzymatic mechanism underlying the synthesis of adenosine triphosphate (ATP);" **Jens C. Skou** (b. 1918), Denmark, "for the first discovery of an ion-transporting enzyme, Na+, K+-ATPase."

1998 ● **Walter Kohn** (b. 1923) U.S., "for his development of the density-functional theory;" **John A. Pople** (1925–2004), United Kingdom, "for his development of computational methods in quantum chemistry."

1995
Paul J. Crutzen

1999   ● **Ahmed H. Zewail** (b. 1946), Egypt and U.S., "for his studies of the transition states of chemical reactions using femtosecond spectroscopy."

2000   ● **Alan J. Heeger** (b. 1936), U.S.; **Alan G. MacDiarmid** (b. 1927), U.S. and New Zealand; **Hideki Shirakawa** (b. 1936), Japan, "for the discovery and development of conductive polymers."

2001   ● **William S. Knowles** (b. 1917), U.S.; **Ryoji Noyori** (b. 1938), Japan, "for their work on chirally catalysed hydrogenation reactions;" **K. Barry Sharpless** (b. 1941), U.S., "for his work on chirally catalysed oxidation reactions."

2002   ● **John B. Fenn** (b. 1917), U.S.; **Koichi Tanaka** (b. 1959), Japan, "for their development of soft desorption ionization methods for mass spectrometric analyses of biological macromolecules;" **Kurt Wüthrich** (b. 1938), Switzerland, "for his development of nuclear magnetic resonance spectroscopy for determining the three-dimensional structure of biological macromolecules in solution."

2003   ● **Peter Courtland Agre** (b. 1949), U.S., "for the discovery of water channels [in cell membranes];" **Roderick McKinnon** (b. 1956), U.S., "for structural and mechanistic studies of ion channels [in cell membranes]."

2004   ● **Aaron Ciechanover** (b. 1947), Israel; **Avram Hershko** (b. 1937), Israel; **Irwin Rose** (b. 1926), U.S., "for the discovery of ubiquitin-mediated protein degradation."

2005   ● **Yves Chauvin**, France (b. 1930); **Robert H. Grubbs**, U.S. (b. 1942); **Richard R. Schrock**, U.S. (b. 1945), "for the development of the metathesis method in organic synthesis."

2003
Peter C. Agre

SECTION SIX
SIX
CHARTS & TABLES

Elements

In the following table elements are listed by letter symbol. The list includes the atomic number, element name, and the atomic weight of each element.

* indicates the atomic weight of the isotope with the lowest known half-life.

Periodic table of the elements

Letter symbol	Atomic number	Name	Atomic weight
Ac	89	actinium	227.0278*
Ag	47	silver	107.868
Al	13	aluminum	26.98154
Am	95	americium	243.0614*
Ar	18	argon	39.948
As	33	arsenic	74.9216
At	85	astatine	209.987*
Au	79	gold	196.9665
B	5	boron	10.81
Ba	56	barium	137.33
Be	4	beryllium	9.0128
Bh	107	bohrium	264
Bk	97	berkelium	247.0703*
Bi	83	bismuth	208.9804
Br	35	bromine	79.904
C	6	carbon	12.011
Ca	20	calcium	40.08
Cd	48	cadmium	112.41
Ce	58	cerium	140.12
Cf	98	californium	251.0796*
Cl	17	chlorine	35.453
Cm	96	curium	247.0703*
Co	27	cobalt	58.9332
Cr	24	chromium	51.996
Cs	55	cesium	132.9054
Cu	29	copper	63.546
Db	105	dubnium	262
Ds	110	darmstadtium	271
Dy	66	dysprosium	162.5
Er	68	erbium	167.26
Es	99	einsteinium	254.088*
Eu	63	europium	151.96
F	9	fluorine	18.9984
Fe	26	iron	55.847
Fm	100	fermium	257.0951*
Fr	87	francium	223.0197*
Ga	31	gallium	69.72
Gd	64	gadolinium	157.25
Ge	32	germanium	72.59
H	1	hydrogen	1.0079
He	2	helium	4.0026
Hf	72	hafnium	178.49
Hg	80	mercury	200.59
Ho	67	holmium	164.9304
Hs	108	hassium	269
I	53	iodine	126.9045
In	49	indium	114.82
Ir	77	iridium	192.22
K	19	potassium	39.0983
Kr	36	krypton	83.8
La	57	lanthanum	138.9055
Li	3	lithium	6.941
Lr	103	lawrencium	260.105*
Lu	71	lutetium	174.967
Md	101	mendelevium	258.099*
Mg	12	magnesium	24.305
Mn	25	manganese	54.938
Mo	42	molybdenum	95.94
Mt	109	meitnerium	268
N	7	nitrogen	14.0067
Na	11	sodium	22.98977
Nb	41	niobium	92.9064
Nd	60	neodymium	144.24
Ne	10	neon	20.179
Ni	28	nickel	58.69
No	102	nobelium	259.101*
Np	93	neptunium	237.0482*
O	8	oxygen	15.9994
Os	76	osmium	190.2
P	15	phosphorus	30.97376
Pa	91	protoactinium	231.0359
Pb	82	lead	207.19
Pd	46	palladium	106.42
Pm	61	promethium	144.9128*
Po	84	polonium	208.9824*
Pr	59	praseodymium	140.9077
Pt	78	platinum	195.08
Pu	94	plutonium	244.0642*
Ra	88	radium	226.0254*
Rb	37	rubidium	85.4678
Re	75	rhenium	186.207
Rf	104	rutherfordium	261
Rg	111	roentgenium	272
Rh	45	rhodium	102.9055
Rn	86	radon	222.0176*
Ru	44	ruthenium	101.07
S	16	sulfur	32.064
Sb	51	antimony	121.75
Sc	21	scandium	44.9559
Se	34	selenium	78.96
Sg	106	seaborgium	266
Si	14	silicon	28.0855
Sm	62	samarium	150.36
Sn	50	tin	118.69
Sr	38	strontium	87.62
Ta	73	tantalum	180.9479
Tb	65	terbium	158.9254
Tc	43	technetium	96.9064*
Te	52	tellurium	127.6
Th	90	thorium	232.0381
Ti	22	titanium	47.88
Tl	81	thallium	204.383
Tm	69	thulium	168.9342
U	92	uranium	238.029*
Uub	112	ununbium	285
Uuh	116	ununhexium	292
Uup	115	ununpentium	288
Uuq	114	ununquadium	289
Uut	113	ununtrium	284
V	23	vanadium	50.9415
W	74	tungsten	183.85
Xe	54	xenon	131.29
Y	39	yttrium	88.9059
Yb	70	ytterbium	173.04
Zn	30	zinc	65.381
Zr	40	zirconium	91.224

Elements by groups

A Group 4 element

A The eight groups read downward.
B The groups rank elements by number of electrons (**a**) in an atom's outer shell (**b**): Group 1, one electron; Group 2, two electrons, and so on through Group 8. Elements with the same number of outer shell electrons share similar properties. (Note: hydrogen fits no group, and helium,

although in Group 8, has only two electrons.)
Group 1 Alkali metals, the sodium family, with one electron in the outer shell. These are similar, very active metals.
Group 2 Alkaline-earth metals, the calcium family, with two electrons in the outer shell.
Group 3 Nonmetallic through metallic

elements, with increasingly complex atoms. All have three electrons in the outer shell, and stable inner shells.
Group 4 Nonmetallic through metallic elements, also with increasingly complex atoms. All have four electrons in the outer shell, and stable inner shells.
Group 5 The nitrogen family—from nonmetallic nitrogen and phosphorus to metallic bismuth. All have five electrons in the outer shell, and stable inner shells.
Group 6 The oxygen family—from oxygen to metallic polonium. All have six electrons in the outer shell, and stable inner shells.
Group 7 The halogen family of active nonmetals. All have seven electrons in the outer shell, and stable inner shells.
Group 8 The inert gases. None chemically combines with any element. All (except helium) have eight electrons in the outer shell.

Electron arrangement of atoms

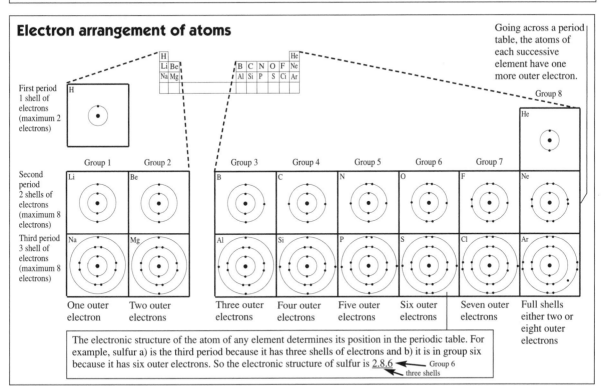

Going across a periodic table, the atoms of each successive element have one more outer electron.

First period 1 shell of electrons (maximum 2 electrons)

Second period 2 shells of electrons (maximum 8 electrons)

Third period 3 shell of electrons (maximum 8 electrons)

| Group 1 | Group 2 | Group 3 | Group 4 | Group 5 | Group 6 | Group 7 | Group 8 |
| One outer electron | Two outer electrons | Three outer electrons | Four outer electrons | Five outer electrons | Six outer electrons | Seven outer electrons | Full shells either two or eight outer electrons |

The electronic structure of the atom of any element determines its position in the periodic table. For example, sulfur a) is the third period because it has three shells of electrons and b) it is in group six because it has six outer electrons. So the electronic structure of sulfur is 2.8.6 ← Group 6
three shells

Discovery of the elements

Element	Date	Discovered by
Actinium	1899	André-Louis Debierne (France)
Aluminum	1825	Hans Christian Ørsted (Denmark)
Americium	1944	Glenn Seaborg (U.S.), Ralph James (U.S.), Leon Morgan (U.S.), and Albert Ghiorso (U.S.).
Antimony	ancient	unknown
Argon	1894	Lord Rayleigh (U.K.) and William Ramsay (U.K.)
Arsenic	ca. 1250	Albertus Magnus (Germany)
Astatine	1940	Dale R. Corson (U.S.), Emilio Segrè (U.S.), and K.R. Mackenzie (U.S.)
Barium	1808	Humphry Davy (U.K.)
Berkelium	1949	Glenn Seaborg (U.S.), Stanley Thompson (U.S.), and Albert Ghiorso (U.S.)
Beryllium	1798	Louis-Nicolas Vauquelin (France)
Bismuth	ca. 1400	unknown
Bohrium	1981	Gesellschaft für Schwerionenforschung [GSI] (Germany); Yuri Oganessian and colleagues at the Joint Institute for Nuclear Research [JINR] (USSR)
Boron	1808	Humphry Davy (U.K.); Joseph-Louis Gay-Lussac (France) and Louis-Jacques Thénard (France)
Bromine	1826	Antoine-Jérôme Balard (France)
Cadmium	1817	Friedrich Strohmeyer (Germany)
Calcium	1808	Humphry Davy (U.K.)
Californium	1950	Glenn Seaborg (U.S.), Albert Ghiorso (U.S.), Stanley Thompson (U.S.), and Kenneth Street (U.S.)
Carbon	ancient	unknown
Cerium	1803	Jöns Jakob Berzelius (Sweden) and Wilhelm Hisinger (Sweden); Martin Klaproth (Germany)
Cesium	1860	Robert Bunsen (Germany) and Gustav Kirchhoff (Germany)

Element	Date	Discovered by
Chlorine	1810	Humphry Davy (U.K.)
Chromium	1798	Louis-Nicolas Vauquelin (France)
Cobalt	1735	Georg Brandt (Sweden)
Copper	ancient	unknown
Curium	1944	Glenn Seaborg (U.S.), Albert Ghiorso (U.S.), and Ralph James (U.S.)
Darmstadtium	1994	Peter Armbruster and colleagues at the GSI (Germany)
Dubnium	1967	Albert Ghiorso and colleagues at the Lawrence Berkeley National Laboratory [LBNL] (U.S.); Georgy Flerov and colleagues at the JINR (USSR)
Dysprosium	1886	Paul-Émile Lecoq de Boisbaudran (France)
Einsteinium	1952	Albert Ghiorso (U.S.), Stanley Thompson (U.S.), Gregory Choppin (U.S.), and Glenn Seaborg (U.S.).
Erbium	1843	Carl Gustaf Mosander (Sweden)
Europium	1901	Eugène Demarçay (France)
Fermium	1952	Albert Ghiorso (U.S.), Gregory Choppin (U.S.), Stanley Thompson (U.S.), and Bernard Harvey (U.S.)
Fluorine	1886	Henri Moissan (France)
Francium	1939	Marguerite Perey
Gadolinium	1880	Jean-Charles de Marignac (Switzerland)
Gallium	1875	Paul-Émile Lecoq de Boisbaudran (France)
Germanium	1886	Clemens Winkler (Germany)
Gold	ancient	unknown
Hafnium	1923	Dirk Coster (the Netherlands) and Georg von Hevesy (Hungary)
Hassium	1984	Peter Armbruster, Gottfried Münzenberg and colleagues at the GSI (Germany)
Helium	1868	Pierre Janssen (France); Joseph Norman Lockyer
Holmium	1878	Marc Delafontaine (Switzerland) and Jacques-Louis Soret (Switzerland); Per Theodor Cleve (Sweden)
Hydrogen	1766	Henry Cavendish (U.K.)

Element	Date	Discovered by
Indium	1863	Ferdinand Reich (Germany) and Theodor Richter (Germany)
Iodine	1811	Bernard Courtois (France)
Iridium	1803	Smithson Tennant (U.K.)
Iron	ancient	unknown
Krypton	1898	William Ramsay (U.K.) and Morris Travers (U.K.)
Lanthanum	1839	Carl Gustaf Mosander (Sweden)
Lawrencium	1961	Albert Ghiorso (U.S.), Torbjørn Sikkeland (U.S.), Almon Larsh (U.S.), and Robert Latimer (U.S.)
Lead	ancient	unknown
Lithium	1817	Johan August Arfvedson (Sweden)
Lutetium	1907	Georges Urbain (France)
Magnesium	1755	Joseph Black (U.K.)
Manganese	1774	Johan Gottlieb Gahn (Sweden)
Meitnerium	1982	Peter Armbruster, Gottfried Münzenberg and colleagues at the GSI (Germany)
Mendelevium	1955	Albert Ghiorso (U.S.), Bernard Harvey (U.S.), Gregory Choppin (U.S.), Stanley Thompson (U.S.), and Glenn Seaborg (U.S.)
Mercury	ancient	unknown
Molybdenum	1781	Peter Jacob Hjelm (Sweden)
Neodymium	1885	Carl Auer (Austria)
Neon	1898	William Ramsay (U.K.) and Morris Travers (U.K.)
Neptunium	1940	Edwin McMillan (U.S.) and Philip Abelson (U.S.)
Nickel	1751	Axel Cronstedt (Sweden)
Niobium	1801	Charles Hatchett (U.K.)
Nitrogen	1772	Daniel Rutherford (U.K.); Joseph Priestley (U.K.)
Nobelium	1958	Albert Ghiorso (U.S.), Torbjørn Sikkeland (U.S.), John Walton (U.S.), and Glenn Seaborg (U.S.)
Osmium	1803	Smithson Tennant (U.K.)
Oxygen	1772	Carl Scheele (Sweden)

Element	Date	Discovered by
Palladium	1803	William Hyde Wollaston (U.K.)
Phosphorus	1669	Hennig Brand (Germany)
Platinum	pre 1700	unknown (South America)
Plutonium	1940	Glenn Seaborg (U.S.), Arthur Wahl (U.S.), and Joseph Kennedy (U.S.)
Polonium	1898	Marie and Pierre Curie (France)
Potassium	1807	Humphry Davy (U.K.)
Praseodymium	1885	Carl Auer (Austria)
Promethium	1945	Jacob Marinsky (U.S.), Lawrence Glendenin (U.S.), and Charles Coryell (U.S.)
Protactinium	1917	Lise Meitner (Austria) and Otto Hahn (Germany); Frederick Soddy (U.K.) and John Cranston (U.K.)
Radium	1898	Pierre and Marie Curie (France)
Radon	1900	Friedrich Dorn (Germany)
Rhenium	1925	Walter Noddack (Germany), Ida Tacke (Germany), and Otto Berg (Germany)
Rhodium	1803	William Hyde Wollaston (U.K.)
Roentgenium	1994	Peter Armbruster and colleagues at the GSI (Germany)
Rubidium	1861	Robert Bunsen (Germany) and Gustav Kirchhoff (Germany)
Ruthenium	1808	Jedrzej Sniadecki (Poland)
Rutherfordium	1964/1969	Georgy Flerov and colleagues at the JINR (USSR); Albert Ghiorso and colleagues at the LBNL (U.S.)
Samarium	1879	Paul-Émile Lecoq de Boisbaudran (France)
Scandium	1879	Lars Fredrik Nilson (Sweden)
Seaborgium	1974	Georgy Flerov, Yuri Oganessian and colleagues at the JINR (USSR)
Selenium	1817	Jöns Jakob Berzelius (Sweden)
Silicon	1824	Jöns Jakob Berzelius (Sweden)
Silver	ancient	unknown
Sodium	1807	Humphry Davy (U.K.)
Strontium	1790	Adair Crawford (U.K.)

Discovery of the elements: Palladium – Strontium **CHARTS & TABLES**

Element	Date	Discovered by
Sulfur	ancient	unknown
Tantalum	1802	Anders Ekeberg (Sweden)
Technetium	1925	Walter Noddack (Germany), Ida Tacke (Germany), and Otto Berg (Germany)
Tellurium	1783	Franz Joseph Müller (Austria)
Terbium	1843	Carl Gustaf Mosander (Sweden)
Thallium	1861	William Crookes (U.K.)
Thorium	1829	Jöns Jakob Berzelius (Sweden)
Thulium	1879	Per Theodor Cleve (Sweden)
Tin	ancient	unknown
Titanium	1791	William Gregor (U.K.)
Tungsten	1783	José and Fausto d'Elhuyar y de Suvisa (Spain)
Ununbium	1996	Peter Armbruster, Sigurd Hofmann and colleagues at the GSI (Germany)
Ununhexium	1999	Kenneth Gregorich, Victor Ninov and colleagues at the LBNL (U.S.)
Ununoctium	-	NOT YET OBSERVED a claim was made in 1999 but later retracted
Ununpentium	2004	Scientists at the LBNL (U.S.) and the JINR (Russia); not yet ratified
Ununquadium	1998	Yuri Oganessian, Vladimir Utyonkov and colleagues at the JINR (Russia)
Ununseptium	-	NOT YET OBSERVED
Ununtrium	2004	Scientists at the LBNL (U.S.) and the JINR (Russia); not yet ratified
Uranium	1789	Martin Klaproth (Germany)
Vanadium	1801/1830	Andrés Manuel del Rio (Mexico); Nils Gabriel Sefström (Sweden)
Xenon	1898	William Ramsay (U.K.) and Morris Travers (U.K.)
Ytterbium	1878	Jean-Charles de Marignac (Switzerland)
Yttrium	1794	Johan Gadolin (Finland)
Zinc	ca. 1200	unknown (India)
Zirconium	1789	Martin Klaproth (Germany)

Metals and alloys

All but 25 of the known elements are metals. Metals are elements whose atoms can lose one or more electrons to form electrically positive ions. Most metals are good conductors of heat and electricity. They are malleable (can be beaten or rolled into a new shape) and ductile (can be pulled out into long wires). All metals are shiny, crystalline solids, except mercury, which is a liquid.

Activity series

Some metals form positive ions more easily than others, and so are more chemically active. Sixteen common metals are listed in the order of their activity. Lithium is the most active of all the metals, and gold is the least active.

Native metals

Only four of the least active metals – copper, silver, platinum, and gold – commonly occur in the Earth's crust as native metals (i.e. as free elements). All the others are found in compounds, called ores, which must be chemically treated to obtain the pure element.

Metalloids

These elements are "halfway" between metals and nonmetals. Depending on the way they are treated, they can act as insulators like nonmetals or conduct electricity like metals. This makes several metalloids extremely important as semiconductors in computers and other electronic devices. The eight metalloid elements are boron, silicon, germanium, arsenic, antimony, tellurium, polonium, and astatine.

Most active

Lithium
Potassium
Calcium
Sodium
Magnesium
Aluminum
Zinc
Chromium
Iron
Nickel
Tin
Lead
Copper
Silver
Platinum
Gold

Least active

Alloys

An alloy is a mixture of two or more metals. Here we list some everyday alloys, the metals from which they are made, and examples of their use.

Alloy	Metals	Examples of use
Bronze	copper, tin	"copper" coins
Brass	copper, zinc	doorhandles, buttons
Cupronickel	copper, nickel	"silver" coins
Pewter	tin, lead	tankards
Stainless steel	iron, chromium, nickel	cutlery, pots, etc.
Sterling silver	silver, copper	jewelry
9, 18, and 22 carat gold	gold, silver, copper	jewelry
Dental amalgam	silver, tin, copper, zinc, mercury	filling cavities in teeth
Solder	lead, tin	joining metals

Chemical reaction types

In a chemical reaction, molecules of a substance gain or lose atoms or atoms are rearranged. There are four main kinds of chemical reaction.

1 Combination: Two or more substances combine, forming a compound

2 Decomposition: A chemical compound breaks up into simpler substances

3 Replacement (substitution): A compound loses one or more atoms but gains other atoms instead

4 Double decomposition (double replacement): Two compounds decompose, exchanging atoms to form two new compounds

1

2

3

4

Biochemical cycles

Oxygen cycle Oxygen plays a vital part in the respiration of animals and plants.
1 Oxygen in air
2 Oxygen breathed in by animals
3 Carbon dioxide (a carbon-oxygen compound) breathed out by living things as waste
4 Carbon dioxide absorbed by plants and used in photosynthesis to make carbohydrate foods
5 Surplus oxygen released into the air by plants as waste

Carbon cycle Plant material is a valuable source of carbon. Oxidizing carbon compounds provide energy for animals and plants.
1 Carbon dioxide (a carbon-oxygen compound) in air
2 Carbon dioxide absorbed by plants for making food
3 Plants eaten by animals
4 Carbon dioxide waste breathed out by animals and plants
5 Dead organisms broken down by bacteria
6 These give off carbon dioxide waste
7 Remains of long-dead plants and microscopic organisms forming hydrocarbon fossil fuels: coal, oil, and gas
8 Carbon dioxide released back into the air by burning fossil fuels

Nitrogen cycle As an ingredient in proteins and nucleic acids, nitrogen is vital to all living things.
1 Nitrogen in air
2 Atmospheric nitrogen trapped by some plants' roots
3 Nitrogen used by plants for making proteins
4 Plant proteins eaten by animals
5 Proteins in dead organisms and body wastes converted to ammonia by bacteria and fungi
6 Ammonia converted to nitrate by other bacteria
7 Nitrate taken up by plant roots

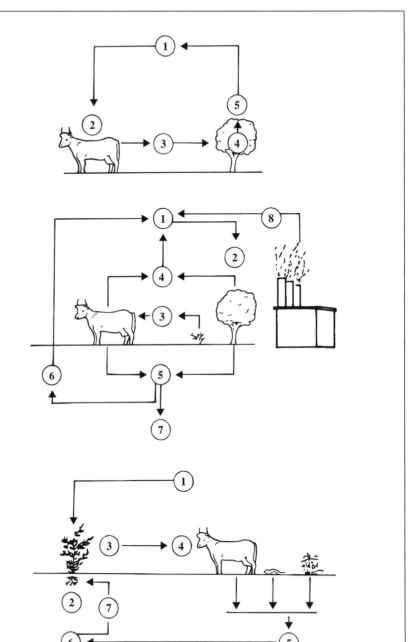

Sulfur cycle Sulfur is in two of the 20 amino acids that are used by the body to make proteins.
1 Sulfates (sulfur-oxygen compounds) absorbed by plant roots
2 The oxygen in the sulfate is replaced by hydrogen in a plant process that produces certain amino acids
3 Plants eaten by animals
4 Sulfur-containing amino acids of dead plants and animals broken down to hydrogen sulfide (which gives off a rotten egg odor) by decomposer microorganisms
5 Sulfur extracted from sulfides by bacteria
6 Other bacteria combine sulfur with oxygen, producing sulfates

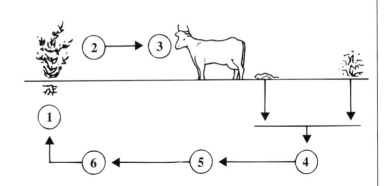

Phosphorus cycle Phosphorus is a vital ingredient of proteins, nucleic acids, and some other compounds found in living things.
1 Phosphates (compounds of phosphorus, hydrogen, and oxygen) absorbed by plant roots
2 Phosphates used by plants in making organic phosphorus compounds
3 Plants eaten by animals
4 Compounds in dead plants and animals broken down to phosphates by microorganisms

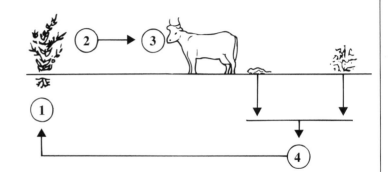

Krebs cycle The Krebs or citric acid cycle is the second stage of aerobic respiration in which living things produce energy from foods. It requires oxygen; enzymes (proteins that promote but are not used up in chemical changes) create successive compounds, thus transforming pyruvate to carbon dioxide and water and releasing energy.
1 Acetic acid combines with . . .
2 Oxaloacetic acid to form . . .
3 Citric acid. Later changes produce . . .
4 Aconitic acid
5 Isocitric acid
6 Ketoglutaric acid
7 Succinic acid, carbon dioxide, and energy-rich ATP (adenosine triphosphate)
8 Fumaric acid
9 Malic acid

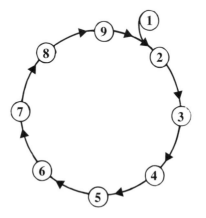

Hydrocarbons

ALKENES These contain only carbon and hydrogen. There are four main types: Alkenes, Alkanes, Alkynes, and Aromatic hydrocarbons. Contain double bonds between carbon atoms.

Name	Molecular formula	Structural formula
Ethene	C_2H_4 or $CH_2=CH_2$	
Propene	C_3H_6 or $CH_3CH=CH_2$	
Butene	C_4H_8 or $CH_3CH_2CH=CH_2$ or $CH_3CH=CHCH_3$	

ALKYNES Contain triple bonds between carbon atoms.

Name	Molecular formula	Structural formula
Ethyne	C_2H_2	
Propyne	C_3H_4	
Butyne	C_4H_6	

ALKANES Contain only single bonds.

Name	Molecular formula	Structural formula
Methane	CH_4	
Ethane	C_2H_6 or CH_3CH_3	
Propane	C_3H_8 or $CH_3CH_2CH_3$	
Butane	C_4H_{10} or $CH_3CH_2CH_2CH_3$	
Pentane	C_5H_{12} or $CH_3CH_2CH_2CH_2CH_3$	

AROMATIC HYDROCARBONS Have six-sided rings with alternating double and single bonds.

Name	Molecular formula	Structural formula
Benzene	C_6H_6	
Toluene	$C_6H_5CH_3$	
Naphthalene	$C_{10}H_8$	

Isomers

These are compounds with the same molecular formula but different structural formulas.

H   H   H   H
| | | |
H–C –C –C – C–H
| | | |
H   H   H   H

Butane

H   H   H
| | |
H–C – C – C–H
| | |
H   H–C–H   H
        |
        H

2 – methylopropane

Structural isomers of the hydrocarbon C_4H_{10}

Cl   Cl
  \   /
    C = C
  /   \
H   H

Cis – 1, 2 dichloroethane

Cl   H
  \   /
    C = C
  /   \
H   Cl

Trans – 1,2 – dichloroethane

Cis-trans isomers differing in arrangement about a double bond

---

H   H
| |
H –C – C – OH
| |
H   H

Ethanol

H   H
| |
H–C– O –C–H
| |
H   H

Dimethyl ether

Structural isomers differing in functional groups

Cis

Trans

Cis-trans isomers differing in arrangement about a single bond with restricted rotation

---

H   H   H
| | |
H – C – C – C – OH
| | |
H   H   H

Propan-1-ol

H   H   H
| | |
H–C – C – C–H
| | |
H   O   H
    |
    H

Propan-2-ol

Structural isomers differing in the position of the functional group

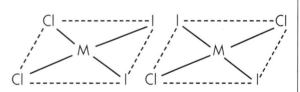

Cis

Trans

Cis-trans isomers differing in a planar metal complex

Polymers

Polymers
These are very large, usually long-chain, molecules made by linking together numbers of small molecules called monomers.

$$n\,A \rightarrow -A-A-A-A$$

Monomers   Polymer

Natural Polymers
These occur in all plants and animals.

Carbohydrates
In carbohydrates glucose is linked to make starch or cellulose.

Proteins Amino acids link to make up proteins

$$n\;NH_2\,CHCOOH \rightarrow$$

Synthetic polymers
Many different types exist.

Polyethene

Polypropene

Polyvinyl chloride

Chemicals from oil

Gases
(bottled gas)

104°F
(40°C)

Petrol
(car fuel)

Kerosene
(jet fuel)

Diesel
(truck, bus fuel)

Light oil
(lubricants)

Fuel oil
(heating oil)

Wax
(candles)

Bitumen
(road surfaces)

Decreasing boiling point

752°F
(400°C)

Crude oil (petroleum) is a valuable fossil fuel. It is formed from the remains of marine organisms. Oil is a mixture of hydrocarbons, which are separated in a refinery by distillation. The oil separates into fractions, which have mixtures of hydrocarbons with similar boiling points.

Fractional distillation takes place in a fractionating column, which separates the crude oil. The fractions are used for:
● fuels
● lubricants
● sources of other chemicals

Water as a solvent

Water can dissolve a greater range of substances, in greater amounts, than any other common liquid. Its dissolving power is related to its small molecular size and to the water molecule's polar nature.

● Polar and ionic substances tend to be soluble in water; covalent substances are generally less soluble in water.
● A crystal of sodium chloride dissolves readily in water because positively charged sodium ions tend to

be pulled into solution by the slightly negatively charged oxygen atoms of water molecules.
● Negatively charged chloride ions are pulled into solution by the hydrogen atoms in water with a slight positive charge.

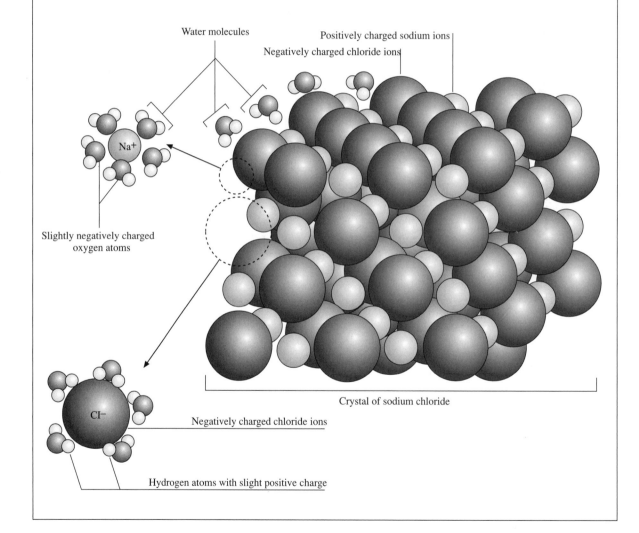

Water molecules

Positively charged sodium ions

Negatively charged chloride ions

Na+

Slightly negatively charged oxygen atoms

Crystal of sodium chloride

Cl−

Negatively charged chloride ions

Hydrogen atoms with slight positive charge

SECTION SEVEN
SEVEN
ASSOCIATIONS

CHEMISTRY

American Association for Clinical Chemistry
International society of clinical laboratory professionals, physicians, and research scientists involved with clinical chemistry and related disciplines.
> 2101 L St., N.W., Washington, DC 20037
> Tel. 202-857-0717; 800-892-1400
> http://www.aacc.org

American Chemical Society
Member organization promoting scholarly knowledge and providing professional services and support in all fields of chemistry.
> 1155 16th St., N.W., Washington, DC 20036
> Tel. 202-872-4600; 800-227-5558
> http://www.acs.org/

American Chemistry Council
Organization representing chemical businesses.
> 1300 Wilson Blvd., Arlington, VA 22209
> Tel. 703-741-5000
> http://www.americanchemistry.com/

American Crystallographic Association
Group dedicated to "the study of the arrangement of the atoms in matter, its causes, its nature and its consequence, and of the tools and methods used in such studies."
> PO Box 96, Ellicott Station, Buffalo, NY 14205
> Tel. 716-898-8690
> http://www.hwi.buffalo.edu/ACA/

American Institute of Chemical Engineers
Professional organization "fostering chemical engineering knowledge, supporting the professional and personal growth of its members, and applying the expertise of its members to address societal needs throughout the world."
> 3 Park Ave., New York, NY 10016
> Tel. 212-591-8100; 800-242-4363
> http://www.aiche.org/

American Institute of Chemists
Association representing the professional interests of chemists and chemical engineers and promoting the advancement of chemical professions in the U.S..

> 315 Chestnut St. , Philadelphia, PA 19106
> Tel. 215-873-8224
> http://www.theaic.org/

American Microchemical Society
Nonprofit society formed to encourage the advancement of microchemistry in its broadest sense.
> c/o Herk Felder, 2 June Way, Middlesex, NJ 08846
> http://www.microchem.org/

American Nuclear Society
Nonprofit organization established to unify the professional activities within the diverse fields of nuclear science and technology.
> 555 N. Kensington Ave., La Grange Park, IL 60526
> Tel. 708-352-6611
> http://www.ans.org/

American Society for Biochemistry and Molecular Biology (ASBMB)
Society formed to advance the science of biochemistry and molecular biology through scholarship, advocacy, support of science education at all levels, and encouragement of diversity of individuals entering the scientific workforce.
> 9650 Rockville Pike, Bethesda, MD 20814
> Tel. 301-634-7145
> http://www.asbmb.org/ASBMB/site.nsf?Open

American Society for Mass Spectrometry
Professional organization formed to promote and disseminate knowledge of mass spectrometry and allied topics.
> 2019 Galisteo Street, Santa Fe, NM 87505
> Tel. 505-989-4517
> http://www.asms.org/

American Society for Neurochemistry
Society formed to advance and promote the science of neurochemistry and related neurosciences through scientific meetings, seminars, publications, and related activities.
> 9037 Ron Den Lane, Windermere, FL 34786
> Tel. 407-876-0750
> http://www.asneurochem.org/

AOAC International (formerly Association of Official Analytical Chemists)

Organization "committed to be a proactive, worldwide provider and facilitator in the development, use, and harmonization of validated analytical methods and laboratory quality assurance programs."

> 481 North Frederick Ave., Gaithersburg, MD 20877
> Tel. 301-924-7077; 800-379-2622
> http://www.aoac.org/

Chemical Heritage Foundation

Organization dedicated to preserving and sharing the history and heritage of the chemical and molecular sciences, technologies, and allied industries.

> 315 Chestnut St., Philadelphia, PA 19106
> Tel. 215-925-2222
> http://www.chemheritage.org/

The Electrochemical Society, Inc.

The leading society for solid-state and electrochemical science and technology.

> 65 South Main St., Pennington, NJ 08534
> Tel. 609-737-1902
> http://www.electrochem.org/

The Federation of Analytical Chemistry and Spectroscopy Societies

Federation of professional societies representing 9,000 analytical chemists and spectroscopists.

> PO Box 24379, Santa Fe, NM 87502
> Tel. 505-820-1648
> http://www.facss.org

Geochemical Society

Professional society founded to "encourage the application of chemistry to the solution of geological and cosmological problems."

> Department of Earth and Planetary Science, Washington University, One Brookings Dr., St. Louis, MO 63130
> Tel. 314-935-4131
> http://gs.wustl.edu/

Institute for Sustainability

Organization of chemical engineers formed to "develop and implement cost-effective technologies, processes, and practices needed to meet global societal and marketplace challenges."

> 3 Park Ave., New York, NY 10016
> Tel. 212-591-7462; 800-242-4363
> http://www.aiche.org/IFS/index.aspx

International Association of Environmental Analytical Chemistry

Professional association formed to promote environmental analytical chemistry and its use in assessing the impact of substances on the environment.

> c/o Marianne Frei-Hausler, Allschwill 2, Postfach 46, CH-4123 Allschwill, Switzerland
> Tel. 41-61-4812789
> http://www.iaeac.ch/

International Society of Chemical Ecology

Organization formed to promote "the understanding of interactions between organisms and their environment that are mediated by naturally occurring chemicals."

> c/o Dr. Stephen Foster, Dept. of Entomology, North Dakota State University, Fargo, ND 58105
> Tel. 701-231-6444
> http://www.chemecol.org

International Union of Pure and Applied Chemistry

The authority on chemical terminology, measurement, and other evaluated data.

> IUPAC Secretariat, PO Box 13757, Research Triangle Park, NC 27709
> Tel. 919-485-8700
> http://www.iupac.org/

National Organization for the Professional Advancement of Black Chemists and Chemical Engineers

Organization dedicated to increasing the number of minorities in science and engineering through diverse programs designed to foster professional development and encourage students to pursue careers in science and technical fields.

> PO Box 77040, Washington, DC 20013
> Tel. 202-667-1699; 800-776-1419
> http://www.nobcche.org/

Society for Applied Spectroscopy

Professional organization formed to disseminate knowledge and information on spectroscopy and other allied sciences.

> 201 B Broadway St., Frederick, MD 21701
> Tel. 301-694-8122
> http://www.s-a-s.org/

Society of Environmental Toxicology and Chemistry

Society promoting the development of principles and practices leading to sustainable environmental policy and research on contaminants and other stressors in the environment.

> 1010 North 12th Ave., Pensacola, FL 32501
> Tel. 850-469-1500
> http://www.setac.org/

Society of Toxicology

Society formed to advance the science and application of toxicology in order to enhance human and environmental health.

> 1821 Michael Faraday Dr., Reston, VA 20190
> Tel. 703-438-3115
> http://www.toxicology.org/

GENERAL SCIENTIFIC

American Association for the Advancement of Science (AAAS)

Organization formed to "further the work of scientists; facilitate cooperation among them; foster scientific freedom and responsibility; improve the effectiveness of science in the promotion of human welfare; advance education in science; and increase the public's understanding and appreciation of the promise of scientific methods in human progress."

> 1200 New York Ave., N.W., Washington, DC 20005
> Tel. 202-326-6400
> http://www.aaas.org/

Association of Science–Technology Centers

Organization of science centers and museums dedicated to "furthering the public understanding of science among increasingly diverse audiences."

> 1025 Vermont Ave., N.W., Washington, DC 20005
> Tel. 202-783-7200
> http://www.astc.org

Association for Women in Science

Organization formed to "achieve equity and full participation for women in science, engineering, technology, and mathematics."

> 1200 New York Ave., N.W., Suite 650,
> Washington, DC 20005
> Tel. 202-326-8940
> http://www.awis.org

The National Science Foundation

An independent agency of the U.S. government whose mission is to promote the progress of science; to advance the national health, prosperity, and welfare; and to secure the national defense. It is a major source of research grants and funding in the sciences.

> 4201 Wilson Blvd., Arlington, VA 22230
> Tel. 703-292-5111
> http://www.nsf.gov/

National Science Teachers Association

Professional organization dedicated to "excellence and innovation in science teaching and learning for all."

> 1840 Wilson Blvd., Arlington, VA 22201
> Tel. 703-243-7100
> http://www.nsta.org

Society for Amateur Scientists

Collaboration between world-class professionals and citizen scientists to "remove the roadblocks that prevent ordinary people from participating in scientific adventures of all kinds."

> 5600 Post Rd., East Greenwich, RI 02818
> Tel. 401-398-7001
> http://www.sas.org/

SECTION
EIGHT
WEB SITES

CHEMISTRY

About Chemistry
About.com Includes links to a glossary, encyclopedia, experiments, periodic table, chemical structure archive, chemistry problems, and articles.
http://chemistry.about.com/?once=true&

Chem4Kids
Accessible information on matter, atoms, elements, reactions, biochemistry, and much more, for grades 5–9.
http://www.chem4kids.com/

Chemistry Carousel: A Trip Around the Carbon Cycle
Oracle ThinkQuest Education Foundation Site explaining the carbon cycle.
http://library.thinkquest.org/11226/index.htm

Chemistry Central
WebRing Offers basic atomic information, information on the periodic table, chemical bonding, and organic chemistry as well as extensive links to a wide variety of other resources.
http://users.senet.com.au/~rowanb/chem/

Chemistry.org
American Chemical Society Offers publications, career advice, information, and curriculum materials for K–12.
http://www.acs.org/

The Chemistry Research Center
Oracle ThinkQuest Education Foundation
Offers high school students links to useful sites for help with homework.
http://library.thinkquest.org/21192/lowg/index.html

Chemistry Tutor
Oracle ThinkQuest Education Foundation
Help for high school students with chemistry homework. Includes an introduction to chemistry, equations, calculations, types of reactions, information on lab safety, and links to other sources.
http://library.thinkquest.org/2923/

ChemSpy.com
Links to chemistry and chemical engineering terms, definitions, synonyms, acronyms, and abbreviations.
http://www.chemspy.com/

CHEMystery
ThinkQuest A virtual chemistry textbook, providing an interactive guide for high school chemistry students and links to other resources.
http://library.thinkquest.org/3659/

Common Molecules
Indiana University Information and 3-D presentation on molecules studied in chemistry classes or of interest for their structural properties.
http://www.reciprocalnet.org/common/index.html

Delights of Chemistry
Department of Chemistry, University of Leeds
Presents more than 40 chemistry demonstrations and 500 photographs/animations of experiments and chemical reactions.
http://www.chem.leeds.ac.uk/delights/

EnvironmentalChemistry.com
Kenneth Barbalace Includes a chemical and environmental dictionary; a detailed periodic table of elements; articles on environmental and hazardous materials issues; a geologic timeline.
http://environmentalchemistry.com/

Eric Weisstein's World of CHEMISTRY
Online encyclopedia, still under construction, with excellent graphics; good source for chemical reactions.
http://scienceworld.wolfram.com/chemistry/

General Chemistry Online
Professor Fred Senese Contains searchable glossary, frequently asked questions, database of compounds, tutorials, simulations, and toolbox of periodic table and calculators.
http://antoine.frostburg.edu/chem/senese/101/index.shtml

The Learning Matters of Chemistry
Knowledge by Design Offers visualizations of molecules and atomic orbits, interactive chemistry exercises, and links to other resources.
http://www.knowledgebydesign.com/tlmc/tlmc.html

The Macrogalleria: A Cyberwonderland of Polymer Fun
Department of Polymer Science, University of Southern Mississippi An Internet "mall" for

learning about polymers and polymer science.
http://www.pslc.ws/macrog/

Nuclear Chemistry and the Community

Kennesaw State University Introduction to nuclear chemistry and its impact on society.
http://www.chemcases.com/nuclear/index.htm

The pH Factor

Miami Museum of Science Introduction to acids and bases for middle school students.
http://www.miamisci.org/ph/

PSIgate: Chemistry

Resource Discovery Network Offers interactive tutorials, timeline, and links, in many areas.
http://www.psigate.ac.uk/newsite/chemistry-gateway.html

Reactive Reports

David Bradley Web chemistry magazine offering news stories and links to sites.
http://www.reactivereports.com/index.html

The Science of Spectroscopy

Introduction to spectroscopy with descriptions of common spectroscopic analysis techniques, as well as applications of spectroscopy in consumer products, medicine, and space science.
http://www.scienceofspectroscopy.info/

Virtual Chemistry

Oxford University 3-D simulated laboratory for teaching chemistry, with links to an online encyclopedia, tutorials, and close-ups of molecules.
http://neon.chem.ox.ac.uk/vrchemistry/

A Visual Interpretation of the Table of Elements

Chemsoc Striking visual representations of 110 elements. Site includes detailed information on the elements and on the history of the periodic table.
http://www.chemsoc.org/viselements/index.htm

Web Elements™ Periodic Table Scholar Edition

Mark Winter, University of Sheffield High quality source of information about the periodic table for students. There is also a professional edition.
http://www.webelements.com/webelements/scholar/index.html

What's that Stuff?

Chemical & Engineering News Explores the chemistry of everyday objects.
http://pubs.acs.org/cen/whatstuff/stuff.html

GENERAL WEB SITES

American Association for the Advancement of Science (AAAS)

Information on scientific developments and education programs for all ages.
http://www.aaas.org

Exploratorium

Produced by San Francisco's interactive Exploratorium science museum, the site contains experiments, exhibits, and sound and video files exploring hundreds of different topics.
http://www.exploratorium.edu

How Stuff Works

HSW Media Network Extensive resource of individual tutorials in Earth science, engineering, physical science, life science, and space.
http://science.howstuffworks.com/

National Science Digital Library (NSDL)

National Science Foundation Giant database of links to quality resources and services supporting science education at all levels.
http://nsdl.org/

NOVA: Science in the News

Australian Academy of Science Information on scientific principles and concepts in theheadlines.
http://www.science.org.au/nova/

Quiz Hub

Schmidel & Wojcik Learning center with quizzes, homework help, resources, and interactive games.
http://quizhub.com/

Science Learning Network (SLN)

Links to an international group of inquiry-based science museums and Web sites as well as educator hotlists.
http://sln.fi.edu/org/

ScienceMaster

News, information, links, columns, and homework help in all major areas of science.
http://www.sciencemaster.com/

Science News for Kids

Science Service Suggestions for hands-on activities, books, articles, Web resources, and other useful materials for students ages 9–13.
http://www.sciencenewsforkids.org/

Scientific American.com

Scientific American Latest news in science as well as an "Ask the Experts" feature.
http://www.sciam.com

Society for Amateur Scientists

Hotlists for a variety of disciplines as well as science hobbyists, science suppliers, science education stores, scientific organizations, science books, magazines, and newsletters.
http://www.sas.org/

ThinkQuest Library

Oracle ThinkQuest Education Foundation Links to hundreds of scientific sites on the Web.
http://library.thinkquest.org

TEACHER RESOURCES

Curriculum Center: Discoveryschool.com

Classroom activities for core curriculum topics.
http://school.discovery.com/curriculumcenter/

Education World: The Educator's Best Friend

Links, lesson plans, practical information for educators, information on integrating technology in the classroom, articles by education experts, site reviews, and daily features and columns.
http://www.education-world.com

Element

Jacqueline Floyd Includes links to science news sites, research labs, educational resources, scientific data, freeware for data analysis, and chat forums.
http://www.elementlist.com/lnx/index.php

Middle School Physical Science Resource Center

North Carolina State University Hands-on science experiments, book reviews, a newsletter, relevant essays, and a discussion forum.
http://www.science-house.org:8530/middleschool/

National Science Teachers Association

Information on the teaching of science, including links to teacher recommended Web sites.
http://www.nsta.org

Resources for Teaching Chemistry

Norman Herr, Ph.D. Links to professional organizations, information on chemical chemicals reference data, chemical demonstrations, laboratory safety, science museums, and lesson plan ideas.
http://www.csun.edu/~vceed002/chemistry/

EQUIPMENT SUPPLIERS

Carolina Biological Supply Company

Online catalogue of science equipment and teacher resources.
http://www.carolina.com

Fisher Science Education

Online catalogue of science equipment and teacher resources.
http://www.fishersci.com/education/index.jsp

Frey Scientific

Online catalogue of science equipment and teacher resources.
http://www.freyscientific.com/index.jsp

NSTA's Suppliers Guide

National Science Teachers Association Listing of suppliers of textbooks, reference works, computer programs, curriculum kits, and lab equipment.
http://suppliers.nsta.org

RadioShack

Online retailer of electronic parts, batteries, and accessories.
http://www.radioshack.com/home/index.jsp

ScienceLab.com

Discount supplier of science education materials and laboratory equipment.
http://www.sciencelab.com

Ward's Natural Science

Supplier of materials for high school- and college-level biology and geology classes, and life, environmental, Earth, and physical science studied in grades 5 through 9.
http://www.wardsci.com

INDEX

The A–Z Glossary and other thematic Sections provide direct access to information. The Index offers supplementary access to Sections 2 to 6. Page numbers in **bold** type indicate the main biographical note on individuals.